Day of Reckoning

DAY
of
RECKONING

The Consequences of
American Economic Policy
Under Reagan and After

Benjamin Friedman

 Random House New York

Copyright © 1988 by Benjamin M. Friedman
All rights reserved under International and Pan-American Copyright
Conventions. Published in the United States by Random House, Inc.,
New York, and simultaneously in Canada by Random House of Canada
Limited, Toronto.

Library of Congress Cataloging-in-Publication Data

Friedman, Benjamin M.
Day of reckoning / by Benjamin Friedman.
p. cm.
ISBN 0-394-56553-3
1. Fiscal policy—United States. 2. Debts, Public—United States.
3. Loans, Foreign—United States. 4. United States—Economic
conditions—1981- I. Title.
HJ257.2.F75 1988
336.3'4'0973—dc19   88-11693
CIP

Manufactured in the United States of America
2 3 4 5 6 7 8 9
First Edition

In Memory of My Father
And with Love for My Sons

Acknowledgments

This book is about debt: debt and the material and moral impoverishment that inevitably follow, no less for a nation than for an individual or a family, from continually borrowing for no purpose other than to live beyond one's means.

There is also another kind of debt. Debts of personal gratitude are often enriching, not impoverishing, and it is my good fortune to have accumulated many of these in the course of writing this book. I want here to acknowledge the most important among them.

The greatest of these debts is to David Laibson and Jeffrey Wolk, two Harvard College seniors who devoted much of the past year to assisting me in the research for this book. Their work was as creative and insightful as it was diligent and resourceful. They are surely two of Harvard's finest.

Many colleagues and friends have also contributed to this effort. Robert Solow read the entire manuscript and made many useful suggestions. Rudiger Dornbusch and Peter Temin read parts of the manuscript and provided further helpful comments. Alan Auerbach, Richard Cooper, Arthur Dubow, James

Duesenberry, John Gorman, William Helkie, Richard Herrnstein, Charles Kindleberger, Lawrence Kotlikoff, Paul Krugman, Kenneth Kuttner, Lawrence Lindsey, John Musgrave, James Poterba, Robert Roosa, Jeffrey Sachs, Francis Schott, Robert Solomon, Lawrence Summers, Stephen Taylor, Jeffrey Williamson Thierry Wizman, and Judith Ziobrow—and too many others to mention individually—each helped by discussing ideas with me, by helping me to interpret empirical evidence, or by providing me with relevant data. Jason Epstein closely read and commented on two full manuscript drafts, and also helped me to distinguish what was and was not likely to be useful (not to mention intelligible) to the general reader. Helen Deas efficiently and cheerfully typed the manuscript, then did so again, and then again, and then again. I am grateful to all of these for the assistance and support that they have given my effort.

Harvard University provided a sabbatical during which I wrote most of this book, and also supported my research with grants from several university funds, including especially the Harvard Program for Financial Research. Over a period of years, the National Science Foundation and the Alfred P. Sloan Foundation also supported my research on many of the issues with which I have dealt here. I am grateful for all of this support.

None of these institutions, however, nor any other organization with which I am associated, nor any of the many individuals from whose help I have benefited bears any responsibility for the contents of this book. The opinions and interpretations I have expressed here are mine, and so too is the responsibility for any errors they may contain or any controversies to which they may give rise.

And finally, for the support that has mattered the most in

my efforts, I thank Barbara for her encouragement, John for his curiosity, and Jeffrey for his company.

Benjamin M. Friedman

Cambridge, Massachusetts
June 1988

Contents

Day of Reckoning

Chapter I

BROKEN FAITH

A good man leaveth an inheritance to his children's children.

—PROVERBS, XIII:22

What can you say to a man on a binge who asks why it matters? Flush with cash from liquidating his modest investment portfolio and from taking out a second mortgage on the inflated value of his house, he can spend seemingly without limit. The vacation cruise his family has dreamed about for years, the foreign sports car he has always wanted, new designer clothes for his wife and even his children, meals in all the most expensive restaurants—life is wonderful. What difference does it make if he has to pay some interest? If necessary, next year he can sell his house for enough to pay off both mortgages and have enough left over to buy an even faster car. What difference does it make whether he owns a house at all? For the price of the extra sports car, he can afford the first year's rent in the fanciest apartment building in town. Why worry?

Americans have traditionally confronted such questions in the context of certain values, values that arise from the obligation that one generation owes to the next. Generations of Americans have opened up frontiers, fought in wars at home and abroad, and made countless personal economic sacrifices because they knew that the world did not end with themselves and because they cared about what came afterward. The American experiment, from the very beginning, has been forward looking—economically as well as politically and socially. The earliest Americans saw this experiment as an explicit break with the past and devoted their energies to constructing the kind of future they valued both individually and collectively. The generations that followed accepted their debt to the past by attempting to repay it to the future.

The thesis of this book is that the radical course upon which United States economic policy was launched in the 1980s violated the basic moral principle that had bound each generation of Americans to the next since the founding of the republic: that men and women should work and eat, earn and spend, both privately and collectively, so that their children and their children's children would inherit a better world. Since 1980 we have broken with that tradition by pursuing a policy that amounts to living not just in, but for, the present. We are living well by running up our debt and selling off our assets. America has thrown itself a party and billed the tab to the future. The costs, which are only beginning to come due, will include a lower standard of living for individual Americans and reduced American influence and importance in world affairs.

For many Americans, the sudden collapse of stock prices in October 1987 punctured the complacency with which they had accepted a national policy based on systematic overconsumption. After all, the resulting economic environment had looked pretty appealing to the average citizen. Jobs were plentiful in most areas, inflation and interest rates were both down from the frightening levels that had marked the beginning of the decade, and taxes were lower. Plenty of foreign-made goods were still available at cheap prices despite the falling dollar. Most companies' profits were high and going higher. The business recovery that began at the end of 1982 had already become the longest sustained economic expansion in American peacetime history, and there was no recession in sight. The phenomenal stock market rally, with the average share price almost tripling in just five years, seemed both to reflect this prosperity and to foretell its permanence.

By now it is clear that this sense of economic well-being was an illusion, an illusion based on borrowed time and borrowed money. Jobs are plentiful and profits are high because we are spending amply, but more than ever before what we are spending for is consumption. Prices have remained stable in part because business was depressed at the beginning of the decade, and also because until recently the overpriced dollar delivered foreign-made cars and clothes and computers more cheaply than the cost of producing them in America. Our after-tax incomes are rising because we are continuing to receive the usual variety of services and benefits from our government, but we are not paying the taxes to cover the cost.

In short, our prosperity was a false prosperity, built on borrowing from the future. The trouble with an economic policy that artificially boosts consumption at the expense of investment, dissipates assets, and runs up debt is simply that each of these outcomes violates the essential trust that has always linked each generation to those that follow. We have enjoyed what appears to be a higher and more stable standard of living by selling our and our children's economic birthright. With no common agreement or even much public discussion, we are determining as a nation that today should be the high point of American economic advancement compared not just to the past but to the future as well.

The decision to mortgage America's economic future has not been a matter of individual choice but of legislated public policy. Popular talk of the "me generation" to the contrary, most individual Americans are working just as hard, and saving nearly as much, as their parents and grandparents did. What is different is economic policy. The tax and spending policies that the U.S. government has pursued throughout Ronald Reagan's presidency have rendered every citizen a borrower and every industry a liquidator of assets. The reason that the average American has enjoyed such a high standard of living lately is that since January 1981 our government has simply borrowed more than $20,000 on behalf of each family of four.

Worse still, we owe nearly half of this new debt to foreign lenders. At the beginning of the 1980s, foreigners owed Americans far more than we owed foreigners. The balance in our favor, amounting to some $2,500 per family, made the United States the world's leading creditor country, enjoying the advantages of international influence and power that have always accompanied such a position. Today, after a half dozen years in which our government has borrowed record sums on our behalf, we owe foreigners far more than they owe us. The balance against us, already amounting to more than $7,000 per family, now makes the United States the world's largest debtor. Foreigners have already begun to settle these debts by taking possession of office buildings in American cities, houses in American suburbs, farm land in the heartland, and even whole companies. We are selling off America, and living on the proceeds.

Our unprecedented splurge of consumption financed by borrowing has broken faith with the future in two ways, each of which carries profound implications not just for our standard of living but for the character of our society more generally. Whether we continue or reverse our current economic policy will determine how Americans in the future will think of themselves and their society, whether the free ideals and democratic institutions at the core of the American experiment will continue to prosper, and whether America as a nation will be in a position to advance these ideals and institutions beyond our own borders.

The cost of the economic policy we have pursued in the 1980s is no more than what any society pays for eating its seed corn rather than planting it. With the federal deficit averaging 4.2 percent of our total income since the beginning of the decade, compared to a net private saving rate of just 5.7 percent, our rate of investment in business plant and equipment has fallen beneath that of any previous sustained period since World War II.[1] So has our investment in roads, bridges, airports, harbors, and other kinds of government-owned infrastructure. Our investment in education has also shrunk compared to our total income despite the urgent need to train a work force whose opportunities will arise more than ever before from industries oriented to technologically advanced production and the processing of information.

With so little investment in the basic structure of a strong economy, our ability to produce the goods and services that people want has been disappointing in the 1980s despite a marked improvement in some of the other factors that affect business performance. Workers on average are older and more experienced, business is spending more on research and development, and most of the investment needed to meet environmental regulations is already in place. But these favorable developments have been swamped by the weakness of business investment, so that there has been no significant increase in the amount of capital at the disposal of the average American worker. Since 1979, the last year of full employment before the pair of business recessions that began this decade, our overall productivity growth has averaged just 1.1 percent per annum.[2] If productivity growth continues at this pace, we shall, at best, be able to do no more than pay the interest on our mounting foreign debt. On our current trajectory, there will be no margin to provide for increases over time in our standard of living.

To persist in our present policy is therefore to risk the material basis for the progress that has marked Americans' perceptions of themselves and their society since its very beginnings. Forging a great nation from a raw continent within just a few centuries provided the momentum, the spirit of progress, the dynamic, that by de Tocqueville's day had already come to characterize the American outlook. This sense of America as a dynamic and progressive society has always had an economic basis. Economic incentives motivated the first explorers to seek out what were then unknown lands, and economic incentives also led many of the earliest settlers to establish themselves here. Subsequent waves of immigration swelled the population with men and women led here by aspirations for political freedoms and for economic opportunities, often opportunities that only their children would be able to exploit fully. The conquest of the frontier, the building of a nation that was at first mostly rural and agricultural, and the subsequent development of that nation into a largely urban and industrial power, all required tangible and visible economic progress.

The idea of progress for the nation as a whole both reflected and demanded continual economic betterment for the individual citizen. As Americans' standard of living doubled roughly once every thirty years—not as a one-time phenomenon but as an ongoing process that compounded itself from one generation to the next—the assumption of a better life as time passed became a basic element in the outlook of Americans who lived out their lives here, no less than of those who came from elsewhere. The idea that each generation of Americans would enjoy a noticeably greater level of material well-being was a fact, not just a hope.

And over time, the fact of continual economic progress shaped the character of American society more broadly. A rising standard of living is worth having not only on its own account but even more so because it provides the material basis for a free and democratic society. The nature of the choices any society has to make is different when its citizens' incomes are regularly doubling every generation than when incomes stagnate. The openness, the social mobility, the breadth of individual opportunity, and the tolerance of diversity that have given American society its unique flavor are inseparable from a continually rising overall living standard. So is the ability to make crucial choices, which in the end determine the shares that individuals and groups can claim from what the nation produces, without destructive social conflict.

But all this depends on progress and continuity. In the simplest terms, that means adequate saving, investment in productive assets and housing for a growing population, and in general, sufficient attention to creating new wealth rather than living off the endowments left by prior generations. There is no evidence of a breakdown of the deep-rooted inhibitions against abandoning these obligations to the future on the part of individual Americans. As we shall see, Americans have not suffered an attack of laziness in the 1980s or a sudden urge to burn up their savings or even a failure of foresight. Yet as a nation, we are consuming more than we earn, investing less than we used to, and all the while borrowing from abroad and selling off our property.

Economic policy, not individual behavior, has made the difference. The fact that this new policy came clothed in a rhetoric appealing to traditional values that most Americans hold important and that we typically identify with our fundamental aspirations for the country's future has not prevented it from violating those values and denying those hopes. By now we should realize that being in favor of saving and investment or work effort or competitiveness is not the same as actually advancing these objectives. The ax on the chain of progress and continuity has been the nation's new fiscal policy.

Continued government spending not matched by the taxes to restrain private consumption is eroding the material basis for American society as we know it. What would America be like —what would Americans be like—without the fact, and consequently the idea, of progress? How long will it take before the rigidity, complacency, and mediocrity characteristic of economically stagnant societies set in? Which of our open and democratic institutions will survive the more fractious disputes over shares of a national product that is not increasing? We simply do not know. But now that the implications of our new fiscal policy are clear, it is hard to believe that anyone wants to stay the course in order to find out.

The second way in which this policy has broken faith with future generations is by sacrificing a part of America's sovereignty. It is no accident that the great sums we have borrowed to finance our overconsumption have included large amounts borrowed from abroad. As we shall see, the link connecting the government's fiscal deficit—the difference between federal spending and federal revenues—and our international trade deficit—the difference between what we import and what we export—is real enough. With government borrowing absorbing nearly three fourths of our private saving, heightened competition among business and individual borrowers for the remainder has raised our interest rates, in relation to inflation, to record levels—and, importantly, to levels well above what investors could get in other countries. For half a decade, therefore, the dollar became ever more expensive in terms of other countries' currencies, as foreign investors competed among themselves to acquire dollars with which to buy high-interest debt instruments in America. As the dollar rose, the ability of our industries to compete with foreign producers all but collapsed not only in world markets but even here in America.

With the dollar so overvalued, we increased what we consumed faster than what we produced not only because the deficit absorbed our potential investment capital but because we increasingly imported more than we exported. As we paid for our growing excess of imports over exports, we sent ever more dollars abroad for foreigners to invest in our financial markets. Indeed, because so little of what we save is left over after the government has financed its deficit, this reinvestment of our own dollars by foreign lenders now finances most of what little investment we are able to do.

As our trade deficit has continued to grow, the great accumulation of dollars in foreign hands has increasingly saturated the foreign appetite for dollar-denominated assets. As a result, the dollar has now fallen back almost to where it started. Our ability to compete will therefore improve, and our trade deficit will shrink. But a significant correction will take time, in part because we have neglected our industries during these years. We have underinvested in our economy as a whole and especially in our manufacturing sector.

Even more important, as a result of the borrowing we have done along the way, to finance the imports we have not paid for with exports, within less than a decade we have dissipated our net international holdings and run up the world's largest debt. As a further result, we have not one debt problem but two: the debt that our government owes as a result of borrowing to finance its string of record budget deficits and the debt that we as a nation owe as a result of borrowing from abroad to finance our record string of trade deficits. Each has separate implications for our future well-being, but the root of both, as we shall see in some detail, is our new fiscal policy.

One worrisome implication of America's becoming a debtor nation is simply our loss of control over our own economic policies. Losing control over one's affairs is, after all, what being in debt is all about—no less for a nation than for an individual or a business. The era when other countries surrendered autonomy over their monetary policies in order to peg their currencies to the dollar is already giving way to an era in which we contemplate sacrificing the independence of our monetary policy in order to fix the dollar's value in marks or in yen.

The stock market crash in October 1987 highlighted the tension that can arise, when a nation's fiscal policy is far out of balance, between a monetary policy designed to support its currency and a monetary policy designed to prop up its economy. In the wake of the crash, the Federal Reserve System promptly lowered interest rates so as to prevent the stock market collapse from bringing about an economic collapse. That choice was clearly the right one, but the resulting further drop in dollar exchange rates as interest rates fell created problems of a different kind and risked a renewed decline in the prices of stocks or other assets denominated in dollars: a risk more severe than it would have been a decade or two earlier, precisely because of the new reliance of our financial markets on foreign lenders and investors.

Here too, however, the most important implications of our new fiscal policy extend beyond narrow economic considerations. Foreign investors who may become nervous about holding deposits issued by U.S. banks and securities issued by the U.S. Treasury are perfectly free to buy up our businesses and our real estate instead. As we shall see, they are already doing so in increasing volume, and given the vast amounts of dollars held abroad, it is clear that the process has only begun. We are surrendering the ownership of our country's productive assets, not in exchange for assets we will own abroad but merely to finance our overconsumption. The realization that we increasingly live in foreign-owned buildings and work for foreign-owned firms, once it dawns, will jar harshly with our traditional perception of America as a nation of owners.

World power and influence have historically accrued to creditor countries. It is not coincidental that America emerged as a world power simultaneously with our transition from a debtor nation dependent on foreign capital for our initial industrialization, to a creditor supplying investment capital to the rest of the world. But we are now a debtor again, and our future role in world affairs is in question. People simply do not regard their workers, their tenants, and their debtors in the same light as their employers, their landlords, and their creditors. Over time the respect, and even deference, that America had earned as world banker will gradually shift to the new creditor countries that are able to supply resources where we cannot, and America's influence over nations and events will ebb.

Most Americans continue to think of themselves as creditors. We readily offer unsolicited advice to other debtor countries, as if they had fallen into a trap that we had successfully avoided. Meanwhile, the Japanese and Germans appear still to think of themselves as debtors. As a result, world leadership arrangements do not yet reflect our changed circumstances or theirs. But self-perceptions on both sides will soon catch up to the new reality, in which our financial problems circumscribe our scope for maneuver in world affairs while other countries' financial strength does the opposite. Just how large a departure from recent history that reality represents will depend in part on whether, and how, we change our economic policy.

. . .

The challenge to American economic policymaking is two-fold. We must first set a new fiscal policy that commits most if not all our saving to investment in productive capital rather than to funding the government deficit. That means paying more taxes or cutting back on government spending or both. Second, we must adjust our economic policy in the broadest sense to confront the debt left by the Reagan era. Even a complete reversal of our current fiscal policy beginning immediately will not magically wipe away the legacy of almost a decade of overconsumption and excessive borrowing. But it will be a start, and the sooner we start the smaller the sacrifices we shall eventually be forced to make.

Neither of these tasks will be accomplished simply. The agonizing bipartisan negotiations that finally delivered a $30 billion grab bag of small tax hikes, small spending cuts, and assorted accounting gimmicks in the wake of the October 1987 stock market crash showed once again that there are no easy solutions to our current problem. But then why should there be? Nobody enjoys consuming less. Nobody likes doing without the services or the benefit payments that our government provides. And nobody wants to pay more taxes. Our new fiscal policy abandoned the long-standing American commitment to paying our government's way, and the excess consumption that resulted sacrificed our future prospects, but few Americans found the experience unpleasant along the way. To correct course will now require a retrenchment from the combined levels of private consumption and government services to which we have become accustomed.

Moreover, we missed the opportunity to begin this retrench-ment when our economy was vigorous and resilient. By 1984 business was solidly recovering from the unusually severe 1981–82 downturn. Unemployment had already dropped from 11 percent of the labor force to 7 percent, and business activity overall had grown by an average 5.6 percent per annum, after inflation, since the recession's end.[3] The economy no longer needed the continued stimulus provided by government spending far in excess of revenues. But instead of acting then to bring spending and taxes into line, we mindlessly continued a policy that raised the deficit to yet a new record level the next year and again the year after that.

By the end of 1987, prospects for continuing economic growth were less sure. The aging business expansion had already gone on longer than any sustained upturn since the Vietnam War. Along the way it had built up the usual potentially retarding forces plus record accumulations of public and private debt as well as a record volume of business bankruptcies. Too great a government retrenchment, implemented too rapidly, might halt the expansion altogether. Whatever lingering effect the sudden disappearance of a trillion dollars' worth of accumulated stock market wealth could have on spending by individuals and businesses would only make matters worse.

These concerns are valid, but they do not lessen our need to restore fiscal policy to a stable trajectory so that we shall hereafter live within our means and invest adequately for the future. Instead, the prospect that a new fiscal policy to correct the excesses of the Reagan era may coincide with a downturn in the business cycle makes it all the more important to conceive the policy transition with keen attention to the subtle connections between fiscal and monetary policies. The right response to the risk of a business slowdown compounded by fiscal retrenchment is to link that retrenchment firmly to an expansionary monetary policy, fully reversing the combination of expansionary budgets and tight money that prevailed over much of the Reagan era, rather than to defer action indefinitely and let the costs of our current irresponsibility continue to mount.

The connections between our policies and those of our international trading partners are important in this regard too. The widely publicized meetings held by the finance ministers of the principal trading countries in recent years, beginning long before the collapse of world stock prices intensified the high drama of these sessions, have mostly led to short-term fixes for the exchange markets, accompanied by empty statements of principle. America's refusal to correct its fiscal imbalance has been a major cause of the shallowness of these efforts at international policy coordination. Although it is never possible to rely fully on other governments, which inevitably face their own domestic problems and political pressures, the removal of this impediment will improve the prospects for genuinely constructive policy coordination, including the adoption of more stimulative fiscal and monetary policies abroad. Especially with the dollar's sharp decline, other countries now have a great incentive to avoid forcing America into a business downturn that will only reduce still further what they can export to us and to others.

But the large fiscal retrenchment that America needs in the post-Reagan era is possible only if most Americans perceive it to be necessary. From this perspective, the stock market crash may have been helpful, for American politics is often activated only by crisis. The drop in stock prices was not itself enough to force a serious fiscal solution, but it did begin to awaken both government officials and the general public to the need for a major change. We must still find a new policy, but the issue remains lost in a cloud of empty rhetoric about how well off we are, while no one asks how we are going to pay for what we consume.

Retrenchment on the necessary scale must also be perceived by Americans to be fair, if it is to be successful. When times are good, "fairness" to most Americans means fairness to others. When times are not so good, "fairness" no longer means "them" but "us." Because the essence of the required policy change means giving something up—consuming less and investing more—the fairness question will also be critical.

As we shall see, there is no shortage of obvious ways to cut the deficit, each of which involves significant sacrifice and all of which are roughly equivalent in economic terms. But they are not equivalent politically. Picking the right combination from the list of possible choices is therefore not a matter of economic analysis. On economic grounds there is no uniquely right combination. But politically it is clear that some combinations have a chance of succeeding while others do not. The only ones that do are those that citizens will regard as broadly equitable.

How have we gotten into such a mess? It is tempting, of course, simply to blame what has happened on shortsightedness, or greed, or even sheer folly on the part of the American public. Or to suppose that there is some inherent flaw in the American system of representative government. But claims of public irrationality or of shortcomings of the democratic process fail to explain this decade's sudden departure from America's prior fiscal conduct.

If Americans as a political body are somehow incapable of following an economic course that pays adequate attention to their and their children's future, why did our fiscal posture remain as stable as it did for so many years until the 1980s? If the American system of government is inherently faulty, why did federal revenues sufficiently cover spending over two centuries, so that until the 1980s our national debt never rose faster than the country's income except in wartime and at the bottom of the Great Depression? If the entire system is prone to overconsumption and dissipation, why did Americans throughout this century steadily build their net international asset position, rather than spend it away? The sharpness of the discontinuity that has occurred in the 1980s calls for more than vague laments about the inadequacy of the American character or the failure of our form of self-government.

The place to begin to understand what happened is to remember that Americans chose the fiscal policy their nation has followed in the 1980s, at least in part because its architects had assured them that it would lead to a better future, not mortgage that future or squander it. It is safe to say that few Americans who welcomed Ronald Reagan's election victory over Jimmy Carter in 1980 or applauded his string of legislative victories in 1981 foresaw fully what his fiscal policy would bring. The persistent argument used to sell this policy to the public—and at the same time to market the candidates who proposed it—was that it would revive America's economy and provide what Reagan billed as a "New Beginning for the Economy" after the harsh experience of the mid- and late seventies.[4]

No one asked Americans to vote for doubling our national debt or diverting our saving away from productive investment or making our industry uncompetitive or turning our country into the world's largest debtor, all within less than a decade. Yet the policy that Americans were asked to endorse and that they did endorse has had just that effect.

Above all, Reagan was explicit and emphatic, both as a candidate and then as President, that his policy would deliver a balanced budget. Throughout the campaign he held forth the prospect of balancing the budget by 1983. This was a central objective that his fiscal policy, in contrast to Carter's, would achieve. In the very first minute of his first televised address to the nation after taking office in January 1981, he pointed to that year's "runaway deficit of nearly $80 billion" as evidence that "the federal budget is out of control."[5] And two weeks later in his first address to Congress, he echoed the same warning in a different way. "Can we, who man the ship of state, deny that it is somewhat out of control?" he asked. "Our national debt is approaching one trillion dollars."[6]

As Reagan's presidency ends, it is difficult to recapture the sense of alarm that these numbers aroused so few years ago. The $79 billion budget deficit that Reagan took over from Carter in 1981 was the last he would ever be able to express in two digits. Over the next six years the deficits ranged from a low of $128 billion in 1982 to a high of $221 billion in 1986. The average for the six years 1982–87 was $184 billion.[7] By 1988 the idea that the U.S. government might complete a year having spent only $80 billion more than its revenues has come to represent almost hopeless optimism. When Reagan leaves office, the national debt he leaves to his successor will not be the $914 billion he inherited from Carter but $2.6 *trillion.*

Moreover, it is foolish to pretend that there has been any major disagreement between President Reagan and the Congress over the total amount—in contrast to the composition—of federal spending. For the six fiscal years 1982–87 (the 1981 budget was still Carter's), savings on defense spending came sufficiently close to offsetting the excess spent on nondefense programs, so that total government outlays for all purposes other than interest on the national debt were only $90 billion more than what Reagan requested. But the accumulated deficit for those six years was more than $1.1 trillion. The deficit has resulted mostly from the fact that federal revenues have consistently fallen far short of the administration's early projections. Disagreements over spending priorities notwithstanding, the fiscal policy we have pursued during the 1980s—including the deficits, and with them the damage they have brought and are yet to bring to our economic prospects—has been Reagan's fiscal policy. This new policy, which Americans overwhelmingly endorsed in 1980 and again in 1984, has simply failed to deliver what Reagan and its other advocates claimed it would bring.

The essence of the "supply-side" argument that Reagan advanced in 1980 (and to which he has resolutely clung ever since) is that the incentive effects of across-the-board cuts in personal tax rates would so stimulate individuals' work efforts and business initiatives that lower tax *rates* would deliver higher tax *revenues*. Lower tax rates, according to this notion, would help balance the federal budget, despite sharp increases in military spending, without requiring cuts in the nondefense programs that people genuinely valued. Americans could therefore enjoy both continued government spending and lower tax rates too. There was no need to worry about what deficits meant for the nation's future, because under this policy the government would run no deficits.

The idea that lower tax *rates* meant higher tax *revenues* neatly severed the link between the inherent attraction of easier taxes and the economic consequences of tax cuts without spending cuts—which Americans had traditionally regarded as irresponsible—because the theory promised that lower tax rates would *prevent* deficits and that the government would therefore borrow less, not more. The investment needed to renew America's productivity growth and restore competitiveness abroad would not wither but flourish. The costs of Reagan's new fiscal policy were not an issue, because it would bring only benefits, both immediately and in the future.

But is it realistic to suppose that American voters really believed this fairy tale just because Ronald Reagan asked them to? Did the 323 congressmen and the 67 senators who voted for the Kemp-Roth tax cut in the summer of 1981 actually believe that lowering tax rates would increase tax revenues? No one who examined the available evidence in 1980 would have made or accepted such a claim, and there was surely no lack of opponents—including George Bush, who proclaimed it "voodoo economics"—who bluntly said that it made no sense. Further, once record deficits began to emerge, as they were bound to under this bizarre policy, no one who examined the Kemp-Roth experiment in progress would have expected that the economy could simply grow its way out of the deficits that that policy had created.

It is a fact nonetheless that Ronald Reagan persistently advanced these ideas and the policies they implied, and it is also a fact that Americans elected him president by huge majorities in 1980 and again in 1984. To be sure, Reagan's forceful advocacy was a persuasive, even beguiling, influence for many Americans. But was there more to our breaking faith with future generations than that we were gulled by an exceptionally attractive politician? Was there also something disingenuous about it, either on the part of those who called for this new policy or among the majority of the citizenry who were so willing to acquiesce?

The most favorable construction to place on this extraordinary abdication of our long-standing commitment to the future is that the architects of the new fiscal policy genuinely believed the claims they made for it, and that the level of economic frustration on the part of voters was sufficient to induce them if not entirely to believe, then at least to suspend their disbelief. Reagan's startling question in 1980—"Are you better off than you were four years ago?"—tapped a frustration that had been building for more than a decade. Failure in Vietnam during the sixties and more recently the drawn-out hostage crisis in Iran had harshly demonstrated the limits of American military power. Inflation, high oil prices, flagging productivity growth, and repeated business recessions had likewise emphasized the limits of American economic power. But the very idea of limits, and especially a limit to economic progress, was foreign to a nation whose traditions and self-perceptions had arisen from the experience of pushing back the frontier at home and then extending America's reach abroad. Reagan's supply-side economics, with its promise of unbounded growth if only individual incentives and entrepreneurial efforts could be freed from the shackles of high taxes and oppressive regulation, was in many ways a direct response to the "limits of growth" ideas that reflected in part the repeated economic failures that had marked the seventies. In their frustration, Americans seem to have gambled on hope rather than analysis, on a willing suspension of disbelief.

Moreover, even if no one except Ronald Reagan thought it was literally true, the claim that lower tax rates would generate higher tax revenues at least seemed credible enough to make both policymakers and the general public less sensitive to how much reduced tax rates *would actually lower* tax revenues. The real issue in 1980 and 1981 was not whether the 25 percent Kemp-Roth tax cut would actually raise revenue but whether the resulting revenue losses would be large enough so that, in the absence of major reductions in core programs like Social Security or defense, the resulting deficits would threaten the nation's economic future. By even partially suppressing their doubts that Kemp-Roth would help *balance* the budget, people could convince themselves that the likelihood of huge deficits and their consequences was less real—and if it was real, less threatening.

But if the ready acceptance by the voters of the supply-side promise contained at least some element of self-deception, it is also possible, as Reagan's Budget Director David Stockman later alleged, that the claims offered on behalf of the new fiscal policy were disingenuous in the first place. If the most favorable construction we can put on this policy after the fact is that it vastly overestimated the incentive effects of lower tax rates while vastly underestimating our commitment to the activities our government undertakes, a darker assessment is that its hidden agenda was deliberately to mortgage the nation's future as a means of forcing Americans to give up government activities which they would otherwise have been able to afford.

Especially once the Kemp-Roth tax cut had clearly failed to deliver either the sustained economic growth or the additional tax revenues its proponents had promised, an increasingly familiar claim has been that this had been the real intention all along: that the policy of running up ever larger deficits and government debt, with whatever costs have occurred and are still to follow, was not a failure of economic thinking but a carefully calculated plan for forcing the government to reduce its role in American life. And further, that the economic costs of this subterfuge were not a surprise but the inevitable and fully foreseen by-products of a more important campaign in which the issue at stake was not economic well-being but the character of American life in broader terms and in which our economic prospects (not to mention our government's fiscal position) were merely a hostage.

It would be sad—far worse than sad—if that were so. Just on practical grounds, the notion that higher taxes simply lead to more government spending is at best an unsubstantiated claim and more likely a myth.* But even if that claim bore

---

*Studies comparing the implications of different kinds of tax structures among the fifty states show no evidence of faster growth of the public sector in states with tax structures that automatically generate rising tax revenues as a share of statewide income (for example, a progressive income tax) than in states with tax structures that keep the revenue share flat (for example,

some validity, a deliberate policy aimed at forcing Americans to accept a smaller role for government, by deceitfully adopting a fiscal policy that imposes ever mounting economic costs until we do, runs against the grain morally.

Citizens in a free society, and especially one as rich as ours, should have the right to choose how much of their income to devote to strictly private pursuits and how much of it to spend on public goods like defense or highways or parks or law enforcement. Citizens in such a society should also have the right to choose how generously they want to support their elders who have retired and how much of that support they want to share on a public basis. A policy that intentionally provides too little tax revenues to pay for the cost of government, as determined by the voters, while accumulating ever greater debt both at home and abroad amounts to willful bankruptcy: the deliberate curtailment of our economic growth for fear of how the next generation of Americans will choose to use it.

We shall probably never know which of these alternative accounts of the origins of the Reagan fiscal policy better describes what really happened. On one construction, it was an intellectual error of the first magnitude. On the other, it was deliberate moral irresponsibility on a truly astonishing scale. But from the perspective of where to go from here, just what combination of forces was at work nearly a decade ago hardly matters.

------

a sales tax). Instead, states where taxes grow faster than incomes regularly offset that growth by tax "cuts," so that on average their spending growth is no faster than that of other states.[8] Similarly, the experience of the twelve European countries that introduced value-added taxes in the late sixties and early seventies showed no systematic tendency for the resulting access to new tax revenues to increase the growth of their public sectors, compared to what happened in other industrialized countries over the same period.[9]

. . .

What does matter is that we now call a mistake a mistake and fix it.

It would be simplistic to pretend that the deficit has been responsible for all our economic disappointments in the 1980s. We have also faced forces that are beyond our control, like the spread of advanced technologies to countries where labor is cheaper than we would ever want ours to be, or the steady shift of our economic activity from the production of goods to the provision of services, or the ongoing agricultural revolution which has already rendered countries like India and Bangladesh self-sufficient in food. Other major impediments to our productivity and competitiveness may stem more directly from our own decisions but still have little to do with the deficit. No doubt much of our difficulty has reflected such factors as poor product design, lack of innovation, an inadequately trained and motivated work force, and short-sighted management. We can and we should address each of these problems.

But it is fair to say that the deficit has been the greatest single force underlying the most severe failures of our economic performance in the 1980s, especially those with the most troubling implications for the future. The realization that our fiscal policy is a failure is now spreading rapidly. So is the desire, at some abstract level, to change it. Yet even in the aftermath of the stock market crash, which brought these concerns to the top of the public policy agenda, we did not do so to any meaningful extent.

Ironically, because of how our crisis-activated political machinery works, it might be better if our fiscal policy produced some highly visible cataclysm sufficient to rivet attention and demand an immediate response, something even more arresting than the stock market crash. Instead, the damage that this policy inflicts is subtle, intangible, and corrosive. Its full impact, as seen from any moment, always lies in the future. Because most of its consequences will occur only gradually—indeed they are already occurring, but only gradually—they are likely to remain mostly imperceptible from day to day or even year to year. And because this gradual decay preserves the illusion of prosperity today at the expense of the generation that is too young to vote, not to mention the generation that is not yet born, it is harder still for the nation's political system to address.

The situation has therefore resulted in inaction that would have seemed unthinkable not long ago: first the pretense that there was no problem, next the wait for others to make the necessary sacrifices, and finally the complacent conclusion that nothing could be done because nothing would be done. But Americans who voted for a new economic policy in the belief that it would balance the federal budget surely had the right to think this new policy would be changed if instead it delivered a never-ending series of budget deficits bigger than ever before. Americans who voted for a new policy because it was supposed to bolster our international competitiveness had the right to think it would be changed if it increased our export-import gap by an order of magnitude.

It has been too easy to rationalize continued allegiance to a failed policy by pointing the other way, by citing the fact of higher consumption while ignoring lower investment, and by hailing the illusion of fatter incomes and profits while forgetting about the swollen debts and the assets surrendered to foreigners. Even as the true shape of our false prosperity has become unmistakable, it has then been too easy to complain that there is no conclusive evidence, no proof beyond the shadow of doubt, that the spreading disorder has anything to do with fiscal policy in the first place.

These attitudes work well for professional sports and the

criminal justice system, but they are disastrous for economic policy. Boosterism that systematically sees only the bright spots makes for fine home-team loyalty. Maintaining that the accused is innocent until proven guilty beyond any doubt ensures careful trials and cautious punishments. But few families run their personal economic affairs by clinging indefinitely to ill-based hopes as they become ever more patently out of touch with reality, and few owners or executives manage their businesses by refusing to cut their losses until the failure of a new venture is proven with absolute certainty. For our government to persist in the kind of attitudes that people would immediately shun in their own affairs is irresponsible. When the burden of such irresponsibility falls mostly on our children, it is immoral.

As we shall see, fixing the problem will mean making genuine sacrifices, not just gestures. Because of the accumulated damage that our binge of overconsumption has already done, those sacrifices must now be greater than they need have been if we had corrected course by the middle of the decade. What is economically necessary will therefore be politically possible only if Americans fully comprehend what is at stake.

Chapter II

AMERICA IN
ECONOMIC DECLINE

Be not made a beggar by banqueting on borrowing.

—ECCLESIASTICUS, XVIII:33

Any country's ability to sustain economic growth over time depends critically on a proper balance of economic activity in the short run. Because we have invested so little during the 1980s, it is hardly surprising that our productivity gains have continued to be disappointing despite favorable tendencies in other factors that also affect business performance. If we continue along the fiscal trajectory that we have followed in this decade, productivity gains will be weak indefinitely and we will lose our traditional ability to achieve a rising standard of living from one generation to the next.

The chief counterpart to our overconsumption in the 1980s has been underinvestment. On average during the prior three decades, we invested 3.3 percent of our total income in net additions to the stock of business plant and equipment. Moreover, for periods long enough to average out the ups and downs of the business cycle, our investment rate showed little variation. Net business capital formation was 3 percent of total income on average during the fifties, 3.5 percent during the sixties, and 3.3 percent during the seventies. Thus far during the 1980s, the average has been just 2.3 percent. In no single year since 1981 have we achieved even 3 percent.[1]

As a result of this underinvestment, the historical trend toward more capital-intensive production—that is, more capital on average for each worker—has all but stopped. Between 1950 and 1980 the amount of plant and equipment behind the average American worker outside agriculture, measured at today's prices, rose from $26,000 to $43,100.[2] Even during the years when the work force grew at an extraordinary rate as the postwar baby boom generation came of age, growth of the capital stock more than kept pace. Growth of the work force has slowed since 1980, but we have invested so little that growth of our business capital stock has slowed by even more. By 1987 the average American worker had just $45,900 of plant and equipment behind him, barely more than in 1980. The rate at which the capital intensity of America's production rose had been cut by half.

At the same time, we have also systematically slighted other aspects of our investment which might have compensated for our lack of new plant and equipment. When production technologies are changing rapidly, investment in training the labor force can be just as important as investment in new factories for advancing the productivity of key industries that are at the forefront of a country's competitiveness. Even within the more limited context of physical investments alone, better roads and port facilities can sometimes do as much for a nation's productivity and competitiveness as new buildings and machines. As we shall see, however, in the 1980s we have neglected these aspects of our investment too.

Differences that may seem small in how much a nation invests can build up to large differences in economic well-being over time. If net business capital formation had merely continued during the 1980s at the average pace of the prior thirty years, so that the nation's stock of plant and equipment had grown at 3.9 percent per annum instead of the 2.9 percent that actually occurred, by 1987 the average worker would have had not $45,900 in capital behind him but $49,100. If overall business activity continues to expand in line with recent trends, the gap between the capital that American workers will have under these two investment rates will widen (in today's prices) to $47,100 apiece versus $52,000 by 1990 and $51,500 versus $62,600 by the end of the century: a difference of 20 percent.

Seemingly small differences in productivity growth build up over time as well. In 1987 the average American worker outside agriculture made $312 a week.[3] If business had managed since 1979 to achieve even the same 2 percent per annum productivity advance that had prevailed on average over the prior three decades—including the high growth years of the fifties and early sixties, the years of less rapid growth in the late sixties and early seventies, and the dry years of the mid- and late seventies —and if real wage gains had reflected this higher productivity, as they usually do, by 1987 the average pay would have been $336 a week instead. If the same 1.1 percent per annum productivity gain that has actually prevailed since 1979 continues, the average weekly pay (in today's prices) will rise merely to $323 by 1990, $341 by 1995, and $360 by the end of the century. Starting from the same base level in 1987, but with a 2 percent per annum average productivity gain, average weekly pay would instead be $332 by 1990, $366 by 1995, and $404 by the year 2000.

In the absence of significant progress in reducing the deficit, our investment will continue to fall short of even the modest average pace of the post-World War II period before the 1980s. So will our productivity performance and with it our economy's ability to deliver real income growth. Because the high rate of consumption encouraged by our new fiscal policy has left disproportionately little for investment, we may expect a lower standard of living for ourselves and for our children in the not so distant future.

If a lower investment rate and hence a lower rate of productivity growth were the only cost of our current fiscal policy, the case for a change might not be as compelling as it is. But our new fiscal policy has left another economic legacy which will depress Americans' real incomes even further: a growing foreign debt. Because of the need to service that debt, we will have to live on less than what we produce and earn. That the incomes from which we will have to pay interest on this debt will already be diminished, as a result of inadequate capital formation and sluggish productivity growth, will make the resulting deterioration in the standard of living still worse— probably enough so that without a change of policy real incomes in America will stagnate altogether.

By year-end 1986 America was a net debtor to other countries in the amount of $264 billion, or more than $1,000 for every citizen.[4] This debt has continued to accumulate as we have continued to import foreign-produced goods in excess of what we sell abroad. By year-end 1987 our net debt to foreigners was probably near $400 billion, or about $1,650 per citizen. By 1987 the sharp decline in the dollar exchange rate had finally begun to spur American exports, although it had not yet slowed our imports. The nation's trade deficit and hence our further accumulation of foreign debt therefore remain huge. Even on an optimistic reading of the prospects for further improvement in our trade position, by the end of the decade our net foreign indebtedness will be some $800 or even $900 billion. The swing in our net international investment position which has occurred just since 1980 will have amounted to a trillion dollars, or some $4,000 for every American.

Like the world's other debtors, whether large ones like Brazil and Mexico or small ones like Bolivia and Peru, America for the foreseeable future has no way to pay off this debt. The issue is instead how to pay the interest. Even at fairly modest interest rates, the interest on America's debt by the end of the 1980s will take between 1 and 2 percent of our total income *each year.* To prevent the debt we owe to foreigners from rising even further—in other words to pay the interest we owe rather than piling debt on debt by borrowing that too—our exports will have to exceed our imports by approximately that margin.

America as a debtor nation will therefore have to maintain a continual trade surplus. But the proceeds of that surplus will neither accumulate as wealth held abroad by Americans nor reduce America's international indebtedness. Net proceeds from international trade in the amount of 1 percent to 2 percent of our total income will merely pay the interest on the debt we will already owe by the end of the 1980s. To reduce this debt will require an even larger trade surplus.

What will moving to a trade surplus of this magnitude mean? In 1987 America's imports exceeded exports by $159 billion, or 3.5 percent of income.[5] To do no more than *balance* imports and exports will therefore require an adjustment equal to 3.5 percent of our yearly income—to which we will have to add another 1 percent to 2 percent, for the net interest due foreign lenders. To move from the 1987 trade *deficit* to a trade *surplus* of the size needed to service our foreign debt at the end of the decade will therefore require an adjustment equal to approximately 5 percent of each year's national income.

Some part of this 5 percent adjustment will necessarily consist of goods and services from abroad that we will do without. Fewer Americans will be able to buy foreign-made cars or cameras or watches or VCRs, or be able to travel abroad. The rest will consist of additional goods and services that we will produce not for our own use but for export. More American-made products will go abroad, and more Americans will work to provide hotel rooms and restaurant meals for foreign tourists.

When and how we will make this huge adjustment will not be entirely or even largely up to us. Like any borrower, our ability to keep borrowing more depends mostly on the lenders. How soon we must reduce our current high rate of consumption and how severe the adjustment will be will depend largely on how much appetite foreign investors have for owning assets in this country.

As long as foreign investors as a group continue to want to increase their holdings of assets in the United States more rapidly than we are increasing our holdings abroad, we can continue to borrow the interest on our outstanding debt and perhaps also finance an ongoing excess of imports over exports. But our ability to do so will depend on foreigners' continuing desire to own ever more American assets—including not just debt instruments, both public and private, but also stocks in American companies and the full range of direct investments in American business and real estate. As long as foreigners are willing, we can continue to finance what we owe by borrowing more and by selling off our assets.

No one can say confidently how long we can continue to run an international deficit in this way. But even America cannot increase its foreign debt indefinitely, any more than the world's other debtor countries can—nor, as we shall see, should we want to do so if we could. Even if our annual imbalance completely disappears by the end of the decade, so that our net foreign debt stabilizes at $800–900 billion, that sum will represent 15 percent to 20 percent of our yearly income. If our foreign trade deficit persists longer, our net debt position will grow larger still. But foreigners care about what their investments are worth in their own currencies—yen for Japanese investors, marks for German—and what the returns on these investments will buy in world markets. Foreign lenders will not continue indefinitely to accumulate our IOUs, without growing fears that we will not pay or that when we do it will be in inflated dollars. Foreign investors will not continue indefinitely to accumulate stocks and real estate and other assets in America, when the incomes and prices that matter for their own standard of living are those of their home countries.

Once foreigners accumulate enough American holdings so that they are unwilling to increase their net investments in the United States except to the extent of collecting the interest, dividends, and other returns that they earn on their American assets, the dollar will finally fall by enough to bring our imports and exports into balance. Any continuing excess of imports over exports at that point will just send more dollars abroad than the amount that foreigners want to put into additional holdings of American assets. As foreign investors collectively try to sell their extra dollars in the foreign exchange market, with no one to whom to sell except each other, they will only drive the dollar still lower. Attempts to support the dollar by our Federal Reserve System or by the central banks of other countries will prove futile. Concerted government action can temporarily arrest the decline of an overvalued currency, as we and our allies have done several times during the past few years. But as the repeated collapse of these stabilization efforts has demonstrated, the international dollar market is simply too big to be manipulated indefinitely by official intervention.

And once foreign investors have accumulated enough holdings in America that they are unwilling to increase their net position at all—in other words, when they are willing to increase their ownership of assets here no more rapidly than we are increasing our ownership of assets abroad—we will not even be able to borrow the debt service we owe. It is at this point that our trade balance will have to move into surplus in order for us to earn, rather than borrow, enough to pay the interest and dividends we will owe to foreigners. The dollar will then have to fall still further, to whatever level will enable American exports to exceed American imports by at least enough to earn each year's debt service. Otherwise, even the payment of interest and dividends would only send more dollars abroad than foreign investors need in order to buy American goods or want in order to buy American assets. And once again, the collective effect of the effort by foreigners to sell these extra dollars in the foreign exchange market will just push the dollar still lower. The dollar will finally stop falling only when it is low enough to enable America to earn a trade surplus.

In the aftermath of the spectacular collapse of our competitiveness in the 1980s, the notion of an American trade surplus any time within the foreseeable future seems fanciful at first thought. American industry has for all practical purposes abandoned to foreign producers many of what used to be its staple home markets. Most of the cameras and television sets, many of the computers and air conditioners, and an increasingly large share of the watches and automobiles that Americans buy, all come from other countries. American producers have also fallen progressively further behind in the international competition for many markets abroad, ranging from telephones to industrial equipment to project engineering. How can we not only bring our exports into line with imports but even go beyond that in order to service our huge foreign debt? With American manufacturing on the decline and the rest of the world increasingly able to feed itself, what can America make that the rest of the world will want to buy?

Putting the question this way loses sight of the essential role of the declining dollar in the international adjustment process we have already begun to undergo. And therefore it also misses the potential seriousness of this adjustment for our future standard of living and the risks it poses for the international trading community more generally.

It is difficult to escape the conclusion that the 74 percent average *increase* in dollar exchange rates between 1980 and early 1985—an increase largely driven by the budget deficit as we shall see—was the greatest single factor eroding the competitiveness of our industry. Other factors played a role, to be sure. The record of many of our major industries is studded with evidence of shortcomings of one form or other. But the turnaround in our export sales that has already begun in our manufacturing industries in the wake of the dollar's 43 percent decline since 1985, affecting such industries as aerospace, telecommunications equipment, electrical machinery, and computers, belies the sometimes fashionable view that our recent inability to compete has stemmed only from chronic failures on the part of management and labor rather than from our fiscal and monetary policies and the resulting overvaluation of the dollar during the first half of the decade.

With a lower dollar, American industries will once again be able to compete more effectively, even if there is no improvement in the other factors that have also hindered their performance in the past. Just as the dollar at its high point put even our most efficient industries at a competitive disadvantage, a far lower dollar can at least partly offset cost advantages that foreign producers enjoy from lower wages or even from more efficient production.

But to whatever extent rising exports do *not* bring our trade balance into surplus, shrinking imports will, once foreigners no longer want to increase their net holdings of American assets. Should American industry remain uncompetitive abroad even at a lower exchange rate, or should the American appetite for foreign-made goods persist even at higher prices, then the dollar will have to fall so much further. If enough Americans are still eager to buy Toyotas when the dollar is worth just 125 yen or Volkswagens when the dollar is worth only 1.70 marks, then the dollar will have to decline by even more. At some point—perhaps not until the price of a Toyota or a Volkswagen in dollars is twice that of a Cadillac—we will finally cut back on what we import from abroad.

Having to make do without all those Toyotas and Volkswagens, as well as the thousands of other imported products that made up our $159 billion trade deficit in 1987, will mean a sharp reduction in our standard of living. Having to suppress imports by still more, to generate a trade surplus large enough to service our outstanding debt, will depress living standards even further. Because we are not so indebted in relation to our income as most developing debtor countries—at least not yet —we need not anticipate all the costs these countries have had to pay in the attempt to meet their obligations, costs such as sharply depressed incomes, hyperinflation, capital flight, and the inability to make new investments. But the fact that we are not yet as indebted compared to income as Argentina or Mexico does not mean that our own adjustment will be free of costs.

The more we increase our exports of course, the less we shall have to reduce our imports. For this reason, our efforts to persuade our trading partners to remove restrictions that bar our goods from their markets, or to increase their own rate of overall economic expansion so that their appetite for our goods will be greater, are potentially important ways to make the necessary adjustment less harmful—and not just for us but for countries whose prosperity depends on their ability to sell us their goods. But our adjustment to a trade surplus will take place anyway, with or without growing exports, on whatever schedule foreign investors' asset preferences dictate.

And the longer we continue to borrow from abroad, for no other purpose but to pay for our overconsumption, the farther our living standards will ultimately have to fall. If our net foreign debt stabilizes by the end of the decade at almost $1 trillion, or about $4,000 per American on average, the required reduction in our total spending compared to our total income will amount to a once-for-all, permanent drop of about 5 percent. But if our binge of overconsumption continues into the 1990s with our annual trade imbalance still running at $100 billion, by 1995 our net foreign debt will be greater by not only $500 billion of accumulated export-import deficits but also the debt service payments we will have borrowed along the way. In that case our net foreign debt will approach $2 trillion, and the swing in our trade balance required to service this amount will be more like 6 percent or 7 percent of our yearly income than "only" 5 percent. Further prolonging our overconsumption until the end of the century would force us to accumulate still more debt and make the required adjustment, once it happens, more like 8 percent of our income.

What will make servicing this foreign debt all the harder, once we begin to do it, is that in the 1980s America has borrowed not to invest but to consume. After all, issuing debt in order to build new facilities is standard practice for most soundly run businesses. Most developing countries rely heavily on foreign capital to finance their early industrialization—as America did during several key periods of especially rapid investment in the nineteenth century. If a business is successful, it will earn enough from its new facilities to service its debt and add to its profits too. If a country's economic development is successful, as America's was, it will generate enough income to service its foreign debt and also raise its citizens' standard of living.

But America in the 1980s is accumulating foreign debt while decreasing domestic investment. Whether or not the returns from additional capital formation would be sufficient to service our new foreign debt is not an issue, because there is no additional capital formation in the first place. Because of our new fiscal policy, the share of income that we devote to net business investment in the 1980s is not greater than it used to be but smaller.

As we shall see, Americans in the 1980s are borrowing from foreign lenders on a scale that exceeds what their great-grandparents borrowed during the country's peak period of foreign borrowing for industrial expansion in the late 1860s and early 1870s, when borrowing from abroad averaged 2.2 percent of America's annual income. Since 1984 when Reagan's fiscal policy hit full stride, each year's net borrowing from abroad has exceeded that mark, averaging 3 percent of yearly income. In 1986 the net inflow was 3.4 percent of our income. In 1987 it was 3.5 percent.[6] But in America in this decade there is no equivalent to the expanding railroad system or the new steel industry that accounted for much of the foreign borrowing a century ago. There are only higher levels of consumer spending compared to our income than ever before. We are not borrowing against the future earning power of our new industries, for there are none. We are simply mortgaging our future living standard.

Regardless of when it occurs therefore, the reduction of American incomes required to restore international equilibrium will have an even harsher effect, because it will take place in a context of little real growth in any case. Even apart from the need to service our debt to foreigners, our new fiscal policy has left a lower stock of productive capital and therefore a

lower level of productivity than we otherwise would have had.*
Having to give up 5 percent of our income each year to balance
our accounts and pay interest to foreigners will depress our
prospects still further.

What will it actually mean to reduce our standard of living
by 5 percent—or even by 8 percent—when our income will
already be growing only slowly? And what are the risks that
such a reduction will touch off a spreading business contraction
that will have still further damaging consequences here and
perhaps abroad as well?

Recent history provides little guidance. No business downturn since World War II has involved a decline in our national
income of even half the magnitude at issue here, much less a
comparable decline in the consumption of the average citizen.
Moreover, even the more modest declines in our income that
have occurred have been short lived, with recoveries following
in fairly rapid order. The business recession that successfully
halted inflation at the outset of the Reagan presidency, for
example, was by many measures the most severe of the postwar
period. Even so, the fall in America's total income from the
peak quarter in 1981 to the trough quarter in 1982 was just 3.3
percent after allowing for inflation, and income had already
regained its early 1981 peak by mid-1983. Averaged over whole
years, the drop in real income from 1981 to 1982 was just 2.5
percent.[7]

More important, nationwide consumer spending never declined at all during the 1981–82 downturn. Some families had
to cut back, to be sure, but on average for all Americans, we

---

*In addition, as we shall see, even if we now change that policy by narrowing
the deficit, the 1986 "tax reform" has now dampened business incentives to
undertake new capital formation in the future.

absorbed the entire decline in our income by reducing what we invested, not by cutting back our standard of living. Aggregate consumer spending showed no growth throughout 1981 and very little growth in 1982 until nearly year-end when the recession ended. But at least spending did not decline, nor has it substantially declined in any of the other business recessions that have occurred since World War II.

The distinction between declining incomes and declining consumption is critical, because balancing our trade and servicing our foreign debt by cutting back on our already meager investment would be precisely the wrong way to salvage what is left of our future economic prospects.* The effect of our new fiscal policy on our spending patterns is systematic overconsumption. The path to a stable economic trajectory that does not lead to secular economic decline must involve reducing our consumption, at least relative to our income.

The most recent instance in which Americans sustained an actual decline in living standards was the Great Depression of the 1930s. Nationwide income, measured in after-inflation dollars, fell by 30 percent between 1929 and 1933. Consumer spending fell by 20 percent. A decline in average living standards of this magnitude is far greater than what is now required to restore our international balance, and so the horrors of the 1930s in any detail are not a good guide to what lies in store,

---

*To a large extent, that is what the debtor countries of Latin America have done to right their accounts. Mexico, for example, cut its imports from 14.1 percent of national income on average during 1979–81 (before the debt crisis) to 7.1 percent of income on average during 1983–85. It did so primarily by reducing imports of capital goods, which declined from $5.4 billion per year to $2.7 billion per year. As a result the share of Mexico's income devoted to gross investment of all forms declined from 23.6 percent to 16.4 percent on average during these two periods.[8]

even if market forces compel us to complete our required adjustment abruptly. But at the very least, the fact that we have not sustained an actual reduction in our average standard of living since the 1930s, not even temporarily, indicates the extent to which whatever decline we undergo in order to reverse the excesses of the 1980s will present a new experience for many Americans.

Just how much our standard of living will have to fall to right our international imbalance will depend in part on how productive and competitive we can be. Especially if events in the foreign exchange markets allow us to accomplish this adjustment over a period of years, growth of what we produce can take the place of a decline in what we consume, and growth in what we export can take the place of a decline in what we import. In the wake of the underinvestment that our new fiscal policy has brought however—including the failure to increase capacity in many of the industries that offer the best prospect of increasing our exports now that the dollar has fallen—more of the burden will have to fall on our standard of living than we otherwise might have hoped.

A continuation of our current trajectory until 1990, with productivity gains averaging 1.1 percent per annum as they have since 1979 and real wage gains running parallel, implies an average wage of $323 a week (at today's prices) in 1990. But that extrapolation does not reflect our need to begin exporting more than we import rather than vice versa. If the increase in our standard of living falls short of the increase in what we produce by an amount equal to 5 percent of our income, about enough to stabilize our international debt position, the average American worker's effective wage in 1990 will fall to $307 a week, well below the 1987 level. Part of the difference between $323 and $307, the part that corresponds most directly to our cutting imports, will come from higher prices for imported goods. With a cheaper dollar, foreign goods will cost more, so that what will look like a rising wage will not support a higher standard of living. The rest of the difference will reflect a shortfall of wages themselves from the level that otherwise would have been consistent with our productivity gains. Zero growth in our standard of living over four years (actually a slight decline), despite continuing productivity gains, will simply be part of the price we shall have to pay for the excessive consumption of the Reagan years.

Worse still, it is by no means clear that we can accomplish this adjustment without setting off a contraction of business activity that will make its consequences far worse. As we shall see, it is no simple matter for a nation to achieve a realignment of its economic policies and a reorientation of its domestic and international economic posture on the scale that is now required. If American business responds to the absence of consumer spending growth by cutting investment, a recession could follow, perhaps a severe one. If other developed countries act to block rising imports of our goods or if they allow their own economies to contract as the cheaper dollar prevents them from selling as much to us as they have in recent years, these actions could result in a worldwide economic contraction from which we could hardly isolate ourselves. If our overall income stagnates during this period because of either sluggish domestic investment or the contraction of foreign markets, then reducing our consumption compared to what we produce will mean not just the absence of any increase in the average American's standard of living but an outright decline, for the first time since the 1930s.

For example, it is certainly possible that any of these reactions to our economic adjustment, or all in conjunction, could induce a business contraction in America comparable to the pair of recessions we experienced in 1980 and in 1981–82. In that case, our real income in 1990 would be no greater than in 1987, and a 5 percent reduction in our consumption compared to our income would mean an outright reduction of what we consume by that amount. Five percent of national income is about two fifths of what we spend each year on all the food we eat, or about two thirds of what we spend for all our medical care. But meals and doctor bills are not the marginal items in most families' budgets. Five percent of national income is modestly more than what we spend each year for new cars or for clothing, or to run our houses and apartments. Five percent of our income is almost twice what we spend each year to buy new furniture and household appliances.

Just which items the average American family would cut back if it had to reduce its spending by this amount is impossible to say, in part because we have had no recent comparable experience. Nor is it possible to predict how the businesses that make and sell the products people do cut out would change their work force or their investment spending in response. What our experience of business recessions has shown, however, is that the resulting dislocations would not fall in equal proportion on all families or on all companies. Inequalities, both real and perceived, would multiply enormously. In any economic downturn, but probably even more so in this instance, economywide averages mask the real story of what happens to large numbers of Americans. Though *aggregate* consumer spending never declined during the 1981–82 recession, unemployment rose by five million and the number of Americans living below the poverty line rose by six million. Though *aggregate* income fell by only 3 percent, more than seventy thousand businesses failed just during 1981–83 alone.[9] The concrete implications of a 5 percent cut in our consumption—if that is the form our adjustment takes—would be even harsher.

. . .

If we can right our international balance more slowly, there-fore, we would reduce the likelihood of an outright decline in our living standard—though we would still have to face the consequences of little or no increase. Retarding this adjustment would also reduce the risk of an international business contrac-tion. But because our own international debt position would continue to deteriorate along the way, in the end a slower adjustment would increase the overall cost we would have to sustain.

For example, on our current 1.1 percent per annum produc-tivity growth trajectory, with comparable gains in real wages, the average American worker's weekly wage (in today's dollars) will be $360 by the year 2000. By then however, the adjust-ment needed to restore our international balance will be more like 8 percent of our income than 5 percent. That 8 percent would leave effective weekly income at the end of the century at only $331 a week, up from $312 a week in 1987 but not by much. By contrast, if we complete our adjustment by 1990, the average wage would rise to $342 a week (again, in today's dollars) by the year 2000, even apart from any gains that a new economic policy would bring in productivity growth. And if returning to a more normal investment rate also enables us to return in the 1990s to the more typical 2 percent per annum productivity gain that we maintained before the 1980s, the average wage at the end of the century would be $374: greater by well over 10 percent compared to what would follow from a slower adjustment.

In evaluating the respective risks and rewards of faster versus slower adjustments however, we should distinguish two aspects of what our overconsumption has meant in the 1980s and what reversing it will mean in the future. One consequence of our new fiscal policy, as we have seen, is that we have run a huge and chronic trade imbalance which has made us a net debtor country. The adjustment from an American trade deficit to an American trade surplus, which will stabilize our international debt position, will occur on a schedule mostly not of our own choosing. By acting in concert with other countries to affect the attractiveness of dollar assets relative to assets denominated in other currencies, we can influence the dollar's value and hence exert at least some influence on the speed of this adjustment. But for the most part it will be beyond our control.

By contrast, there is a second consequence of our new fiscal policy which we can correct on whatever schedule we choose: our persistent failure to invest adequately in productive assets at home. There is no reason that we must let the pace at which foreign investors drive down the dollar determine the pace at which we return to our historical average level of net investment—or better yet, to an above-average level so as to make up for what we have failed to do during the Reagan years. The first adjustment is a matter of our economic posture with respect to that of our trading partners. Even under less burdened circumstances, it would not be ours to determine alone. The second adjustment is a matter of dividing what we spend in America between consuming and investing. We *can* determine that allocation on our own. Even if events abroad somehow greatly increased the desire of foreign investors to hold assets in America, so that the dollar began to rise again and our trade to deteriorate further, we could still choose to cut back on our consumption and increase our investment. Even if our imports are rising, there is no reason for us to import cameras and VCRs instead of machine tools and steam turbines.

It is important to understand this distinction as we chart a new policy course in the aftermath of the Reagan years. Reducing the federal deficit will free up our saving and allow our real interest rates to fall and therefore will encourage capital formation. The decline in real interest rates will also probably help the dollar reach a level consistent with stabilizing our net foreign debt position if it has not already done so. But even if the dollar remains overvalued and our trade continues in deficit, reducing our *government* deficit will still be essential to replacing our overconsumption with renewed net investment. Whenever the transition to international equilibrium is complete, the faster productivity growth that follows from greater investment will support increased growth in our standard of living. But even if our foreign debt continues to accumulate for some years, with faster productivity growth we will at least be better able to pay the interest we owe without reducing our living standard still further.

Moreover, our ability to return to international balance by increasing our exports rather than shrinking our imports will also depend to a significant degree on investment in new capacity. Even the limited increase in export sales that has already occurred as a result of the cheaper dollar has begun to strain capacity in some of our key export industries, as faster order flows have led to lengthening backlogs rather than rising sales. After almost a decade of high real interest rates and a half-decade of an overvalued dollar, our ability to deliver these products has dwindled. Rebuilding capacity in these industries will require new investment in productive plant and equipment. It will also permit the return to higher-paying manufacturing jobs by at least some of the nearly two million workers who have moved to the service sector, usually at much lower pay.

Increasing our investment and hence our productivity growth is fully within our capacity. It is also necessary if America is not to slide into permanent economic decline, with all the social and political consequences that follow. What most

Americans think of first when asked how their country's economic system differs from anyone else's is their high and continually rising standard of living—in other words, the traditional American belief in the inevitability of economic progress. It is central to our belief that our system is better. It is no coincidence that the most serious erosion of confidence in this system in our history occurred during the Depression of the 1930s, when forward economic progress had stopped and prospects for its renewal appeared dim.

Our rising standard of living has not only made each generation of Americans materially better off than their forebears but, more important, has enabled each generation to afford a way of life more consistent with American cultural, social, and political ideals. One generation abolished slavery. Another eliminated sweatshops. Another relieved the degradation of poverty in old age. Another acted to bring blacks and other racial minorities, as well as a surge of new immigrants, into the American mainstream. In each case a rising level of material well-being for the country as a whole made the improvement in the character of American society significantly easier to achieve. Economic growth has historically proved a powerful solvent for social rigidities.

The material basis for this sustained combination of economic growth and social progress has been a steady rise in our productivity. Even before the 1980s however, our productivity gains slowed from the pace that not long ago we had taken for granted. After decades of growth averaging about 3 percent per annum, the output produced by the typical worker advanced by only 2 percent per annum in the late sixties and early seventies and then by only .5 percent per annum in the late seventies. It is hardly surprising that the slowdown in American productivity growth, especially from the mid-seventies on, rapidly became a major public policy issue. The halt in the traditional secular climb of living standards threatened basic assumptions that generations of Americans had made about their country, about their families, and about themselves. These anxieties were not frequently expressed publicly, probably because the values now suddenly at risk cut too deeply for comfortable airing. But the concern was there nonetheless. The prospect of a whole new generation of Americans who might live less well than their parents, had become distressingly real.

Ronald Reagan's 1980 call for a "New Beginning for the Economy" directly addressed just these fears. His economic program called for actions on a variety of fronts, intended to restore America's productivity growth to prior levels. Eliminating nettlesome regulations would free both workers and management to get on with the business of producing whatever they made. Relaxing environmental restrictions would free them still further, not just in smokestack industries but in primary production areas like mining and farming too. Most important of all, new incentives would encourage individual Americans to save and American businesses to invest. New plant and equipment would modernize production facilities and enhance the average worker's output. With productivity on the rise again, our standard of living would renew its traditional climb.

In his first televised address after his inauguration, President Reagan put America's productivity problem in stark terms: "Today this once great industrial giant of ours has the lowest rate of gain in productivity of virtually all the industrial countries with whom we must compete in the world market. We can't even hold our own market here in America against foreign automobiles, steel, and a number of other products."[10]

And in his first budget report to Congress, the new president clearly set out the objective of restoring America's productivity growth and pinpointed the central role of business capital formation in achieving that objective: "Since the late 1960s the rate of net capital formation (excluding spending mandated to meet environmental standards) has fallen substantially. For the five years ending in 1979, increases in real net business fixed capital averaged just over 2 percent of the Nation's real net national product, or one half the rate for the latter part of the 1960s. One of the major tasks facing the U.S. economy in the 1980s is to reverse these trends and to promote more capital investment. To combat the decline in productivity growth, to hasten the replacement of energy-inefficient machines and equipment, to comply with government mandates that do not enhance production, we must increase the share of our nation's resources going to investment. Both improvements in productivity and increases in productive jobs will come from expanded investment."[11]

It sounded inspiring. And as an abstraction it still does. But the promise of increased investment collided with the reality of Reagan's fiscal policy, centered on major tax cuts without significant restraints on government spending. As the growing federal deficit absorbed ever more of the country's saving, net business capital formation sagged instead of increased. And after a remarkably short spurt due to the upward turn of the business cycle, productivity resumed the sluggish growth pace that had stirred such widespread concern in the first place. What is different now is that we are nearly a decade further down the road of sustained low growth in our productive capacities and owe to foreigners a large and growing slice of even what our diminished capacities can produce.

Chapter III

AMERICA'S PLACE IN THE WORLD

The rich ruleth over the poor,
and the borrower is servant to the lender.

—PROVERBS, XXII:7

Economically stagnant countries cannot lead the world, no matter what their military strength. In time, other nations with stronger economies first match and then surpass their ability to produce goods and services for internal use as well as for export. Eventually these materially more successful nations become dominant in international affairs. Even if the sole economic effect of America's new fiscal policy were to cripple our growth, in time that wholly internal failure would constrain our international relations as well. But because we have also become a net debtor heavily dependent on foreign lenders, the implications are more serious than what inevitably follows from an isolated country's economic decline.

To begin, a fall in the dollar sufficient to enable us to switch from accumulating ever more international debt to servicing what we owe abroad would have an immediate impact on the trading patterns of other countries. America cannot export more unless our trading partners import more or export less. Likewise, if we cut our imports, other countries must suffer a reduction in their exports. The adjustment required to restore

America's international balance after the debacle of the 1980s will be so large as to force major changes in other countries' trading patterns as well, even if that adjustment occurs smoothly. But in all likelihood, the transition will not be smooth, and the sharp discontinuities along the way will pose still further difficulties both here and abroad. A return to high inflation in America—an ironic though not unlikely side effect of Reagan's economic policy as we shall see—would pose a perhaps even sharper dilemma for many of this country's major trading partners and competitors.

But like the domestic costs of this new policy, the more important international implications are likely to be intangible, hard to discern as they occur, and harder still to quantify. The key question is whether an indebted America can continue to play the central role in global economic and political affairs that we have now enjoyed for nearly half a century. And if not, what then? How will the international order rearrange itself to fill the resulting vacuum? And are we prepared—politically, militarily, even psychologically—for the shrunken role that our diminished wealth and power will bring?

America remains the largest single participant in world commerce, though not by much. In 1987 our $410 billion of imports and $251 billion of exports accounted for 15 percent of the world's recorded international merchandise trade.[1] America's share of world trade has declined irregularly ever since the end of World War II as other major trading nations have completed their postwar reconstruction programs and then gone on to achieve faster rates of overall economic growth, built in many cases around a special emphasis on producing for export. Even so, West Germany, the second largest participant in world trade, still accounted for only 14 percent in 1987, and Japan, the next largest, for just 9 percent.[2]

Though American exports have stagnated, our total international trade flows—including both exports and imports—remain the largest for any country, and by a sizable margin.*

Moreover, because global trade patterns are uneven, America bulks especially large as a trading partner for particular countries and regions. Our $85 billion of imports from Japan in 1987 represented more than a third of Japan's total merchandise exports. The $74 billion of goods that we bought from Canada accounted for more than three fourths of all Canada's exports. Even for Western Europe, which is far less dependent on sales to this country, America's $96 billion of imports in 1987 accounted for about a fifth of the total merchandise exports for the region considered as a whole.

The swing in America's trade balance required to stabilize our net international debt will amount to about 5 percent of our total income if the adjustment to a new equilibrium takes place by the end of the decade, and still more if—as is likely—it takes longer. In the context of the trade flows that occurred in 1987, a change equal to 5 percent of our income would have meant an American export-import *surplus* of some $65 billion instead of a $159 billion deficit. To have effected such an adjustment, we would have had to import $224 billion less or export $224 billion more or done some combination of the two. By 1990 or even later, the dollar totals involved will be correspondingly greater.

An adjustment in America's trade flows on this scale will not only lower our standard of living but also impose major burdens

*Some other countries' trade flows bulk larger in relation to their respective economies, however. Our $661 billion of merchandise imports and exports in 1987 amounted to 15 percent of our total income that year versus more than 50 percent for West Germany (but only 16 percent for Japan, now that the dollar is so cheap compared to the yen.)

on many if not most other countries participating in international commerce. For some of these countries the implications of this realignment are profoundly threatening. Much of the prosperity of Japan and the newly industrialized Asian countries has resulted from their ability to sell to American buyers a large share of what they export and hence a substantial share of what they produce overall. In 1987 exports to America equaled more than a fifth of total economywide production in the four "Asian tigers": Taiwan, South Korea, Hong Kong, and Singapore. Canada is likewise dependent on U.S. markets, so much so that the two countries are for many practical purposes economically integrated. Even in Western Europe, the industries that sell to American markets are in some cases heavily dependent on those sales, even if their economies more broadly are not. A dramatic decline in our imports from any of these countries would remove a basic pillar supporting their prosperity.

Eventually of course, these countries will presumably be able to redeploy their productive resources. But because of the huge amounts involved, what is at stake is more than the ordinary ebb and flow of world commerce. The implosion of our trade deficit from $26 billion in 1980 to $159 billion in 1987 bankrupted American companies, displaced American workers, in some cases eliminated entire industries, and depressed whole regions of the country. Reversing the process, and then some, by cutting back our imports by enough to deliver a substantial trade surplus, is likely to have corresponding effects on export industries abroad. And because no other country is as large as America and few countries are as economically diversified, balancing the damage to some industries against gains elsewhere will doubtless be an even more difficult challenge than it has been here.

These problems will be even more staggering for the fifty or so developing countries that already carry excessive debts denominated not in their own currencies but in dollars. The largest of these debtors, and the only ones whose defaults could plausibly endanger the world's financial structure, are in Latin America. These countries depend especially heavily on U.S. markets to earn dollars to service their debts. Brazil, for example, which suspended all interest payments to its foreign creditors in February 1987 (and then resumed payments a year later, after receiving a new $6 billion package of bank loans), heads the list of developing country debtors with $110 billion owed abroad.[3] The $8 billion of goods that we imported from Brazil in 1987 accounted for more than a fourth of Brazil's total exports.[4] Mexico, with $100 billion of foreign debt, has thus far kept its payments current but only through an extraordinary series of special arrangements coordinated and supported by the U.S. government. In 1987 the United States imported $20 billion of goods (about half of which was oil and gas) from Mexico, accounting for more than two thirds of Mexico's entire exports.

Because of the severe implications of a massive reduction in American imports, not just America but the world trading community as a whole has every reason to hope that we will eliminate our trade imbalance primarily through mechanisms that will involve our exporting more rather than importing less. A business recession in Europe or Asia brought about by shrinking exports could lead to a severe world economic contraction, while debt defaults by developing countries, if not handled adeptly, could threaten our banking system. American efforts to persuade other countries to eliminate barriers that close their markets to our goods therefore make sense in broader terms than merely our own self-interest. So do recent American efforts to persuade other industrialized countries to seek faster rates of overall business expansion and thereby increase their imports more generally.

The reluctance of these countries to adopt a more stimulative posture, articulated most clearly by the Germans, stems primarily from the fear that doing so would cause their spending to grow faster than their productive capacity, at the risk of inflation. It is increasingly questionable that these economies, which now suffer extremely high rates of unemployment by their own historical standards, could not safely increase their own production. But more important, this objection ignores the potential role that American exports could play if these countries did adopt more expansionary policies. Because we must make such a large trade adjustment and because with the dollar now cheap it is in so many countries' interest that we do so by boosting exports rather than slashing imports, creating a gap between demand and production that American goods can fill in other countries is precisely the point.

But this strategy will make sense only if American industry can produce goods that these other countries will want. And so here we do face the nagging question of what America can make that other countries will want to buy.

From the narrow perspective of whether or not America adjusts its trade balance, once foreigners tire of adding to their mountain of weakening dollars and real assets that they can sell only for dollars, it does not matter whether we can succeed in boosting our exports. If we can, so much the better. But if we cannot, the falling dollar will eventually do the job simply by making a wide variety of everyday imports too expensive for Americans to afford.

From the perspective of the severe costs that so large a decline in American imports would impose, however, not just here but abroad—not just on the Americans who buy the VCRs but on the Japanese who make them as well—the ability of American industry to compete successfully in world markets remains crucial. The cheaper dollar will be a great advantage. But the decline of American competitiveness has more diverse roots than merely an overvalued exchange rate. Our failures in this regard have hardly been a matter of fiscal policy only.

Our inadequate capital formation during the Reagan years, including especially the absence of any significant growth in investment in our manufacturing industries even after the 1981–82 recession ended, will make it all the harder for us now to increase our exports, no matter how Germany and Japan run their economies. So will the impact of the 1986 tax legislation, which has sharply increased the cost to American business of investment in new equipment. By impeding the ability of American industry to compete effectively in world markets, these policies have raised the real cost of this adjustment not only for us but for other countries too. On neither side are the required transitions likely to be smooth.

The longer this adjustment takes and the more problematic it is along the way, the greater is the threat that protectionist measures—either here or abroad—will constrict the world's trading system. President Reagan's consistent rhetorical devotion to free trade notwithstanding, America during the 1980s has taken more steps away from genuine free trade than in any comparable period since World War II. Outright duties, like the 100 percent tariff imposed on some electronic and semiconductor products in 1987, have been infrequent. But protectionism built on back-door devices like "voluntary" export restraints, which exclude foreign-made goods while maintaining the fiction of free trade, is protectionism nonetheless. The share of America's nonoil imports subject to such nontariff restriction has already grown from 17 percent in 1981 to 25 percent in 1986.*5 And now businessmen abroad are conclud-

*This measure includes the "voluntary" restraints that Japan has imposed since 1981 on automobile exports to the United States, despite the fact that

ing that the decline in the dollar since early 1985 is a modern equivalent to the Smoot-Hawley tariff we imposed in 1930.

The protectionist steps that America has taken so far have been small and incremental, however, compared to what they might have been—and under some circumstances, what they might still be. Proposals for more general trade barriers, or for import surcharges specifically directed against countries with which we run large bilateral trade deficits, have repeatedly failed to attract sufficient support in Congress. In 1986 for example, the House of Representatives passed an Omnibus Trade Bill which would have required any country running a surplus of more than $3 billion against America (not counting oil exports) to cut its exports to this country by 10 percent each year; but the bill failed in the Senate. The trade bill passed by both houses of Congress in 1988 contained no such provision. In light of the damage that some of our industries have suffered from the abrupt collapse of their ability to compete, it is re- markable that our own slide toward protectionism has not been more precipitous.

If America's trade adjustment proceeds smoothly, protec- tionist sentiment will probably soften further. The cheaper dollar, functioning in place of a general tariff, will make foreign products more expensive for Americans, so that American pro- ducers will be more competitive in their home markets. Fewer American industries will claim economic damage from unfair foreign pricing. And once our trade deficit has visibly begun to shrink, the search for dramatic measures to address an econo- mywide imbalance will seem less urgent.

Even so, our progress toward a trade surplus will not neces-

---

since 1985 the United States has not *officially* requested these restraints. They have remained in force nonetheless, with a 1988 quota of 2.3 million vehicles.

sarily be rapid, and it will certainly not be uniform. In industries that are left behind, both management and labor will still have strong incentives to seek protection against foreign competition. Despite the accumulating evidence documenting the astronomical cost that such measures have imposed on America as a whole—$77,000 per year for each job saved in the shoe industry, for example, or $110,000 per year for each job saved by the "trigger pricing" formula on steel—those industries that see potential benefits for themselves and their workers have powerful incentives to push hard for them.[6] The more uneven the adjustment, the greater will be the remaining pressure to impose protectionist measures here in retaliation for real or perceived barriers abroad.

Protectionist solutions are risky. When they are aimed at genuinely restrictive foreign practices, which are subject to government control, they may lead to corrective action abroad. But they may simply provoke retaliation, especially in cases where the allegation of restrictions abroad is mostly a pretext for weak American firms to seek protection against more efficient foreign producers or where an American industry seeks to protect its home market regardless of whether it competes for foreign sales. At least for the immediate future, most of the highly visible economic events likely to provide the momentum behind protectionist pressures in America have already taken place. The challenge to American policymakers will be to contain these pressures as the nation's trade adjustment proceeds.

The real risk now is that protectionist sentiment will arise in other countries. Foreign industries that have invested on the basis of an overvalued dollar will increasingly find their facilities unprofitable as the dollar falls. In the absence of a major world expansion, much of America's increased exports and reduced imports will represent lost sales to producers in other countries. Even with a sustained expansion, the effect will be only modestly less. To the extent that the industrial countries' collective balance of trade in manufactured goods with the developing world is bound to deteriorate in the long run, as new competitors use their far cheaper labor to exploit imported technologies, the lower dollar will only shift this secular adjustment from us to the Japanese, the Germans, and others among today's major exporters.

Even more important, protectionism threatens to erode the fabric of international cooperation in a broader context. After all, America has led the effort toward an ever freer trade system not merely as a matter of commercial policy but in the interest of free-world solidarity more broadly. It is impossible to know how far the economic fragmentation that widespread protectionism would bring might also threaten such other interests as multinational security arrangements.

A further risk to the international economic order and to America's place in it is that we will return to high inflation. Much of the financial instability that emerged in the late sixties and the seventies was the result of inflation both in America and abroad. This instability in turn affected world currency markets as well as markets for financial assets more generally. It caused not just volatile prices, often day to day and even hour to hour, but in some cases the failure of major financial institutions. None of these failures ever developed into a cumulative default to threaten the world financial structure. But market participants and government policymakers were keenly aware of such possibilities nonetheless. That no real disaster actually materialized was largely the result of prompt response, by American authorities among others, to isolate and offset the specific source of major financial disturbances.

Despite the continuing internationalization of the world's financial markets, America's currency remains at the center of the global trading and asset-holding systems. More than half of all recorded international borrowing and lending normally takes place in dollars. The fraction of international commercial transactions settled in dollars is not recorded, but it is almost certainly far greater. Central banks around the world typically hold between two thirds and three fourths of their international reserves in dollars. A return to rapid inflation in America —this time as a by-product of the effort to relieve the burdens of debt owed both at home and abroad, after the extraordinary borrowing of the Reagan years—would pose serious economic and financial problems in the 1990s, no less than it did in the seventies.

The first economic decision that other countries will face if America returns to high inflation is whether to adopt inflationary policies for themselves as well, rather than allow their currencies to rise even further against the dollar. If they do opt to inflate, then the result of our turn to inflation as a way of reducing the value of our debt will be to reintroduce inflation globally. There is no reason to expect the ensuing financial instability to be any less threatening under current circumstances than it was in the seventies. International trading volumes are now much larger. New risk-oriented financial instruments like futures and options have proliferated. More institutions than ever before are engaged in high-volume trading, often on the basis of razor thin margins. If anything, a return to high inflation in the next decade would pose even greater risks to financial stability than in the seventies.

Alternatively, other countries might resist the temptation to inflate. Despite the series of finance ministers' meetings that began in February 1985 at New York's Plaza Hotel, there is now no commitment to maintain stable exchange rates remotely comparable to the obligations that countries accepted under the Bretton Woods system from the end of World War II until August 1971. Nor are there any commitments comparable to the series of makeshift agreements negotiated during the repeated crises immediately after Bretton Woods collapsed. No country has to import America's inflation (or disinflation, for that matter) unless it chooses. If America returns to high inflation, the pressure for other countries to follow will stem not from international obligations but from the desire to protect their own industries' competitive position, as foreign exchange markets only imperfectly keep the real values of their currencies in line with an increasingly inflated dollar. No doubt some governments will be more susceptible to such pressures, and so more likely to adopt inflationary policies if America does, than others.

If most countries refrain from inflation, however, America's return to high inflation is also likely to erode our ability to remain at the center of the international financial system. Since August 1971, when Richard Nixon terminated the dollar's central role in the Bretton Woods system and thereby effectively abolished the system as a whole, America's central position has been a matter of fact rather than legal obligation. Even so, America has continued to serve as the effective anchor of the international financial system as it had under Bretton Woods. At times of crises, like the failure of Germany's Bankhaus Herstatt in 1974 and of America's own Continental Illinois in 1984, and throughout the series of near defaults by Mexico and Argentina and other debtors that has continued through 1988, the fact of our ability to expand our own economy as needed—and more important to serve as a lender of last resort if necessary—has been essential to international financial stability.

The ability to fill this role has rested on more than the mere size of the American economy or even of American holdings abroad. It has stemmed also from the facts that the dollar is the world's chief vehicle for international trading, financing, and asset holding, and that our Federal Reserve System can instantly create dollars at its discretion to lend to distressed borrowers whose failure might otherwise threaten the financial system as a whole. Until recently, it has also reflected the fact that America, as a growing net creditor country, was already supplying financial resources to foreign markets in excess of what we were borrowing from abroad.

A return to high inflation in America, especially if other countries resist the temptation to follow, will accelerate the erosion of the dollar's central role in the international financial system as well as America's ability to ensure world financial stability. A lender of last resort is effective only if it can lend in the currency that distressed borrowers owe, or at least in a currency that their creditors are willing to accept. The willingness of the State Bank of the U.S.S.R. to lend at its discretion in rubles makes no contribution whatever to international financial stability, because nobody wants rubles. The Federal Reserve's ability to create dollars and place them in the right hands helps in a crisis only if too few dollars in those hands produced the crisis in the first place.

With renewed American inflation, the international financial system would eventually evolve toward a new structure, in which the anchor previously provided by America would be replaced by some new set of arrangements. What these would be is impossible to foresee in any detail. Nations like Japan and Germany, which have maintained the surpluses corresponding to America's deficit in the 1980s and therefore have replaced America as net creditors, will presumably play a major role. Whether that means an enhanced role for their currencies as well or the development of further financing vehicles involving combinations of currencies, or even that these countries would act in a stabilizing role through their willingness to redeploy promptly their own massive holdings of dollars, is unclear. The bank of Japan cannot simply create dollars without limit the way the Federal Reserve can. But it has already accumulated sufficiently large dollar holdings—probably $65 or even $70

billion by year-end 1987—to be able to stem many potential
crises on its own.[7]

Whatever form this evolution takes, however, two unhappy
aspects are probably unavoidable. First, the transition to satisfactory new arrangements will take place too slowly, and with
too little surety, to avoid a substantial interval during which the
international financial system is exposed to distinctly greater
risks. Effective new arrangements may not emerge at all until
the eruption of some fresh crisis precipitates action. Second,
whatever new world financial order may evolve, America's role
in it will be much diminished.

An increasingly popular view in recent discussions of America's trade prospects is that our export-import balance not only
must swing into surplus eventually, but indeed is likely to do
so *soon*, because foreign lenders have by now exhausted their
willingness to hold ever greater amounts of American IOUs
and will henceforth push the dollar ever lower by trying to sell
the dollars our continuing trade deficit sends abroad. Private
foreign investors' virtual boycott of the American securities
markets in early 1987, which forced foreign central banks to
take their place as buyers of our securities in order to arrest the
dollar's fall, appeared to lend credence to this idea. So did the
abrupt further decline of the dollar immediately after the stock
market crashed later that year.

This view would be persuasive if there were nothing other
than American-made goods and American-issued IOUs that
foreigners could take in exchange for their dollars. But foreign
investors can and do use dollars to buy American assets other
than IOUs. Stocks listed on the New York Stock Exchange,
direct ownership interests in American companies, office buildings in New York City, condominiums in Miami, and farm
land in Kansas and California, all must be bought with dollars.

Foreigners are already tiring of accumulating ever greater amounts of certificates of deposit issued by American banks and bonds issued by the U.S. Treasury, but they will still need dollars if they want to buy more of our real assets. There is every reason to believe that they will want to do so, at least until their mix of paper-to-real holdings in the United States returns to a satisfactory balance from the point of view of the risks entailed by holding these assets.

Even in the climate of price stability that has prevailed since the 1981–82 business recession, foreign investors have been increasingly interested in American assets other than deposits and debt securities. Some of this interest has simply taken the form of ordinary stock buying for portfolio purposes. Foreign purchases of American stocks (net of foreign sales) have grown from an average of just $2 billion per year in the late seventies and still only $4 billion per year during the early 1980s to $17 billion in 1986 and more than $15 billion in 1987. Net purchases of American stocks by Japanese investors alone exceeded $3 billion in 1986 and then increased to $11 billion in 1987.[8] With Japanese stocks selling at seventy times earnings on average versus twenty times earnings for American companies before the crash and fifty-five versus thirteen afterward, the American market is clearly attractive.*[9]

Increasingly, however, foreign investors have bought shares in American companies and American real estate to acquire not simply ownership but control. The most highly visible of

---

*Even so, when New York Stock Exchange stocks fell by 29 percent on average in October 1987, Tokyo stock exchange prices fell by only 15 percent. The combined effect of the smaller price decline in Japan and the rising yen-dollar exchange rate made the total value of all stocks traded on the Tokyo market larger than that of all stocks traded on the New York exchange.

these transactions have occurred as part of the more general wave of mergers, acquisitions, and other reorganizations that has swept through corporate America. In 1984 Nestlé (which is Swiss, although most Americans think of the company as our own) paid $3 billion to buy Carnation. In 1986 Unilever (which is Dutch) paid $3 billion for Chesebrough-Pond's, and Hoechst (which is German, but is one-fourth owned by Kuwait) paid $2.8 billion for Celanese. In 1988 Bridgestone (which is Japanese) paid $2.6 billion for Firestone.[10] Other foreign acquisitions of American businesses, in smaller amounts for single transactions, have become commonplace. Foreign purchases of smaller businesses, ranging from manufacturing facilities to gold mines to publishing companies and from agriculture to job placement services to banks are now everyday events.

In some cases, foreign investors have bought significant interests in American firms but have resisted becoming sole owners, arrangements that are often a precursor to ultimate full foreign ownership. For example, beginning in 1969 British Petroleum became the principal shareholder in Standard Oil of Ohio and increased its holdings to 55 percent over the years. In 1987 BP (now one-fifth owned by Kuwait) paid another $8 billion to buy the 45 percent of Sohio it did not already own. Similarly, in 1984 Royal Dutch/Shell (jointly Dutch and British), which had historically owned 70 percent of the American company known as Shell Oil, paid $6 billion for the remaining 30 percent.[11]

Some of the most spectacular foreign purchases of American real assets in the 1980s, especially by Japanese investors, have been major blocks of real estate. In New York alone, Japanese companies have paid $610 million for the Exxon building, $250 million for the Mobil building, $175 million for the ABC building, and $670 million for just thirty-seven floors of the new Citicorp building. With the price of prime commercial real estate approximately ten times higher in Tokyo than in New York on the basis of current exchange rates (in part as a result of Japanese government farm subsidies, which increase land prices generally), office buildings in New York are bargains by comparison. In Los Angeles another Japanese firm paid $620 million for the ARCO Plaza building.[12] Dozens of smaller purchases, as well as partial ownership and financing arrangements, have also proliferated across the country. By 1987 foreign investors owned almost half of the commercial real estate in downtown Los Angeles, more than a third in Houston, and nearly a fourth in New York.[13] Moreover, foreign purchases of American real estate have involved more than just the highly visible transactions done by major financial institutions in the major city centers. As economic distress has driven large amounts of "flight capital" out of Latin America, much of it has found its way into houses, condominiums, and farms throughout this country.

Foreigners have also increasingly moved not just to invest in Wall Street but to own the firms that run it. With American securities firms strapped for capital to support their growing underwriting and trading activities, selling pieces of themselves has been an attractive source of new cash. Foreigners have been ready buyers. In 1986 Nippon Life Insurance bought a 13 percent interest in Shearson Lehman Brothers for $538 million, and the Sumitomo Bank paid $500 million for a one-eighth interest in Goldman Sachs. In 1987 Yasuda Mutual Life Insurance paid $300 million for a one-fourth interest in Paine Webber. At the same time, the four large Japanese securities firms—Nomura, Daiwa, Nikko, and Yamaichi—already account for a fifth of all trading in U.S. Treasury securities *in the United States* and perhaps as much as a tenth of all trading on the *New York* Stock Exchange.[14]

As a result of such major transactions, together with hundreds of others that remain largely invisible, the annual flow of foreign direct investment in America has sharply increased. Including all recorded transactions in which foreign investors have bought real estate or whole companies or more than 10 percent of the stock of a publicly held corporation, foreign direct investment in America (net of sales) rose from just $7 billion per year in the seventies to $20 billion per year in the early 1980s, to $25 billion in 1986, and to $41 billion in 1987.[15] In 1987 alone, there were six separate transactions in which foreign investors spent $1 billion or more at a time on entirely new investments—new for them, that is—in America. There were also 47 such transactions ranging in size from $100 million to $1 billion and another 504 smaller than $100 million, all without even counting transactions in which a foreign partner's investment went to increase its share in a business of which it was already part owner or transactions in which the acquired company's assets came to less than $1 million.[16]

Although some of this investment has represented the creation of new productive assets, at least during the years when the dollar was strong, the great majority of it did not. Everybody knows about the auto plant that Nissan built in Smyrna, Tennessee, and the one that Honda built in Marysville, Ohio, and the new Sony plant in San Diego. These new capital spending projects have been the exceptions, however. For the most part, foreign investors are simply buying up America's *existing* productive assets, not constructing new ones. In 1987 foreign investors spent $26 billion in fresh investment to buy existing American businesses, including $16 billion worth of American manufacturing companies. By contrast, in 1987 foreigners spent only $5 billion to establish new businesses in America, and half of that went into forming new real estate companies.[17] Now that the falling dollar has reduced production costs in America compared to those abroad, more foreign companies are beginning to build new plants here, but the extent of this development remains small compared to each year's total foreign investment in America.

Despite the rapid acceleration of the past few years, foreign purchases of American real assets have not kept pace with the flood of dollars that we have sent overseas to pay for our trade imbalance. Buying a company is usually a slow process. So is buying a major block of real property. Careful investors want to search for potential acquisition targets, evaluate alternatives, and assess their ability to manage a business once they own it. As a result, foreigners have accumulated most of their growing dollar holdings in the form of bank deposits, U.S. Treasury bonds, or other debt securities, as they continue to explore opportunities to buy real assets.

On average throughout the seventies, 47 percent of the assets held in America by foreign investors other than central banks consisted of stocks and direct investment holdings.[18] As of year-end 1980 45 percent of foreigners' American holdings were in stocks and direct investments. Yet despite the acceleration of stock purchases and direct investments in the 1980s and despite the market rally that sharply raised the prices of their stocks after mid-1982, by year-end 1986 only 35 percent of foreigners' holdings here were in stocks and direct investments. And those countries that have been accumulating dollars the fastest have lagged even further behind. Japan's $156 billion of holdings in America as of year-end 1986, for example, included only $6 billion in stocks and another $23 billion in direct investments.[19]

There is every reason to expect that foreign investors will put progressively more of their dollars in America's real assets as time passes. Merely to restore the recent historical balance between what foreigners hold as debt and what they hold in real assets will require vast continuing purchases of stocks and direct investment. The prospect of high inflation, which would erode the value of deposits and debt instruments denominated in dollars, would only make such real assets look all the better.

An unfortunate implication of this foreign appetite for America's real assets is that our avid consumption of foreign goods not paid for by exports may not end as soon as many people expect. Massively shifting our trade so that we export more than we import is one way for us to make good on what we owe to foreigners. But that is not the only way. Another, to which we are increasingly turning, is to hand over our real assets.

Foreigners may not be willing to accumulate American IOUs in exchange for their goods indefinitely, but this does not mean that they will not want dollars for the purchase of other assets. As long as they continue to exchange for American assets the dollars that they receive as a result of our trade deficit, the downward pressure on the dollar that would otherwise result from their trying to sell those dollars will not occur. Just which American assets they take in exchange, our paper IOUs or our productive capacity, is unimportant in this context. What matters is that foreigners will be using their dollars to buy something that America can provide—in this case our industry and real property—instead of selling their dollars in the foreign exchange market.

As a result, it will take us all the longer to stop running up ever larger amounts of foreign debt and start paying the interest on what we already owe. A family with no assets to sell can consume more than it earns only as long as its creditors are willing to keep accepting its IOUs. But a family that owns a house and a car, and some stocks too, can keep excess consumption going longer by selling these assets off one by one. The same principle applies to countries engaging in international finance.

America has plenty of assets to sell. As of year-end 1986, the combined value of all the businesses and privately owned real estate in America was $12 trillion of which foreigners owned only $209 billion.[20] Foreign investors held only 6 percent of the stock in American corporations.[21] And although hard information on who owns land is notoriously difficult to find, studies suggest that foreigners own only about 2 percent of America's farm land.[22]

Selling off our real assets will keep the party going longer, and so the inevitable adjustment will be easier to swallow both for us and for our international trading partners. But it will also make the mortgage on our future and the reduction in our standard of living required to meet the payments all the greater.

Prolonging our overconsumption at the cost of handing over the ownership of ever more of our national assets will affect how we live and how we regard ourselves and our country, in ways that run deeper than a 25 percent or even an 8 percent difference in average living standards.

America has traditionally been a nation of owners. From the earliest days of the European settlement, emigration to America offered individuals the opportunity to own a farm, a business, or a house. So did moving westward, as the country's expansion steadily pushed back the frontier. The values bred in that tradition remain strong, even as the twentieth century nears an end. The two thirds of American families who own their own homes represent a greater share than in any other industrial country, and owning a home is typically the greatest single economic aspiration among the other one third.[23] More Americans own their own cars, their own businesses, and their own farms than the citizens of any other country.

We have always been suspicious of foreign acquisition of American businesses and real property. Twenty-nine states, including practically all that are heavily agricultural, have laws that restrict foreign ownership of farmland in one way or another.*[24] During the mid-seventies, when OPEC's member countries were amassing large amounts of dollar reserves in the wake of sharply higher oil prices, and payments scandals of various kinds reminded us almost daily about differences between our commercial practices and what was standard elsewhere, we were especially apprehensive of foreign control of American businesses. Even so, on the whole we have typically acquiesced in what little foreign ownership there has been.

But foreign ownership of America's real assets was always small compared to what Americans owned abroad. As of year-end 1980, foreigners' direct investments in American businesses and real property amounted to $83 billion, while our holdings abroad came to $216 billion, mostly in primary production and manufacturing facilities.[25] More than half of our direct holdings abroad as of 1980 were in Europe and Canada, but the remainder were spread through developed and developing countries worldwide, including $39 billion worth in Latin America, $23 billion in Asia, and $6 billion in Africa.

Especially since World War II, foreign investment by American business has represented the internationalization of the modern corporation. Producing abroad—using foreign labor and working in close proximity to foreign raw materials—was a rational way for the technological leaders among American business to exploit their superior know-how. Foreign affiliates of U.S. companies primarily served foreign markets, with some two-thirds of their sales typically taking place within the host country.[26] Throughout these years, what continually captured attention both here and abroad was the predominance of *America's* international holdings, not the reverse.

*Because not all of these states have reporting requirements, however, and reporting of land ownership in those that do is often haphazard, the practical effectiveness of these restrictions is questionable.

This imbalance in America's favor has now disappeared. By year-end 1986 foreigners' direct investments here amounted to $209 billion versus $260 billion of our direct investments abroad. Although foreign direct investment in America has lagged behind the accumulation of dollars abroad, and has done so for easily understandable reasons, it has nonetheless trebled while our direct investment abroad has increased by only one fifth. Including ownership of stocks for portfolio purposes, foreigners' 1986 real holdings in this country added up to $377 billion versus only $311 billion of American holdings abroad.

This spectacular reversal does not simply reflect our more stable political environment or even a superior opportunity for business profit here. America has always been politically more stable than most other countries, and at most times our businesses have been more profitable. But until 1981 America was a net creditor country and increasingly so. As we shall see, our new fiscal policy was the principal force that pushed the dollar to such an overvalued level until 1985 and was therefore, after allowing for the lag of commercial flows behind exchange rate movements, the main source of our widening international trade gap through 1987. As we have sent enormous net flows of dollars abroad to pay for the resulting excess of imports over exports, this policy has transformed us from a creditor to a debtor. No wonder that the foreign investors who hold this ongoing accumulation of dollars have gradually moved some of it into stocks and direct investments, instead of leaving it all in bank deposits and Treasury bonds.

Nobody would suggest that increasing foreign ownership of Zaire's assets, or Ecuador's—or for that matter Argentina's or Brazil's—reflects the inherent stability of these countries' political systems or the attractiveness of their business climates, rather than their inability to export enough to finance their imports plus the debt service that they owe. The same circumstances with the same result have suddenly emerged in America.

What is at issue here is more than just the possibility of an irrationally xenophobic reaction to the fact that foreign investors want to hold real assets in America, and that they increasingly do so. During most of the postwar period, world trade has typically expanded more rapidly than the economic growth of individual countries. At the same time, major advances in communications and data processing have fostered the integration of world capital markets. The ensuing international diversification of asset holding helps protect investors from excessively concentrated exposure to risks that are specific to their own country. It also enables countries where the assets are located to gain from experience with different technologies and with new forms of management and entrepreneurship.

But what is happening in America in the 1980s is not just international diversification of the assets that we own matched by a corresponding diversification in the ownership of assets here. Foreign ownership of American assets is rapidly increasing on a *net* basis. Unlike in the past, foreign purchases of American assets for the most part have no counterpart in American acquisitions abroad. As we have seen, the ownership gap in our favor is gone, and the gap in the other direction is rapidly widening.

Ironically, America, with its open financial markets, is servicing foreign debt in precisely the way that debtors like Mexico and Brazil have been mostly unwilling to accept and that we have been reluctant to impose on them. During the 1980s, it has become increasingly clear that many developing countries not only can never repay their foreign debt but cannot practically hope to pay even the interest on what they owe. Their creditors, including American banks, have therefore suggested swapping this debt for ownership shares in the debtor countries' banks, their trading companies, and their productive assets. The volume of such transactions has begun to increase significantly, with some $3 billion authorized in 1985 and more like $6 billion in 1986.[27]

But the debtor countries have rejected most of the more far-reaching debt-for-equity swaps that their creditors have proposed, on the ground that discharging their debts in this way would amount to giving away their national patrimony. Foreign ownership might make the assets of these countries more productive, but the profits in whole or in part would then accrue to the foreign owners. Whether these countries will ultimately have to accept such swaps in amounts large enough to make a major dent in what they owe will depend on what alternatives are available to them: whether creditor country governments or multilateral organizations like the International Monetary Fund and the World Bank are willing to extend new loans, whether the banks will grant debt relief in one form or another, and in extreme circumstances, how severe the penalties are for out-and-out debt repudiation. At least so far, these debtor nations have usually refused to swap their debt for ownership of their productive assets at the prices implicit in the offers they have received.

But what is happening in America's open markets amounts to exactly this kind of exchange. Foreign investors holding deposits in American banks or U.S. Treasury securities or the debt of most other American borrowers can liquidate these assets at any time. They are then free to use the proceeds to buy stocks or whole companies or blocks of American real estate. No official permission is necessary.

Moreover, the falling dollar has now presented foreign investors with the opportunity to pick up American assets cheaply. The decline of the dollar-yen exchange rate from 260 in early

1985 to 130 in 1987 meant that dollars bought 50 percent less in Tokyo than before. But apart from a small amount of inflation, dollars continued to buy the same amount in New York. Little wonder that Japanese insurance companies, which are so flush with dollars that in 1987 one paid $40 million to buy a Van Gogh painting, have begun using their dollars to buy up Manhattan's office towers.

The U.S. government has been unwilling to force the Latin American debtors into accepting significant debt-for-equity swaps, on the ground that the potential consequences for the debtor countries are sufficiently grave that they should enter such arrangements only by their own volition. But at home our own policies have imposed just these consequences on ourselves.

Becoming a nation of tenants rather than owners will jar sharply against our traditional self-perceptions. America will no longer be an owner, directly influencing industrial and commercial affairs abroad. At the same time, we will have to accept the influence and control exercised here by foreign owners. The transition is certain to be demoralizing and probably worse if potentially dangerous frictions also develop as the ordinary resentments of renters against landlords and workers against owners increasingly take on nativist dimensions.

The changes brought about by our new fiscal policy will also affect America's international power and influence in even more general ways. It is not coincidental that America's emergence as a world power in the twentieth century has occurred simultaneously with our transition from a debtor dependent on inflows of foreign capital to a creditor supplying investment capital to the rest of the world.

World power and influence have historically accrued to creditor countries. In the sixteenth and seventeenth centuries,

Spain's preeminent position was based not merely on its armadas but also on its ability to relend the silver that flowed from mines in Mexico and Peru. Tiny Holland became a world-class power in the seventeenth century mostly on the strength of profits from trade that enabled the Dutch to pursue a colonial empire in the East and West Indies and also lend significant amounts in Britain, Austria, and the Baltic countries. The Pax Britannia of the nineteenth century rested not just on the fact that the Royal Navy ruled the seas but also on Britain's ability to supply development capital to other countries. Germany's attempt to emulate Britain at the end of the nineteenth century and in the first decade of the twentieth, and France's efforts on a smaller scale, likewise involved deploying large amounts of capital to investment abroad.

Britain at the outset of what became the industrial revolution was the first country to achieve widespread advances in methods of production. As a result, from the mid-eighteenth century onward Britain achieved consistent trade surpluses and therefore was a steady net lender of financial capital to the rest of the world. Once Britain's foreign holdings had become substantial, British net foreign investment represented not only the proceeds earned from exports in excess of imports but also reinvestment of the interest earned on foreign loans already in place. Net foreign investment grew from about 1 percent of Britain's total income in the closing decades of the eighteenth century to a modestly greater percentage in the period after the Napoleonic Wars and then to 3 percent in the 1850s and 1860s.[28]

By then Britain was running continual deficits in merchandise trade, but the proceeds earned from foreign investments already in place, along with earnings from such activities as shipping, insurance, and banking—all natural ancillaries to being a creditor—were more than sufficient to sustain the momentum. From about 1870 right up to World War I, Britain's net foreign investment averaged 5 percent of income and represented a third of its total gross investment.[29] British investors supplied massive amounts of financing for railroads, mining, and industrial projects in America, Canada, Australia and New Zealand, South Africa, and Argentina, as well as in India, the Middle East, and Hong Kong.

Along the way, the normal desire of borrowers and would-be borrowers to have their creditors think well of them inevitably spread beyond commercial relationships to permeate other aspects of political, diplomatic, cultural, and social intercourse. Britain became the model for these countries' governmental institutions, the source of their social customs, and the place where the elites sent their offspring to be educated. Even in countries not within the empire, Britain played a major role in such episodes as the opening of China in the 1830s and the reform of Turkish finances in the 1860s. Within the empire, the stamp of British influence in countries as disparate as India and South Africa has lasted well beyond the empire itself.

The United States followed much the same course about a century later. In principle the Monroe Doctrine had asserted a form of United States hegemony over Central and South America as early as the 1820s. But what put real flesh on U.S. influence to the south was financing the region's economic development, beginning in the 1890s and continuing well past the turn of the century. American gunboats and marines may have been the most dramatic expressions of this country's interest, but the influence of American capital was more steady and in the end probably more effective. The Panama Canal was only the most visible piece of an enormous program of U.S.-financed development throughout the hemisphere. Theodore Roosevelt, who approvingly presided over the first real crest of this wave, advocated speaking softly and carrying a big stick. He might well have included bringing a big bankroll.

America's growing influence as a genuine world power, not confined to western hemisphere interests, gained further momentum when this country first became a major lender to Britain and France at the time of World War I and then dramatically gained maturity during and after World War II. The $7 billion of Lend-Lease assistance extended to Britain just before the United States entered World War II and the postwar aid to sixteen western European nations under the Marshall Plan permanently shifted the basic presumptions underlying America's international economic relations. The Truman Doctrine, the establishment of NATO, and the assumption of the leadership role in the Korean War were key steps in the development of America's role in the new world order. But throughout this period, both in Europe and in Asia, as well as in the Middle East, that role rested ultimately on the economic preeminence with which this country emerged from World War II.

Throughout the postwar years, American businesses and banks continued to supply private capital abroad, and America's public role as chief financier naturally led to a senior position in the new battery of international organizations, including the United Nations, the World Bank, and the International Monetary Fund. And as in Britain's case a century earlier, the political, cultural, and social position that traditionally accrues to the foreign banker became this country's due not just in Latin America but practically everywhere: so much so that by the sixties growing resentments against the spread of American political and cultural influence increasingly aroused Europeans' reactions to what they saw as "Le Défi Américain" (the American challenge).[30] Friends in America, business connections in America, an education in America, became objects of desire or envy or resentment, but rarely indifference.

.   .   .

Nations can lose influence as well as gain it, however. Britain stopped investing capital abroad after World War I and became a steady borrower in the world's capital markets after World War II. Soon the question was no longer what capital Britain could put up to finance development in what had by then become the Commonwealth nations but what loans those countries could provide to finance Britain's growing payments deficit, no longer what concessions other countries might give in order to make British investors welcome but what arrangements Britain could make to retain the support of foreign creditors. By the sixties this increasing dependence on foreign financing led to periodic "sterling crises," as the ever more fragile willingness of investors in other countries to hold Britain's outstanding debts became central to avoiding precipitous and potentially disruptive declines in the pound. Perceptions of Britain's place in the international order could not help but change in response.

The fiscal policy we have pursued in the 1980s has spawned just such a reversal in our own financial situation. In time the predictable consequences will inevitably follow, as America increasingly depends on foreign capital—a change that cannot help but alter America's international role.

Influence and power will accrue to the new creditor countries more quickly in some areas than in others. The sudden emergence of Saudi Arabia, Kuwait, and other Arabian Gulf states as major net creditors in the mid-seventies almost immediately elevated their position in international financial organizations. Before 1973, no one had thought to assign them major voting rights or board-level representation. The increasing reliance of both the IMF and the World Bank on financing from these countries, especially Saudi Arabia, changed that attitude soon enough. In 1978 Saudi Arabia joined the United States, Britain, France, West Germany, and Japan as one of the only countries represented in the IMF's governance by their own executive directors. In 1986 Saudi Arabia became one of just seven countries (the same six plus China) represented by their own executive directors at the World Bank.

Japan's net foreign investment has increased from less than 1 percent of national income in 1981 to more than 4 percent in 1986. As a result, by year-end 1986 Japan had accumulated net foreign holdings of $180 billion—larger than America's were at their 1981 peak, even after allowing for inflation along the way. Germany's net foreign investment has also grown from less than 1 percent of national income as recently as 1982 to 4 percent in 1986. By year-end 1986, Germany had accumulated net international holdings of $113 billion.[31] Both Japan and Germany are already among the mainstays of the world's international financial organizations and have been so since the sixties. With their emergence not merely as strong economic forces but as the world's largest net creditors, their influence will no doubt grow at a more rapid pace and in a broader sphere.

One example of our diminished abilities is the developing world's debt problem. Because American banks are the principal creditors to the faltering Latin American debtors, the international banking community has repeatedly looked to us for leadership in resolving this issue. Although at first the Reagan administration's fixation with unfettered private market outcomes led it to demur, since 1985 the U.S. government has assumed an increasingly active part in seeking solutions both for specific debtors' embarrassments and in more general terms. At the joint annual meeting of the IMF and the World Bank in Seoul, in October of that year, Treasury Secretary Baker announced a new U.S. government initiative designed to funnel $29 billion of financing to these debtors, including $20 billion from banks in the industrialized countries and another $9 billion from the multinational lending institutions. When Mexico could not meet its scheduled payments in March 1987, the U.S. government brokered the agreement that resulted in the banks' rescheduling Mexico's debt and advancing another $6 billion of new money. The bold proposal announced later that year by New York's Morgan Guaranty Trust Company, to swap $20 billion of Mexico's outstanding debt for half that amount of new debt (in the end the amount actually swapped was only $2 billion), involved a special sale of U.S. Treasury securities to Mexico to secure the new debt.

But despite this show of activity, America is no longer capable of solving the developing country debt problem in ways that would have been straightforward just a decade ago. Talk of another Marshall Plan, for example, this time to benefit the developing world, is hardly realistic. After allowing for both inflation and economic growth, the $12 billion that America dispersed during 1948–50 under the Marshall Plan would come to $200 billion today. With a net foreign debt of $400 billion already, and more to come before we return to international economic balance, the suggestion of a new no-strings program to transfer $200 billion of financial resources to other countries is highly fanciful.

Our situation is not yet so severe that no other debtor country can expect any help at all from this even bigger debtor. When our government and our businesses and our banks borrow, they typically do so in dollars even if the lenders are foreign. The fact that these lenders permit us to borrow in our own currency remains a crucial advantage that the developing countries do not have and may never have. No one will lend to a Brazilian business in cruzados, or to the Bolivian government in the new bolivianos. Because we continue to enjoy this superior ability to garner resources from the world's capital markets, selective transfers from us to other, less privileged debtors are still possible, and no doubt many will take place. But any genuine use of our own resources to help other countries will only increase still further what we will have to borrow or the amount of our assets we will have to sell.

As a result, the developing country debtors will have to search for help elsewhere, wherever they can find it, or make do on their own. We may not like the form in which they do find help, especially if the new creditor countries that provide it tie their financial assistance to trade packages or to other kinds of nonfinancial arrangements. Japanese investors, for example, have already established a significant physical presence in Mexico, including a Honda plant in Guadalajara, a Nissan plant in Aguascalientes, a top-grade Nikko Hotel in Mexico City, and a $700 million pipeline connecting the Gulf Coast oil fields with the Salina Cruz port facilities on the Pacific Coast (financed, but not owned, by Japan's Export-Import Bank).[32] In this way Japan is only repeating the process by which America's international dominance emerged in earlier decades.

For the most part, the dollar's decline since 1985 has been welcomed by American businesses despite its potentially inflationary impact, and many exporters in particular would applaud still further declines. But in time, we, like any other debtor, will become ever more concerned to prevent downward movements in our currency value and anxious in particular to avoid anything that may threaten a sudden collapse. If currency speculation should touch off periodic "dollar crises," then we, like Britain in the sixties, will have to go hat in hand to round up support from other countries' central banks. In a severe enough crisis, we might even have to seek assistance from the IMF and accept whatever changes in economic policy that organization might specify as a precondition for aid. An endless series of ad hoc conciliatory arrangements, and perhaps even the explicit surrender of a degree of sovereignty over our economic policy, will merely be the downpayment asked of us for keeping the dollar afloat. Like British prime minister Harold Wilson in the sixties, American officials can always complain about the fickle portfolio behavior of the "gnomes of Zurich." But this will do little more than help divert attention from the problems that sooner or later go along with being a debtor nation. Creditor countries do not have to worry about gnomes, in Zurich or anywhere else.

Watching our economic power shift to the new creditor countries as they edge into the vacuum left by us—as they begin to cope with the developing world's debt or step in to prevent a "dollar crisis"—will not be pleasant. But it is part of the price we shall pay for our new fiscal policy. Much of this price is already inevitable, a consequence of the diminished capacities that our pursuit of this policy throughout the 1980s has left. But if we continue on the same road, we shall raise the penalty to whole new dimensions and accelerate the pace at which these unhappy transitions proceed.

The rise of Japanese and West European influence will not be a full parallel for America's reduced status. Japan remains demilitarized for most practical purposes and Germany's military establishment is modest. Japan has limited its defense spending to about 1 percent of income and forsworn the use of nuclear weapons altogether as a memorial to the destruction of Hiroshima and Nagasaki. Germany's defense spending is more like 3 percent of income but declining in the 1980s. By contrast, in the 1980s the United States has strengthened its position as a military superpower. For the foreseeable future, America's nuclear and conventional forces will continue to represent the ultimate source of defense capabilities within the non-Communist world.

But to maintain this degree of superiority in military capability indefinitely, as America stagnates while other countries gain in economic and diplomatic stature, is hardly a practical prospect. Without economic growth, supporting our military establishment at the level necessary to provide genuine primacy will become an increasingly unacceptable burden. The historical antecedents behind the moral barriers that still limit the rearmament of the former adversaries who are now our allies will gradually dim with the passage of time, and even now we are encouraging their rearmament as a means of reducing the drain on our own more limited resources. As the popularity of the proposed (but never enacted) Mansfield Amendment first showed in the early seventies, Americans have already tired of bearing so much of the cost of Europe's defenses. Military primacy has its rewards, including the confidence and responsibility that come from full control over its deployment. But it also has its costs. When the costs become too great in relation to a nation's resources, primacy begins to seem less necessary.

More important, military capability in conjunction with economic strength is not the same as military power alone. Among countries whose relations involve such complete interdependence that war between them is practically unthinkable—a condition that fairly describes much of the Western world and its Asian allies today—military power brings influence only in response to external threats.[33] Even under the best of circumstances, for America to earn its international position primarily by military might, as its economic power seeps away, means ultimately that we become a mere policeman, a hired gun. Americans do not want to be the Hessians of the twenty-first century. Genuine influence in world affairs, not to mention the respect and even emulation that can ultimately promote the spread of the free social values and democratic institutions that America represents, requires more than that.

Chapter IV

CORRECTING COURSE

The day is short, and the task great.

—FATHERS, II:15

By now it is clear that Reagan's fiscal policy has achieved none of its advertised economic objectives. The share of the nation's income devoted to investment in business plant and equipment—or for that matter to investment of any kind—is not up but down compared to prior experience. Increases in the productivity of our work force have continued to fall short of our own prior performance as well as that of our foreign competitors. The ability of our industry to compete has suffered on a scale we could not have imagined in 1980.

The contrast between the promise and the reality of this new policy may reflect no more than a failure of economic thinking on the part of its architects as well as a too gullible American public. It may also have stemmed from a willing self-deception on the part of many Americans who were all too ready to believe what they were told. And there may also have been an element of deceit on the part of the policy's proponents. The truth will never be entirely clear. Whatever its origins, however, the consequences of America's fiscal experiment of the 1980s are now known. They add up to a colossal failure, a path on which Americans never would have embarked in the first place had they been told its probable consequences.

America's trajectory as this misguided fiscal policy continues is both unstable in the long run and costly in the meanwhile. No government's debt can rise indefinitely in relation to the income its citizens earn. No nation's debt can rise indefinitely in relation to the goods its businesses produce. By 1987 federal debt was two and a half times what it was in 1980 and almost twice as high relative to income. As we have seen, between 1980 and 1987 America dissipated what had been the world's largest net international investment position and ran up the world's largest net debt. And as of 1988 both the federal debt —the government's accumulated borrowing to finance its spending in excess of revenue—and our net indebtedness abroad—the nation's accumulated borrowing to finance what we import over what we export—are continuing to outpace our economic growth. Neither imbalance can persist forever. As these debts grow, the mortgage against our future prosperity grows proportionately, and so does the threat to American society and America's role in the world.

No change of policy, economic or other, can now neatly restore the damage already done by this radical fiscal policy. Nations, like individuals, often have wished that they could return to whatever positions they occupied earlier, as if their mistakes had never been made. But history runs in only one direction. The assets we have dissipated are gone. The debts we have incurred are real. The capital formation and productivity gains we have forgone are simply lost. The full impact of these new economic facts has not yet reduced our living standards, because the overconsumption that this policy has fostered is still under way. But this cannot go on forever, and at least the international aspects of our inevitable decline are already in motion. The future is beginning to arrive, and it is not what Americans thought they had ordered.

To keep the damage from accumulating further means, in the first place, not committing so much of our private saving and foreign borrowing to finance the federal deficit. Even so, there is nothing magic about a balanced budget. Especially at times when downward shocks like sudden oil price increases depress business activity, government spending not matched by tax revenues can usefully blunt the contractionary effect on output and employment as well as on capital formation. In other circumstances, an outright budget surplus may be more useful. Furthermore, to the extent that part of what the government spends goes for physical investments, like office buildings or interstate highways or military installations, financing such expenditures by borrowing is no more than what any business putting up a new plant typically does—or any family building a new house.

To attempt to match government income and outgo exactly is even less desirable when both are as crudely and arbitrarily measured as they are by the U.S. government. The federal budget, for example, systematically *under*states costs by failing to incorporate the growing liabilities for future payments for the pensions of federal civilian employees and military personnel. At the same time, the budget systematically *over*states costs by including all interest that the Treasury pays on its outstanding securities, while failing to allow for the shrinking real value of those securities due to inflation. And there are many other omissions and mismeasurements. Making serious public policy choices on the basis of seeking precise balance in what the government's accountants arbitrarily include in the budget is not a sensible strategy.[1]

The best measure of a government's fiscal posture over long periods is whether its debt is rising or falling compared to national income. When spending exceeds revenues in a given year, the resulting deficit does not simply vanish with no trace at year-end. Like any business or individual, the government has to pay its bills. It therefore borrows. For the government, borrowing takes the form of selling securities—Treasury bills that come due within a matter of months as well as Treasury notes and bonds not due for some years—to investors who typically include individuals, businesses, banks, and other financial institutions both at home and abroad. Once investors own these Treasury securities, the government is in debt to them (or to whoever in turn buys the securities from them) until the Treasury either repays these obligations as they come due, an action which it usually finances by issuing new securities, or else buys them back.

The debt therefore accumulates over time. When a family borrows in order to live beyond its means, it remains in debt even after it balances its accounts. And it remains in debt unless it saves enough from its income to pay off what it owes. The same is true for any business and for the government too. The only way for the government to reduce its debt is to raise revenues that exceed spending and use the surplus either to pay off securities as they come due or to buy some of them back from whoever then owns them.

The amount of government debt outstanding at any time is the accumulation of all budget deficits the government has run over its entire history, reduced by all of its surpluses. There is no reason that any government would ever need, or even want, to repay its entire outstanding debt in a single year, and no government of any major country has ever done so. But the size of government debt in relation to the national income—that is, how much of the national income it would take to pay off the debt if the government ever chose to do so—is the surest gauge of how indebted a government has become. More important, changes in government debt in relation to the country's income from year to year or even from decade to decade—in other words, the trajectory of the government debt ratio over time—give the best single measure of how its fiscal posture is evolving.

As we shall see, throughout two centuries of America's peacetime experience—until the 1980s—our federal debt was almost always declining in relation to our national income. The ratio of federal debt to income rose, sometimes sharply, in each of the wars we fought. But once these wars ended, we returned to repaying that debt, if not through outright budget surpluses then at least in the economic sense that if the debt rose at all it rose less rapidly than income. The only exception was in the early 1930s at the bottom of the Depression.

The entire federal debt outstanding as of December 1980, accumulated since the founding of the republic, was not quite three quarters of a trillion dollars.* In an economy that was then producing nearly three trillion dollars each year, it would have taken twenty-six cents out of each dollar of income to pay that debt off completely—exactly the same share as in 1920 or for that matter in the 1870s. That the United States entered the 1980s with precisely the same government debt ratio that it had at the beginning of the 1920s, despite the Great Depression and the cost of World War II along the way, demonstrates the remarkable steadiness of the traditional American commitment to paying our own way.

By contrast, the string of seven budget deficits that the government posted between 1981 and 1987 alone added up to

*The gross debt was $937 billion, but the government itself held $194 billion of that in such accounts as the Highway Trust Fund, the Federal Old Age and Survivors Trust Fund (Social Security), and the Federal Hospital Insurance Trust Fund. The debt held by the public at year-end 1980 was therefore $743 billion. The overall federal deficit each year—the "unified budget" deficit—corresponds to the increase in federal debt held by the public.

well over a trillion dollars. Seven years of our new fiscal policy —all years of peacetime—more than doubled federal indebtedness, while the size of the nation's economy increased by barely half. As a result, the nearly two trillion dollars of federal debt in December 1987 amounted to forty-four cents for every dollar of our income.* By year-end 1988 it will probably be nearly forty-six cents per dollar. Our new fiscal policy was new indeed.

Reagan's new fiscal policy was new indeed.

The chief economic criterion governing American fiscal policy in the aftermath of the Reagan years should be to restore the federal debt to a declining trajectory compared to the nation's income—and to do so without inflation. A declining federal debt ratio will mark a return to our traditional fiscal posture, leaving the 1980s as a highly costly, one-time aberration, and put us once more on a course that is not obviously unstable in the long run, a course that will halt the growing mortgage against future American living standards.

A sensible and cautious strategy for the next eight years is to reduce the debt ratio at about half the pace at which it has risen between 1980 and 1988. By 1996 the federal debt will then be no more than thirty-six cents for every dollar of income. Because income will continue to grow in real terms and because there will inevitably be some modest inflation, meeting this target does not mean eliminating budget deficits altogether. But it does mean bringing federal revenues and expenditures closer into line—much closer—than under Reagan.

Between 1980 and 1987, American business expanded by an average 2.4 percent per annum after allowing for inflation: a distinctly disappointing result compared to 3.3 percent per

---

*At year-end 1987 the gross federal debt was over $2.4 trillion, of which $478 billion was held in government accounts and nearly $2 trillion by the public.

annum on average during the prior three decades. Even so, it
would be optimistic at best to rely on a more rapid expansion
in the future. The weakness of net investment in plant and
equipment throughout the 1980s has left us a smaller stock of
productive capital than we normally would have had by now,
and the Tax Reform Act of 1986 has made prospects for
business capital spending even more uncertain. Changing
demographic patterns are also now leading to slower growth of
the labor force, so that it will take faster growth of income *per
worker* just to achieve the same growth of total nationwide
income as before. As a result, 2.4 percent per annum real
growth is a plausible assumption on which to base a sound fiscal
strategy for the next eight years.*

Although prices throughout the American economy rose at
an average 4.6 percent per annum between 1980 and 1987, the
early years of the decade marked the tail end of an experience
few Americans would choose to repeat. The average economywide inflation rate during 1983–87 was just 3.3 percent per
annum. Relying on faster overall price increases than that to
lower the government's debt ratio would be accomplishing one
set of objectives only at the expense of another.

An appropriate benchmark for the coming years is therefore
to narrow the deficit by enough to limit the outstanding federal
debt in 1996 to thirty-six cents for each dollar of income, with
the prospect that on average between 1989 and 1996—including a recession at some point, or more than one, if historical
patterns continue, together with faster growth during recoveries—income will grow by 2.4 percent per annum in real terms
while prices will rise by 3.3 percent per annum. At that rate,

*If the Reagan administration had not relied on its now famous "rosy
scenario," calling for an unprecedented half decade of real economic expansion at 4.4 percent per annum beginning in 1982, perhaps it too would have
followed a different fiscal policy.[2]

total annual income will reach approximately $7.4 trillion by
1996. Debt equal to thirty-six cents per dollar of income would
amount to approximately $2.7 trillion at year-end 1996 com-
pared with a likely debt outstanding (not counting what the
government owes to itself) of some $2.2 trillion as of year-end
1988. Limiting the growth of the federal debt to $500 billion
over eight years means holding the average annual budget
deficit to approximately $60 billion.*

Reducing the federal debt ratio is a matter of basic fiscal
logic. Deciding just how fast to reduce the debt ratio is a matter
of judgment. Reducing the debt ratio between 1988 and 1996
by one half of the increase that has taken place between 1980
and 1988 is probably sensible, especially given the extraordinary risks now associated with an economic downturn either
here or abroad. But other trajectories are possible as well.

*Because the Social Security Amendments of 1983 set contribution rates at
levels high enough that payroll taxes exceed benefits, and are likely to do so
by increasing amounts, the Social Security System will probably run a sizable
and growing *surplus* during these years. (The exact magnitude of this surplus
is a matter of controversy because of disputes over actuarial and other technical assumptions.) The aim of this surplus is to build up a fund that will enable
the Social Security System to cope with the burdens it will face early in the
next century, when the retirement of the baby boom generation sharply
raises the number of retirees receiving benefits compared to the number of
workers making contributions. To let the Social Security surplus mitigate the
deficit that the government incurs in its other activities would vitiate that
purpose, leaving the Social Security System no way to cope with the post-
2000 retirement bulge except to raise payroll taxes to unacceptably high
levels or reduce benefits sharply—just the outcomes that the 1983 amendments were intended to avoid. The target of $2.7 trillion of federal debt
outstanding as of year-end 1996 therefore includes whatever amount of
federal debt the Federal Old Age and Survivors Trust Fund may accumulate.
Likewise, the target $60 billion average annual deficit during 1989–96 in-
cludes whatever part of each year's deficit the Social Security surplus may
appear to offset.

At one extreme, for example, simply to stabilize the federal debt ratio would be a significant change for the better. Doing so would probably mean a debt of some $3.5 trillion as of year-end 1996, a level consistent with an annual deficit averaging just over $150 billion during the eight years 1989–96. By contrast, to reduce the debt ratio as rapidly as it has risen since 1980, so that by 1996 the debt would be back down to twenty-six cents for each dollar of income as it was in 1980 (and 1920 and before), would mean *reducing* the outstanding debt in nominal dollars to below $2 trillion by 1996. This would require a budget *surplus* averaging about $30 billion per year.

There is nothing uniquely right about any of these trajectories. Each would be a clear improvement over present policy, though holding the debt ratio stable at forty-six cents per dollar or reducing it to twenty-six cents per dollar by 1996, would clearly represent the extremes. The chief characteristic of America's peacetime experience until the Reagan years was the tendency for federal debt to grow less rapidly than income. Merely stabilizing the debt ratio over a period as long as eight years would still fall outside this range. Conversely, running nearly a decade of surpluses as large as one half to three fourths of a percent of our income would also be out of character for most of our prior fiscal experience. More important, the economy-wide adjustments required to accommodate so large a policy shift—including, as we shall see, the need to implement an extremely stimulative monetary policy so as to avoid a business downturn in response to such a sharp swing to fiscal stringency—would place needless strains on America's business and financial structure. It makes no sense to adopt a precipitous and extreme policy course from 1989 onward, just because the course we took during 1981–88 was extreme in the opposite direction.

Limiting the federal deficit to an average $60 billion per

year, so as to reduce the federal debt to thirty-six cents per dollar of income by 1996, will already be sharply different from our experience under Reagan. The deficit averaged $169 billion during 1981–87 ($174 billion without the Social Security surplus), with no tendency to shrink over the years.* Though much of the 1987 legislative session was devoted to grappling once again with the deficit, and despite both the $30 billion deficit reduction package put together in the immediate aftermath of the stock market crash, the deficit for 1988 (apart from the surplus of Social Security payroll taxes over Social Security benefits) is likely to be above $175 billion. In the absence of changes in our tax and spending policies—changes that neither the president nor the Congress has yet proposed—the deficit for 1989 will be larger still.

What is necessary is to narrow the deficit by approximately $115 billion: Not by 1996 or at some unspecified date to be determined, but beginning in fiscal year 1989. And not by accounting illusions or by one-shot devices like sales of government-owned assets, which absorb our saving just as if they were sales of Treasury bonds, but by deficit reduction measures that are both genuine and lasting.

That means spending less or taxing more. As we shall see, there is no shortage of ways to do either. What matters is not so much which ways we choose as that we choose at all, in adequate amounts, and act on our choices. Doing so will not

*In the 1987 fiscal year, the deficit narrowed to $150 billion compared to the prior year's record $221 billion, but much of that apparent progress merely represented a temporary bulge in revenues due to the large volume of transactions that both individuals and businesses hastened to conclude before the new, more restrictive tax rules took effect on New Year's Day 1987. Moreover, without a $20 billion surplus in the Social Security System the deficit would have been $170 billion.

be pleasant, both because of the real sacrifices necessary to begin living within our shrunken means and because turning away from a policy oriented toward systematic overconsumption also means abandoning the illusions on which that policy has been based. But we must do so sooner or later, and it is in our own interest, as well as that of our children, to make it sooner.

At the same time, it makes no sense to shift to a new, stable fiscal trajectory, one designed to reduce the debt ratio, in such a way that the transition drives business into recession or worse. Spending cuts and tax increases will serve no purpose if they induce a downturn that lowers revenues and raises expenditures by so much that the deficit instead actually widens. More important, the point of correcting our fiscal trajectory in the first place is to achieve a satisfactory and rising standard of living, now and in the future. Though sacrifices are inevitable, the object is to keep them to a minimum.

Lower spending and higher taxes to the extent of $115 billion could sharply depress business if not offset by other parts of a broader economic policy package. For example, $115 billion is almost one third of the federal government's entire yearly expenditure for employees' salaries (including military) and all the other goods and services that it consumes directly. Cutting the government's own purchases by that amount—all at once and with no offsetting stimulus to private spending—would directly lower nationwide spending by nearly 2.5 percent. Alternatively, $115 billion is more than one fourth of all transfer payments that the government makes to or on behalf of individuals (including Social Security benefits). It is also more than one fourth of all revenues from the personal income tax. Cutting income supports or raising taxes by that amount would lower the aggregate after-tax income of individuals by more than 3 percent. Doing so abruptly without an offsetting stimulus would again sharply reduce overall spending.

Since the demobilization that immediately followed World War II, there have been only two swings of this magnitude in the structural component of the deficit—that is, the deficit as it would be if the economy were always at full employment. Both apparently played some role in causing business recessions albeit fairly mild ones. After allowing for the effects on tax revenues and government spending due to fluctuating incomes and employment, the budget swung from a $5 billion deficit in 1958 to a $5 billion surplus in 1960, a shift equal to nearly 2 percent of that year's income and a move that probably contributed to the recession that lasted through most of 1960. Similarly, a combination of spending restraint and a tax surcharge narrowed the structural deficit from $25 billion in 1967 to $4 billion in 1969, a shift equal to nearly 3 percent of that year's income.[3] A recession began in the autumn of 1969 and lasted throughout 1970. If these two episodes provide a valid guide, a $115 billion narrowing in the deficit in today's economy should be cause for caution if not alarm.

It is incorrect, however, to think that there is any automatic one-to-one relationship between fiscal policy changes and subsequent business fluctuations. Too many other forces also affect the pace of economic activity, including not only influences that arise independently in individuals' and businesses' plans but also, as we shall see, the influence of monetary policy. A shift to tight monetary policy was a key factor in bringing about the downturns in both 1960 and 1969–70, for example. The interest rate on Treasury bills rose from an average 2.77 percent in the first quarter of 1959 to 3.87 percent in the first quarter of 1960, the peak of business activity before the decline, and the growth of money and credit also slowed during this prerecession period.[4] Similarly, the Treasury bill rate rose from an average 5.20 percent in the summer quarter of 1968 to 7.02 percent a year later, at the peak before the 1969–70 recession, and again the growth of money and credit slowed during this period. Disentangling the respective influences of fiscal and monetary policies in these two episodes is impossible in any precise way, but it is clear that both were at work.

Moreover, the three much deeper recessions we have experienced since World War II all occurred with little or no contribution from tighter fiscal policy.* The budget was in surplus throughout 1956 and 1957, but the surplus was shrinking—in other words fiscal policy was becoming more expansionary—in the year or so before the 1957–58 downturn began. Yet that recession was by far the worst of the Eisenhower era, with unemployment rising to levels not reached again for fifteen years. The structural deficit was narrowing when the even more severe 1973–75 recession began, but only modestly so. After allowing for cyclical influences, the 1973 deficit was smaller than in 1972 by only about one fourth of one percent of that year's income. Clearly other factors, including especially the unexpected OPEC price increase, were behind this recession too. Most recently, the structural deficit narrowed between 1980 and 1981 by less than one half of one percent of that year's income, which was less than the amount by which it had widened between 1979 and 1980. It is difficult to attribute the 1981–82 recession to tight fiscal policy either.

Despite the loose historical connection between fiscal policy and recessions, there are reasons to be cautious about the transition to a new fiscal policy now. One is simply the magnitude of the adjustment required. Both postwar fiscal swings on

---

*Before the war the scale of federal government activity was much smaller compared to the size of the economy. In the 1929 fiscal year for example, revenues and expenditures were $3.9 billion and $3.2 billion, respectively, compared to total 1929 income of $104 billion.

this scale presaged business downturns. In addition, the international economic environment is now unusually precarious. Many developing countries are already at the brink of economic collapse, and it remains to be seen how the world's major industrial exporters will respond to the cheaper dollar. Moreover, because in America not just government but business as well have borrowed at an extraordinary pace during the 1980s, our economy's financial structure is now more fragile, and hence less able to absorb downward shocks without the risk of a spreading business contraction, than at any time since World War II.

On average, both American businesses and individual Americans are now more heavily indebted, even in relation to rising income levels, than at any time since before the war. The debt problem is more acute for businesses, however. Individuals have borrowed in record volume during the 1980s, but in large part they have done so to boost their ownership of financial assets—including not just stocks that lost their value in the October 1987 crash but also large amounts of deposits and other liquid instruments—as well as nonfinancial assets like houses. Because the individuals who own these additional assets are often not the same as those who owe the additional debt, it is always possible that these rising levels of mortgage and consumer debt present a problem too. There is no way to know whether the respective distributions of individual assets and individual liabilities are more mismatched than they used to be. But at the aggregate level, the net worth of individual Americans (that is, the difference between the assets they own and the liabilities they owe) has shown no deterioration since 1980 even with recently fallen stock prices.

By contrast, American businesses have borrowed record amounts during the 1980s *without* correspondingly increasing either their physical investment in plant and equipment or their holdings of financial assets. Compared to the size of our economy, American business corporations at year-end 1987 owned no more tangible assets or financial instruments than they did at year-end 1980. Instead, the corporate business sector as a whole has mostly used the proceeds of its extraordinary volume of borrowing to retire its equity securities through the remarkable wave of acquisitions, leveraged buy-outs, and stock repurchases that has transformed American business in this decade. Since 1984, when the corporate reorganization movement gained full speed, U.S. corporations in nonfinancial lines of business have raised a total of $116 billion through new issues of common and preferred stock. During the same period, however, they have retired $432 billion worth of stock. At the same time, they have taken on $726 billion of new debt (net of repayment of old debt).

This massive substitution of debt for equity, in conjunction with the onset of record-high real interest rates, has sharply raised the debt service burden for the average American business. On average in the seventies, interest payments took 33 percent of total corporate earnings (leaving the rest for profit and taxes). On average during the fifties and sixties, interest claimed only 16 percent of earnings. But by 1986, American business corporations needed 56 percent of available earnings just to pay interest. The share of personal income required to pay interest owed by individuals has also risen, but it was still only 8 percent in 1986.[5]

Apart from occasional instances of recklessness, incompetence, or fraud, borrowers typically expect to service their debts on a timely basis. But their ability to do so depends on their earnings and on the value of the assets that they can sell off if in a bind. Both business earnings and business asset values in turn depend heavily on prosperity in the economy at large.

Increased business indebtedness in the 1980s has already led to an extraordinary proliferation of bankruptcies and debt defaults, even during the recent expansion. It was no surprise that in 1982, during the most severe recession since the 1930s, both the number of firms going bankrupt and the volume of business debt declared in default rose to record levels. But remarkably, both bankruptcies and the volume of defaults continued to set new postwar highs in each of the next four years, finally leveling off only in 1987.[6] This experience still falls short of the records set at the bottom of the Great Depression, but the mere fact that 1987 was not 1932 is little comfort. That these failures and defaults have taken place in a time of economic expansion raises serious questions about what would happen in the event of another economic contraction which would again slash earnings and depress asset values. Business bankruptcies would probably increase substantially further: perhaps even enough to threaten the economy as a whole.

Until stock prices fell, it was at least possible to believe that the large share of business earnings required to meet interest payments did not imply a correspondingly large share of debt in business capital structures. For all American corporations engaged in nonfinancial lines of business, the ratio of outstanding debt to equity, measured at market values, was approximately 57 percent in August 1987 when stock prices were at their peak.[7] The debt-equity ratio then was not as low as the 45 percent average for the fifties and sixties, but it represented a large improvement from 78 percent at year-end 1982, and it was far below the postwar high mark of 105 percent (that is, more debt than equity in the average firm's capital structure) set when stock prices fell sharply in 1974. To the extent that stock prices embody the market's beliefs about future earnings, the strong rally that began in mid-1982 and lasted until August 1987 meant that debt levels and interest burdens were not out of line with what investors expected business to earn.

The crash changed all that. By the end of October 1987, the market-value debt-equity ratio for all nonfinancial corporations was back above 75 percent, not far from the 1982 level. By year-end, with continued borrowing and no rebound of stock prices, it was even higher. As a result, the claim that interest payments are high compared to today's earnings but not compared to likely future earnings is far less persuasive than it might have been just a short time ago.

Today's fragile business debt structure is not a result of Reagan's fiscal policy, at least not in any direct way, but it compounds the risks that the transition to a new fiscal policy now poses. Should firms that are otherwise strong begin to fail because their customers and suppliers fail, the cumulative process of defaults could carry the economy far below the level consistent with the nonfinancial factors that ordinarily determine the overall pace of business activity.

A major business recession now would be highly counterproductive for a variety of reasons both domestic and international. Wholly apart from the loss of income (it is not unreasonable to place the cost of the 1981–82 recession at about $1 trillion), the resulting fall in payrolls and profits would widen the federal deficit despite spending cuts or increases in tax rates. Because business investment always falls disproportionately during downturns, at the recession's end our stock of productive capital would be even smaller than on our current low-investment trajectory without a recession. And with the industrial countries that export to us and the developing countries that borrow from our banks both dependent on our prosperity, as we have seen, the combination of the falling dollar and a major recession in America could set in motion a world economic contraction, with consequences that are impossible to predict.

We cannot by any means stay with our current fiscal policy, but we should change it only in conjunction with a significant shift in our monetary policy. After all, our problem since the end of the 1981–82 recession is not that the overall level of economic stimulus delivered by fiscal and monetary policies together has been inappropriate. Business recovered sharply after the recession and then settled into a modest expansion that by the end of 1987 had continued longer than any cyclical upswing since the Vietnam War. The problem is that the *composition* of our economic activity has been wrong, with too much consumption and too little investment, and too many imports and too few exports. The reasons for correcting these imbalances are compelling, but we have no reason to slow the pace at which our economy is growing overall.

A shift to a more expansionary monetary policy is therefore a necessary counterpart to our return to a responsible fiscal policy. Just as it is wrong to think that the business expansion since 1982 could not have happened without the huge federal deficit to fuel it, it is also wrong to think that even a large deficit reduction program will necessarily throw that expansion into reverse. The first error stems from forgetting that if federal spending and revenues had been more nearly in balance as we neared full employment of our resources, the Federal Reserve System could have—and, to judge from Paul Volcker's repeated comments, presumably would have—run an easier monetary policy. The second error amounts to ignoring the possibility of making just such a change in monetary policy now, as we shift to a new fiscal policy.

While the historical connection between business downturns and tighter fiscal policy is at best only loose, the connection with tighter monetary policy is more clear cut. As we have seen, tight monetary policy along with tight fiscal policy preceded the relatively mild recessions that occurred in both 1960 and 1969–70. More to the point, a shift to tight monetary policy preceded each of the three far more severe recessions we have had in the postwar period, when fiscal policy was changing either negligibly or in the other direction.* Interest rates rose sharply, reaching new postwar record levels, and the growth of money and credit slowed, in advance of each of the recessions in 1957–58, 1973–75 and 1981–82. In each case, the record of Federal Reserve meetings and subsequent actions makes clear that the monetary policy squeeze was a deliberate attempt to slow business activity so as to halt an accelerating inflation, even if the resulting recession may have been unintended. And in the latter two episodes, the continuation of this monetary squeeze well past the business peak, resulting in bank failures and other breakdowns in the financial system, helped make these recessions as protracted and severe as they turned out to be.

Higher interest rates and slower growth of money and credit also preceded the relatively mild recession that occurred in 1953–54 and the sharp but short-lived recession in the spring of 1980. In the nearly four decades since its 1951 accord with the Treasury freed the Federal Reserve to conduct an independent monetary policy therefore, America has not experienced even one recession not preceded by a shift to tight monetary policy.

In light of this record, prospects are good that we can implement even the large change in fiscal policy that we now need without necessarily sending business into recession—if we

*Economic historians have long debated whether monetary policy caused the Great Depression, and no doubt they will continue to do so.[8] Interest rates fell sharply after the October 1929 stock market crash, and the volumes of money and credit remained stable until late in 1930. The question at issue is whether the Federal Reserve should have done more, lowering interest rates even further and promoting growth (rather than just stability) in money and credit. After 1930 the collapse of the banking system both here and abroad presumably played a major role in turning the decline into the collapse of 1931–32.

adopt an expansionary monetary policy as a counterbalance. But monetary policy influences economic activity mostly in ways that are less direct than changes in taxes and government spending, and that therefore take longer to have their impact. It would also be prudent, therefore, to adopt an easier monetary policy in advance of the transition to a new fiscal policy.

To ease monetary policy first, in order to reduce the risk of an economic downturn, obviously risks overstimulating the economy and hence increasing inflation if fiscal policy remains on its current highly expansionary course. Even without an easier monetary policy, our hard-won victory over inflation is already in jeopardy. A significant part of the disinflation we achieved in the first half of the 1980s was borrowed against the future, as the increasingly overvalued dollar depressed the prices of foreign-made products sold in America and therefore capped the prices that American producers could charge and still attract customers. Now that the dollar is declining, the price of imports is rising more rapidly, and many American companies are already beginning to take advantage of the resulting room to raise their prices without losing out in competition. Having paid nearly $1 trillion in foregone incomes to bring inflation down from 10 percent in 1981 to 3 percent on average during 1985–87, most Americans would rightly regret a return to high inflation once again.

In the long run, a stable fiscal trajectory is probably the best way to avoid inflation. Both our growing federal indebtedness and growing American indebtedness to foreign lenders will increasingly tempt us to pursue inflationary policies. The federal government's debt consists almost entirely of securities denominated in dollars. So do nearly two thirds of the American assets that foreign investors hold. A solid dose of inflation, sustained over a half decade or so, would shrink both of these burdens in relation to America's income. To be sure, inflation

as a conscious strategy to reduce debt is highly unlikely. Historically countries have not behaved that way. What often
happens instead is that, as the inevitable side effects of heavy
debt burdens become more onerous over time, including high
taxes to service the government's debt as well as the need to
forgo imports in order to service debts owed abroad, the political pressures on monetary policy to blunt these side effects
grow with them. When these pressures become irresistible,
inflation inevitably follows.

For the more immediate future however, the greater threat
to America's new-found price stability is that the Federal Reserve may ease monetary policy in anticipation of a change in
fiscal trajectory that does not occur. In that case we would have
not only Reagan's extraordinarily expansionary fiscal policy but
also an expansionary monetary policy. The two in combination
would rapidly deplete whatever unused labor and capital resources we may have available and then go on to create the
strain of demand against supply that has become all too familiar in inflationary periods ever since World War II.

The way to preclude this tension between the real economic
risks of a tighter fiscal policy without easing monetary policy
and the inflationary risks of easing monetary policy without
fiscal restraint is to legislate our new fiscal policy promptly and
at least partly in advance of its becoming effective. At least in
this respect, the Kemp-Roth tax cut—the root of so much of
our present difficulty, as we shall see—provides a useful model.
Enacted in August 1981, the Economic Recovery Tax Act
lowered personal tax rates by 5 percent in September 1981,
then by another 10 percent in July 1982, and finally by yet
another 10 percent in July 1983. There is no need now to delay
implementing a new fiscal policy by as much as two full years.
But spreading the changes over as much as a year—by defer-
ring spending cuts partly to the 1989 fiscal year and partly to

fiscal 1990, and letting tax increases take effect partly in the 1989 calendar year and partly in 1990—would give the Federal Reserve the window it needs to ease monetary policy ahead of time.

What is essential in such an undertaking, however, is that the shift to a new fiscal policy, on whatever schedule it is implemented, be visibly firm and therefore credible. The main point of phasing in the fiscal changes we need over a year or even more is to provide for an easier monetary policy in advance. It will serve little purpose to stretch out these fiscal changes if that means legislating them in some form—familiar examples are the Gramm-Rudman-Hollings act and each year's congressional budget resolution—that no one will take seriously and that will not give the Federal Reserve sufficient ground on which to act. Legislated promises to find spending cuts or tax increases in the future will not do.

The combination of a smaller deficit and an easier monetary policy will let interest rates fall from the extraordinarily high range, compared to inflation, within which they have fluctuated since 1980. As a result financing will be more affordable for businesses seeking to undertake new capital spending projects, as well as families hoping to build new homes. Just as importantly, in light of the strains that the falling dollar will increasingly place on countries that depend on exports to America, this new combination of monetary and fiscal policies will remove a principal obstacle that has blocked international economic cooperation throughout the 1980s. Developed countries will be freer to ease their own monetary policies and thereby to blunt the contractionary effects on their exports due to the cheaper dollar. And developing countries will face lower debt service costs on their dollar-denominated debts.

As we shall see, there are many options from which we can choose in making the changes in American fiscal policy from which the rest of this process can evolve. But because each will involve sacrifices and hence will require substantial public support, we are likely to be successful in facing these choices only if Americans understand—indeed, understand in some depth —just how sharp a departure from our prior fiscal experience Reagan's policy has been and how it has brought us to our present unhappy situation.

Chapter V

FROM TAX-AND-SPEND
TO SPEND-AND-BORROW

They turned quickly out of the way wherein their fathers walked.

—JUDGES, II:17

The popular view that we have "always" run budget deficits, so that Reagan's fiscal policy was essentially no different from what came before, ignores the great change in scale and the important change in origin of government borrowing that has occurred in this decade. The difference is as great as that between war and peace. In the 1980s the government has borrowed on a scale unprecedented in the nation's prior experience except for wartime. But America has not been at war nor has the acceleration of peacetime defense spending played more than a partial role here. Instead, the government is simply borrowing rather than collecting taxes. For the first time in our peacetime history, we are no longer paying for what our government does.

The reason that most Americans think our government has always run a deficit is that throughout the past half century we nearly always have. The last year that the federal government finished in the black was 1969, when Nixon was President (although the budget was Johnson's). The last surplus year before that was 1960 under Eisenhower. In only eight years since the end of World War II have revenues met expenditures, and three of those eight years were 1947, 1948 and 1949. Before that, the government had run deficits continually during the war of course and throughout the Depression too. The only decade of this century in which surpluses outnumbered deficits was the 1920s, when Andrew Mellon, who served as secretary of the Treasury from 1921 until 1932, decided that sound finance meant paying back what the nation had borrowed during World War I. The government showed a surplus in every year from 1920 to 1930. By the 1980s however, Americans were entitled to think of the twenties as a long time ago —if they thought about the twenties at all.

But through all the decades since, the deficits we ran were starkly different from what has happened in the 1980s. The earlier deficits were different because they were smaller not just in dollar terms but in relation to American business activity. They were different because they sprang from war, or depression and recession, not from a deliberate unwillingness to collect taxes. And they were different because, except for wartime, throughout two hundred years of our history they never placed the United States on a path toward ultimate fiscal instability.

America's First Congress convened in New York in March 1789. The organization of the Treasury was among its first items of business. By September, President Washington had signed the act creating the Department of the Treasury and appointed Alexander Hamilton as its first secretary. When Hamilton issued the department's *First Report on the Public Credit* in January 1790, he reported a total national debt, mostly left over from the Revolutionary War, of $54 million, plus another $25 million of war debts incurred by what were now the United States.* Although Hamilton originally contemplated a sinking fund to retire this debt over time, the government's expenditures over Washington's eight years and Adams's four overran revenues by $900,000. When Thomas Jefferson became president in 1801, the debt was still $80 million. But apart from $13 million to finance Jefferson's purchase of the Louisiana Territory in 1803, the government did no further significant borrowing until the War of 1812. By the beginning of that year the debt was down to just $45 million.[1]

Borrowing to finance the new war and its immediate aftermath ran the debt back up to $123 million by 1816, but once again the government began to pay it off. With the new nation rapidly expanding, this was not difficult. Tariff revenues from growing imports and proceeds from the sale of public lands provided a steady surplus. Despite the decision to plow part of it back into roads, canals, and other forms of "internal improvements," by Andrew Jackson's second term the government had paid off all its interest-bearing debt, leaving only $38,000 in miscellaneous liabilities. The dominant fiscal issue of the day was what to do with the continuing surplus. Jackson proposed to distribute it to the states, and some payments were actually made, but then an economic decline slowed revenue growth and rendered the question moot.[2]

After touching fiscal bedrock in 1835, the government borrowed only on an irregular basis until the need to wage war and pay for the peace arose again. The cost of the Mexican-American War came to $82 million, including $15 million to purchase from Mexico an area as large as modern-day France and Germany combined. As a result, the debt reached $63 million

---

*Hamilton's report recommended that the new government assume these state debts in order to foster confidence on the part of foreign investors. As we shall see, this policy proved successful.

in 1849. And despite some fluctuation, it was still just $65 million when Abraham Lincoln was elected president.

It was the Civil War that first pushed our government debt into the *billions*. During the war both sides borrowed on a previously unimagined scale. Despite the issue of a half a billion dollars' worth of gold certificates, of the kind that circulated as currency in the United States until 1933, plus almost a billion dollars of "greenbacks" (Treasury notes that were not redeemable for gold but circulated as legal tender anyway), the government had to borrow more than $2 billion in interest-bearing debt. The South borrowed an almost identical amount. By 1865 the Confederate debt was worthless, but the Union debt was still good and its total now came to almost $3 billion. By the early 1870s, economic activity had returned to nearly normal, and the government had paid its debt down to just over $2 billion. That sum amounted to about twenty-six cents for each dollar of a year's income.

From the end of the Civil War until World War I, a half century during which America grew from a largely agrarian country of thirty-six states to a world-class industrial power including all forty-eight contiguous states, the government did no further significant borrowing. An unbroken series of budget surpluses running from 1866 to 1893 paid off three fourths of the Civil War debt, as the country expanded and its income grew.* By the beginning of 1917, the entire outstanding debt was just $971 million, less than two cents for every dollar of annual income.

Fighting in a European war was a wrenching experience for a country that had traditionally avoided such entanglements and it was wrenching in a fiscal sense too. Before 1917 the

---

*During the 1880s historians studied the experience of the 1830s for clues about what to do if the surplus continued after the debt was completely paid off, but in the end the debt never fell below half a billion dollars.

government had never spent $1 billion in a single year. That year it spent almost $2 billion. Despite an emergency tax increase, the deficit was $853 million, nearly enough to double the outstanding debt. Just nineteen months' participation in World War I came to ten times the cost of all four years of the Civil War. There was a First Liberty Loan and then a Second, a Third, and a Fourth and finally a Victory Loan in March 1919. By year-end, after all the troops had come home, the debt was $31 billion, equal to thirty cents for every dollar of that year's income.

Like the policy that had emerged more haphazardly during the late nineteenth century, Mellon's deliberate policy of paying down the war debt worked in two ways. First, eleven straight budget surpluses between 1920 and 1930 totaled more than $8 billion, enabling the Treasury to pay off some of its outstanding obligations. And second, the economy grew. Between 1919 and 1929 America's income rose by nearly one third, so that the country would have been paying down its government debt, in the economic sense of reducing the debt in relation to its economic activity, even without the surpluses. With both mechanisms at work, the outstanding debt on the eve of the Great Depression was just sixteen cents for every dollar of America's 1929 income.

The Depression put both of these debt reduction mechanisms into reverse. Ten straight budget *deficits* between 1931 and 1940 added $25 billion of new debt. And until 1934 the economy not only contracted but did so catastrophically. Even by 1940, after six years of a difficult recovery, nearly 15 percent of the labor force remained unemployed, the business bankruptcy rate stood at the highest level since 1933, and the total income produced by American business still fell short of the level reached in 1929. At the end of 1940, the outstanding debt was $43 billion, equal to forty-five cents for every dollar of that year's income.

World War II again led to government borrowing on a whole new scale. During 1941–46 the government spent $367 billion. Apart from interest on the national debt, all but $49 billion went directly into military expenditures, and much of the rest went into war-related activities like shipping. The budgets of more than $90 billion in both 1945 and 1946 were each ten times the government's total spending in any year since World War I had ended. Despite three successive tax increases in 1942, 1943, and 1944, the deficits for these six years totaled $191 billion. To finance this huge shortfall, the government borrowed massive amounts, both absolutely and compared to the economy. By the end of 1946, after seven War Loans and one Victory Loan, its debt was $242 billion.

Two world wars and a depression had built the government's debt from just $.02 per dollar of annual income in December 1916 to $1.02 in December 1946. But with no war and no depression, America spent the next thirty years and more—to be precise until the 1980s—paying down this debt. As the country had done after the War of 1812, after the Mexican-American War, after the Civil War, and after World War I until the Depression, America after World War II reverted to the customary peacetime fiscal stance based on reducing over time the debt left as the war's financial legacy. Surpluses during the first two years after demobilization enabled the Treasury to retire $15 billion of its outstanding securities. The civilian economy added two million jobs between 1947 and 1950, almost half of them in the rapidly expanding service industries. And a burst of inflation after the wartime price controls came off raised prices by almost 14 percent in 1947. By the end of 1950, the government's debt was down to $219 billion, or seventy cents for each dollar of that year's income.

Debt reduction by budget surplus ended as a feature of American fiscal policy after the forties. But debt reduction in the economic sense of income growth that consistently outran the increase in debt, continued for the next three decades. During the fifties, six deficit years and four surplus years added up to just $14 billion in new borrowing for the entire decade, while despite three recessions, business expanded in real terms by more than 3 percent per annum on average. By 1960 the debt had risen to $237 billion, but that was only forty-six cents for each dollar of that year's income—within a penny of the level in 1940. Relative to income, the country had worked off its entire World War II debt in just fifteen years.

During the sixties, nine deficit years and only one in surplus added up to $57 billion of new borrowing. But during those ten years American business expanded even more rapidly than in the fifties. Thirteen million more Americans had civilian jobs in 1970 than in 1960, as real growth averaged nearly 4 percent per annum. And inflation raised prices by an additional 3 percent each year. As a result, the $285 billion of debt outstanding in 1970 amounted to only twenty-nine cents for each dollar of the nation's income that year. Despite Vietnam, America in the sixties had paid down about half of the debt burden left from the Depression.

Finally, ten deficits in a row in the 1970s added up to $436 billion of borrowing—more than double the amount done during World War II. But even this huge increase in debt did not match the combination of business expansion and price inflation. During the seventies American business added an astonishing twenty million new jobs, as real growth fell just short of 3 percent per annum on average despite two recessions. And prices rose on average at more than twice that rate. By the end of 1980, the outstanding debt was $743 billion, or just twenty-six cents for every dollar of that year's income. Government indebtedness in America was, economically, back where it had been in 1920, or for that matter in the 1870s.

But then American fiscal policy reversed gears. The seven successive deficits incurred during 1981 through 1987 added up to nearly $1.2 trillion. By the time Reagan's first term ended, the debt had reached thirty-six cents for each dollar of America's 1984 income, a ratio last seen in 1967. And by year-end 1987 the debt had reached forty-four cents per dollar, a mark most recently passed—not on the way up but coming down—in 1961.

The sustained rise in federal debt in relation to income that our new fiscal policy has brought about is unprecedented in our history. Apart from the wars that every schoolchild recognizes and the Depression that every grandparent remembers, we have always experienced declining government indebtedness. But with a fiscal policy centered on large across-the-board tax cuts, and no real desire in any quarter to cut the core programs like defense and Social Security and Medicare that dominate the government's spending, increasing indebtedness through both peace and prosperity has now become our national policy. In the 1980s, the federal debt ratio is not only rising but rising just as fast as it had fallen in the previous three and a half decades after World War II.

The third of a century running from the post World War II demobilization until the 1980s deserves even closer attention for the light it can shed on traditional American values as expressed in our fiscal policy. One reason is simply that, for most of us, the prewar and pre-Depression experience now seems remote. More important, the enormous growth of the nonmilitary role of government in our society has occurred mostly since World War II. The fact that until the 1980s Americans were prepared to tax themselves for this growth is what makes our present fiscal policy so distinctive.

From the fifties through the early seventies, much of the growth of government spending occurred at the state and local level. The postwar baby boom meant new school buildings and then salaries for teachers to staff the classrooms. Hospital facilities expanded. Cities built roads, states built highways, and thousands of small towns installed sewer systems. By the mid-seventies the baby boomers were beyond high school, and more cities were closing schools than building new ones. Fewer sewers were built because most towns already had them. But although state and local governments were now growing less rapidly than the economy overall, there was no prospect that the postwar increase in their activity might reverse itself. In 1950 spending by all subfederal governmental units in America claimed less than eight cents for every dollar of our income. By 1980 it was over thirteen cents.[3]

State and local governments, however, had no choice but to pay for all this spending. Most states have constitutional provisions severely limiting state or municipal borrowing for current operations. Even during the high-pressure period of the fifties and sixties, our subfederal government more or less balanced its budget. To be sure, there were always some chronic borrowers—New York City and Cleveland were spectacular examples —but they were far outweighed in the aggregate. And especially once the growing future burden of pension obligations became apparent in the early seventies, most cities and states began to set aside increasing sums to provide for the retirement of their teachers and police and their firemen and office workers. Throughout the seventies, most state and local governments were running substantial surpluses.* As we shall see, the resulting rapid growth of state and local taxes during this period was a major engine fueling the "taxpayers' revolt" which helped make Reagan's radical new fiscal policy possible at the federal level.

The federal government faces no formal limits on borrowing

---

*Whether the pension set-asides they made were sufficient to fund the future benefits they had promised was and remains a serious question, but it is a different question.

like those that restrict most states and cities. Congress and the president are free to spend whatever they decide on whatever constitutionally acceptable purposes they choose. They are also free to pay for what they spend by either taxes or borrowing, in whatever combination they choose. The Constitution declares that "the Congress shall have Power to lay and collect Taxes," but it imposes no obligation to do so.

Before World War II, the federal government had been fairly small. There was no standing army to speak of and little civilian bureaucracy. Social Security was in its infancy. Even the New Deal was small stuff by postwar standards, especially after the Supreme Court ruled the National Industrial Recovery Act and the Agricultural Adjustment Act unconstitutional. It was the war that first brought large-scale federal expansion, putting more than sixteen million men and women in uniform and making 42 percent of the entire economy a direct federal activity, while most of the rest came under at least some form of government control.

Demobilization reduced federal activity sharply, but there was no return to the virtual absence of the federal government that had distinguished so many aspects of American life before the war. Now there was a sizable peacetime defense establishment bearing the cost of the nuclear age. Responsibilities to individual citizens had also begun to grow. And the civilian bureaucracy required to carry out the government's new regulatory functions had evolved into a labor market unto itself. In the late 1940s, before the Korean War placed the newly organized Defense Department on a wartime footing, the federal government accounted for fifteen cents of each dollar spent in the United States: less than during World War II, to be sure, but still a long way from the four cents we spent on average in the twenties, or even the eight cents in the thirties.

Over the next three decades, federal spending rose irregularly but on average faster than our income. Throughout these years, the government's chief activities—defense, retirement programs, and other nonmilitary functions—continually changed and changed again in their relative importance. In the fifties defense spending at first grew rapidly but then fell back as the armed services gradually released a quarter of a million men after the Korean armistice. Social Security beneficiaries increased from 2 percent of all Americans in 1950 to 8 percent in 1960, and the average monthly check rose from $22, or just 10 percent of the average worker's pay, in 1950 to $62, or 18 percent of average pay, in 1960.[4] The fifties were also the decade of the interstate highway system, the soil bank for farmers and, after the shock of Sputnik in 1957, a rejuvenated scientific education and research effort including the establishment of the National Aeronautics and Space Administration. In total federal spending amounted on average to 18 percent of our income throughout the decade.

Despite all the attention subsequently paid to the Vietnam War and Lyndon Johnson's Great Society, in retrospect the sixties were not marked by unusual growth of federal spending in relation to income. The war effort peaked in 1968 with three and a half million men and women in the armed services, a half million of them stationed in Vietnam. The next summer Americans landed on the moon—and, what must have been trickier, returned safely to earth. Both the coverage and the generosity of Social Security increased still further, with 13 percent of all Americans receiving benefits by 1970 and the average monthly check up to $100, or 19 percent of the average wage. A burst of new civilian programs included Medicare for the elderly, food stamps for the poor, the Model Cities program for urban renewal, increased aid to primary and secondary education, and public housing on a scale hitherto unimagined.

But even with all that, federal spending rose only to 19 percent of income in the early sixties and 20 percent in the late sixties.

Nor were the seventies all that different either. Under Nixon and Ford, defense spending hit a lower share of income than at any time since before the Korean War, but the Great Society programs were now growing rapidly enough to offset most of the saving on defense.* Medicaid extended to the poor who had not yet reached age sixty-five the same medical services already universally available to the elderly through Medicare. Under Carter defense spending again began to grow about as fast as the economy overall, but nondefense spending continued to grow faster. The slow upward drift in total federal spending as a share of all spending in the United States therefore continued, reaching 21 percent on average in the late seventies.

Yet throughout this third of a century, during which federal spending rose from 15 percent of America's income to 21 percent, federal taxes rose almost as much. And to the extent that there were deficits, they were mostly a temporary result of economic slumps rather than a reflection of basic unwillingness to set taxes equal to spending even when business was strong.

Despite a war in Korea and then three recessions, the fifties saw more or less balanced budgets. The decade's six deficits taken together exceeded the four surpluses by $14 billion, not a large sum in a country whose economy was already producing a half *trillion* dollars of income each year by 1960. And $13 billion of that total occurred in 1959 in the wake of the most

---

*At the same time much of this growth consisted of "revenue sharing" programs, under which the federal government simply passed its tax dollars on to states and local governments, for them to spend either on specific federally endorsed priorities like mass transit or on ordinary operations.

severe of the three Eisenhower recessions. If business had just been up to its average postwar performance, that year's deficit would have been not $13 billion but $4 billion.[5]

The fact that Eisenhower in 1959 did not call for higher taxes or reduced spending, but instead tolerated a peacetime record deficit in response to weakened business, showed that America's fiscal thinking had changed since the 1920s in at least one respect. After the deepening Depression began to erode tax revenues after 1930, Hoover denounced the resulting small deficit (less than half a billion dollars) in 1931, and foolishly under Depression conditions, got Congress to raise taxes.* By contrast, Eisenhower in 1959 not only tolerated the red ink directly due to the business slowdown but actively fought the recession by spending an extra $2.5 billion for defense (mostly on projects like the development and deployment of new ships and missiles, which provided job-creating defense contracts), boosting the Mutual Security aid program by $1 billion, increasing the Atomic Energy Commission budget by $250 million, and trebling the National Science Foundation budget. The $13 billion deficit that ensued was by far the largest for any single year apart from World Wars I and II. It amounted to 2.7 percent of that year's income. But in retrospect it stands out as a unique episode in a decade marked by continuing dedication to fiscal responsibility and approxi-

---

*As the deficit widened in 1932 despite the tax increase, Franklin Roosevelt campaigned for the White House on a platform pledging a return to fiscal austerity and balanced budgets, to be achieved largely through a "drastic reduction of government expenditures."[6] Only after four years in office and one more election, and after a renewed business downturn had shattered hopes of sustained recovery, did Roosevelt firmly abandon his intention to emulate the fiscal policy that Andrew Mellon had steadily pursued under Harding, Coolidge, and Hoover.

mately balanced budgets. For the fifties as a whole, the $14 billion cumulative deficit amounted to less than one third of one percent of America's income.

Eisenhower's response to recession in 1959 set the pattern that subsequent presidents typically followed, in two important ways. First, the government's budget position reflected the ups and downs of the business cycle. In contrast to Hoover's policy, the government did not tighten fiscal policy in an attempt to offset the lower tax receipts and higher spending that recessions brought. Second, most presidents, following Eisenhower's example, took at least some steps—through tax cuts or spending increases or sometimes both—to stimulate business to recover from recessions.

The fiscal record of the postwar years therefore reflected prevailing business conditions, mostly as a result of the government's taxing individuals according to their incomes and corporations according to their profits. A weak economy means disappointing incomes and profits, and the Treasury shares in these disappointments by collecting less taxes. In addition, the steeply progressive structure of tax rates that individuals faced from World War II until 1987 pushed most taxpayers into higher percentage brackets as their incomes rose but dropped them back into lower brackets whenever their incomes fell. During recessions therefore, individuals' tax payments declined even more than in proportion to their incomes.

Business slowdowns also tend to have pronounced, though smaller, effects on several of the government's major spending programs. More workers out of a job means more people drawing unemployment compensation and also more families qualifying for food stamps, Aid to Families with Dependent Children, and other forms of relief. Workers above age sixty-two, who are eligible to retire on Social Security, are more likely to do so if they lose their jobs and discover that new ones are hard to find. Hence Social Security benefit payments also grow faster than normally during recessions. Even health costs reimbursed under Medicare and Medicaid tend to bulge during recessions, as the psychological strains from forced joblessness lead to more sickness, more breakdowns, even more attempted suicides (and sadly, more successful ones too).

These effects of sluggish business on federal revenues and federal spending were the source of most of the federal deficits throughout the next two decades. During the sixties the government managed only one surplus year, but the deficits were mostly small compared to what American business produced. Only once, at the peak of the Vietnam War effort in 1968, did the government overspend revenues by even as much as the $13 billion overage in 1959. Johnson's $25 billion deficit in 1968 was large by any standard, equal to 3 percent of that year's income. But like Eisenhower's single oversized deficit almost a decade earlier, it too stands out in retrospect as an isolated event. The next biggest deficit for any year in the entire decade was only a third as large. And on average over the sixties as a whole, the deficit amounted to less than 1 percent of America's income.*

In the seventies, the government first began not only to run continual deficits but to do so in visibly large amounts in relation to the economy as a whole. But these deficits were still not on a scale comparable to what was to follow, and they still mostly reflected what turned out to be a dismal decade for American business. More than a million workers lost their jobs in 1970 and another million in 1971. The accompanying fall in incomes and profits held federal revenues flat while spending

---

*Measured on a basis that more accurately reflects how much of the nation's saving the deficit absorbs (as in the national income accounts), the average in the sixties was just one half of 1 percent.

continued to grow, so that what had been a small surplus in 1969 became a $23 billion deficit in 1971. A new business expansion, together with the post-Vietnam reduction in military spending, almost succeeded in balancing the budget over the next few years. But instead OPEC struck, and America was back in recession—and the government back in deficit—once again.

Worse still, because higher oil prices not only had depressed business activity but had begun to push up the prices of everything else too, the focus of the nation's economic policy machinery overlooked the developing recession altogether.* Instead of lowering interest rates to encourage a recovery as it had in prior recessions, the Federal Reserve tightened monetary policy further in order to resist inflation. As a result, three million workers lost their jobs, and profits collapsed. The deficit rose to $53 billion in 1975 and to $74 billion, or 4.3 percent of income, in 1976. Deficits that large became not just a moral but an economic issue too. Treasury Secretary William Simon warned that financing them would require so much government borrowing as to "crowd out" needed investment in business capital.[8] But Simon's warning was early by almost a decade, and in the end the seventies too proved to be more or less continuous with prior patterns of American fiscal behavior.

The crucial distinction was, and in the eighties remains, where the deficit comes from. The 1975 and 1976 deficits set records but so did the business downturn that had been induced by high oil prices and worsened by high interest rates. If unemployment had risen only to 6 percent of the labor force,

*In September 1974, almost a year after the business slowdown had begun, President Ford convened a special White House Conference on Inflation, at which the occasional mention of the deepening recession was clearly overshadowed by continuing concerns about rising prices.[7]

instead of a postwar record 8.5 percent—in other words, if another two and a half million Americans had been able to find work—the combined deficit for these two years would have been not $127 billion but $87 billion. Indeed, as business improved, the deficit steadily shrank. By 1979, just before OPEC doubled oil prices yet again, unemployment was back down to 6 percent. Despite continued growth of spending, the resulting growth of tax revenues had reduced the deficit to $40 billion, or just 1.6 percent of that year's total income. On average over the seventies as a whole, the deficit had been 2.4 percent of our total income.* But more than half of that had come from the weak post-OPEC economy in the middle of the decade.

In short, during these decades we did in fact "tax and spend, tax and spend," as Ronald Reagan later complained. Government spending rose faster than people's incomes and so did taxes. Along the way, there was no lack of argument about how much was enough or what was too much. Every president from Truman onward had inveighed against the growth of government spending. Projects cost too much. Agencies were run inefficiently. Transfer programs were too generous, and some recipients were undeserving. Some government efforts turned out to be failures, and others had simply been bad ideas in the first place. There was never any lack of grounds for objecting to the steady climb of government spending or more generally to the increasingly pervasive presence of government throughout our society. But there was general agreement throughout that whatever share of income government spending claimed, taxes should match it. We continued to increase our taxes

---

*Measured on the basis that more accurately reflects the absorption of our saving, the average deficit in the seventies was 1.8 percent of total income.

faster than our incomes, therefore, because government spending was also rising faster. That we did so reflected the deeply rooted moral imperative that we should pay for what we do.

Throughout these years Americans consistently spoke and acted as if they fully understood the difference between paying their own way and laying off their bills on their children, so much so that when Kennedy advocated balancing the government's budget on average over the business cycle but not necessarily in every year—so that there would be deficits during recessions, but surpluses during expansions to offset them—the American public was broadly skeptical, and on what were largely moral grounds. Kennedy's argument was that in 1961 he had inherited a depressed economy with 6.5 percent of its labor force unemployed, far above the fifties' average of 4.4 percent. If the extra two million unemployed workers had jobs, they would be paying taxes instead of cashing benefit checks. Hence Kennedy proposed gauging both spending programs and tax rates to levels that would deliver a balanced budget *if* those two million of unemployed were at work. But everyone was to understand that in the depressed business environment of the day, taxes actually paid would fall short of spending.

In the event, Americans' commitment to paying their own way was great enough that even this persuasive logic failed to command support. In the summer of 1962, when the Gallup poll asked Americans, "Would you favor or oppose a cut in federal income taxes at this time, if a cut meant that the government would go further into debt?" 72 percent of those asked said they were opposed and only 19 percent were in favor. Even among those who had responded to a previous question by saying that they believed taxes were too high, those opposed to cutting taxes if that meant putting the government further into debt outnumbered those in favor by 61 percent to 31 percent.[9]

What was necessary to sell the Kennedy tax cut was the further argument that more spending and less taxes would stimulate business and thereby help raise the depressed incomes and profits that had created the rationale for the deficit in the first place. In Kennedy's naval image, a gap between spending and taxes would help bring the rising tide that would lift all the boats. Americans showed that they would accept lower taxes, leading to unbalanced government budgets, only if they believed doing so was in the public interest.* To lower taxes simply to let people keep more for themselves, instead of paying for what their government undertook, never had much appeal. The moral imperative obligating each generation to the next was too strong.

The vehicle that Ronald Reagan used to set a new course for American fiscal policy was the proposal for across-the-board cuts in individual income tax rates that Congressman Jack Kemp and Senator William Roth had already floated in 1977. Reagan embraced this proposal before taking office, making it a centerpiece of his election campaign, and as president he formally endorsed it within a month of taking office. Congress passed it as the Economic Recovery Tax Act in July 1981. The first tax cuts became effective on October 1.

The measure proposed by Kemp and Roth had called for reducing individual income taxes three times in three successive years by 10 percent each time. For the typical family with two children and income equal to the nation's average, the marginal tax rate would fall from 24 percent to 22 percent, then to 19 percent, and finally to 17 percent. The Kemp-Roth

---

*And even then, as we have seen, the government deficits that ensued after Johnson finally transformed Kennedy's idea into the Tax Reform Act of 1964 were never very sizable anyway.

proposal also called for "indexing" the income levels that determined what tax rate each individual paid, as well as the amount
of each person's income that was automatically exempt from
tax, to offset inflation. Once the lower rate schedule was in
place, people would therefore move into higher tax brackets
only if their incomes grew faster than prices rose, not just
because inflation put higher dollar numbers on the same real
incomes.

The Economic Recovery Tax Act of 1981 included almost
all of these features. It lowered individual tax rates three times,
though the initial reduction which became effective that October was not 10 percent but 5 percent. The next two cuts,
effective as of July 1 in 1982 and again in 1983, were each 10
percent. As a result, the typical family's marginal tax rate fell
from 24 percent to 18 percent. The bill Congress passed in-
dexed both the income levels demarcating the tax brackets and
also the personal tax exemption, although this provision did not
take effect until January 1, 1985. Until then inflation could
(and did) have its usual effect. The Economic Recovery Tax
Act also included several specific measures intended as saving
incentives, like opening to all taxpayers the opportunity to
contribute on a tax-free basis to Individual Retirement Accounts, which were not part of the original Kemp-Roth idea.
Finally, the bill included provisions that cut corporate profit
taxes in a variety of ways, but in dollar terms these were only
one fourth the size of the reductions in individual income
taxes, and Congress reversed most of them the following year
anyway.

The Economic Recovery Tax Act achieved Reagan's goal of
substantially lowering individual income taxes. The Commerce
Department subsequently estimated that because of the 1981
bill, individuals' taxes (including gift and estate taxes) were
lower by $32 billion in the 1982 fiscal year and then by $75

billion in fiscal 1983, $113 billion in 1984, $135 billion in 1985, and $160 billion in 1986.*[10] These are large amounts. In fiscal 1986 for example, personal income taxes paid to the U.S. government totaled $349 billion, while total federal revenues from all sources that year—also including Social Security payroll taxes, corporate profit taxes, and all tariffs and excises— came to $769 billion. By 1986 the federal tax share of America's income had fallen from a postwar high of 20 percent in 1981 back down to 18 percent, the average of the sixties. The Kemp-Roth tax cut had made a big difference, as it was intended to.

But the increased economic activity that Reagan had said would result from lower tax rates simply never happened. Reagan's original budget, submitted in February 1981, projected after-inflation economic growth at an average 4.4 percent per annum during 1982–86. The economy actually expanded by just 2.4 percent per annum on average over these five years. And without major cuts in government programs, the federal spending share of America's income continued to rise even as the tax share fell. When the tax share had peaked at 20 percent in 1981, the spending share had been 23 percent. Now that the tax share had fallen to 18 percent, the spending share had actually risen to 24 percent. The deficit had not steadily narrowed but steadily widened despite the recovery from the 1981–82 recession. Unemployment declined from almost 11 percent of the labor force at year-end 1982 to less than 7 percent in 1986, and most of our industrial capacity was back at work. But the deficit set a new record not just in 1982 and 1983 but again in 1985, and yet again in 1986.

As we shall see, the fact that federal spending as a share of

*In 1987 the tax code changed once again because of the Tax Reform Act of 1986.

the American economy remained high and even rose was due only partly to congressional resistance to the spending cuts that Reagan proposed. The budget fights of the early and mid-1980s were not primarily about the total amount of government spending, because neither Congress nor the president had proposed a major reduction in *total* government spending in the first place. Talking about lower spending was one thing. Actually proposing lower spending was something different. Apart from interest on the national debt, Congress actually voted *less* in total spending than the Reagan administration proposed in both 1984 and 1985 and not all that much more in other years. The issue always was, and still is, about spending priorities—rural versus urban, food stamps versus farm price supports, defense versus everything else—not the total amount the government should spend on all its functions.

The Reagan budget from February 1981 proposed a six-year trajectory ending in 1986 with $849 billion of spending for all purposes other than meeting the net interest payments due on the national debt.[11] The amount actually spent in 1986 was $854 billion, just $5 billion more than proposed five years earlier. To be sure, Congress voted more money for some programs in 1986 than Reagan wanted. But the debate remained one over spending priorities, not spending totals. Non-interest spending for 1986 exceeded the February 1981 Reagan budget projection by $5 billion because the government *underspent* the original Reagan defense proposal for that year by $69 billion and *overspent* the original Reagan proposal for all other government programs by $74 billion. This $5 billion of extra spending for all federal government programs in 1986 was a negligible share of the quarter-trillion-dollar difference between that year's actual budget deficit of $221 billion—fully 5.3 percent of America's income despite four years of business expansion—and the original Reagan estimate of a $28 billion *surplus.*

It was the error in Reagan's economic assumptions that accounted for most of this difference. In the end, lower tax rates simply did not deliver the incentive effects, the growth of incomes, or the higher revenues claimed in advance by Reagan and the other advocates of major tax reduction. As a result, the government's revenues fell short of the original Reagan estimate for 1986 by a startling $171 billion, more than thirty times the spending overage. The rest of the difference simply reflected the fact that with a ballooning national debt, by 1986 the government's net interest bill came to $73 billion more than the administration had expected.

More startling still, the administration's February 1981 budget estimates did not envision the additional revenues generated by the Tax Equity and Fiscal Responsibility Act, which Congress passed in 1982 in the wake of public reaction to the business tax cuts enacted the prior year, and the Deficit Reduction Act, which Congress passed in 1984 after growing deficits had attracted increasing concern. The 1982 bill boosted tax revenues by $52 billion in 1986. The 1984 bill raised 1986 revenues by a further $17 billion.[12] Only with the extra $69 billion of taxes raised by these two later bills, which were not even contemplated during the new administration's first heady months, did revenues in 1986 come within $171 billion of the target. Without this later legislation, the 1986 revenue shortfall would have been an astonishing $240 billion. The 1981 Economic Recovery Tax Act—which by comparison reduced the government's revenues in 1986 by $211 billion—was clearly the central factor accounting for the shortfall.

These comparisons for 1986, the final year covered in the original Reagan budget, are representative. The same failure of tax revenues to meet earlier projections, the same relationship between the missing revenues and the swollen deficit, and the same parallel between the lost revenues and the lower tax rates put in place by Kemp-Roth occurred also in 1983, 1984, and

1985 and again in 1987. In total for the six years 1982–87, the excess of what the government spent over what the Reagan administration requested on a year-by-year basis for all purposes other than paying interest on the national debt came to $90 billion. For the same six years, the government's deficits added up to more than $1.1 *trillion.* Each year, the federal budget was in deficit mostly because tax revenues fell far short of the Reagan administration's early projections, not because total spending exceeded the administration's proposals. And each year, the taxes not paid because of Kemp-Roth made up most if not all the difference between actual revenues and what the administration had projected.

Moreover, unlike the large deficits of 1975 and 1976, this continuing shortfall was not due primarily to economic weakness. Though reduced incomes and poor profits during the business downturn that began shortly after Reagan took office at first accounted for part of the surge in federal borrowing that occurred, active tax and spending decisions, including especially the 1981 tax bill, accounted for still more. By the beginning of the government's 1983 fiscal year, Kemp-Roth had cut individual income taxes by 5 percent and again by another 10 percent. By the time fiscal 1983 ended, it had done so by yet another 10 percent. Even if business had shown no further deterioration after 1981—in other words, even if two and a half million more Americans had been at work—the 1983 deficit would still have been $117 billion.

Under any previous fiscal policy in American history, the business recovery that began at the end of 1982 would have brought the government's revenues more closely into line with its spending within two years or at most three. Not so this time. In 1984 American business added more than four million jobs, profits surged, and the Reagan administration enjoyed a brief moment in which the "New Beginning for the Economy" it had foretold in 1981 seemed perhaps at hand. But with the final 10 percent cut in individual income tax rates under Kemp-Roth, the recovery that would otherwise have reduced the deficit by a substantial amount did so only marginally. And even then, 1984 proved to be only a pause on the road to still new deficit records. As the initial pace of the business expansion slowed, the deficit rose to $212 billion in 1985 and then $221 billion, still 5.3 percent of total income, in 1986. In 1987 a surge of revenues narrowed the deficit to "just" $150 billion, as individuals and corporations accelerated various kinds of transactions in response to the 1986 Tax Reform Act. But even with the $30 billion deficit reduction package negotiated after the October 1987 stock market crash, the deficit in 1988 will again be higher (apart from the growing Social Security surplus), and under our current tax and spending policies it will continue to rise thereafter.

Seven successive deficits in the first seven years of the 1980s constituted a pattern that may have appeared not much different from what we had in the seventies or the sixties. But simply counting minus years and looking in vain for plusses is as far as the resemblance went. The new approach to American fiscal policy in the 1980s produced not just deficits but large deficits: very large—and not just because of inflation but because they were genuinely big compared to what we produced and earned. And although they began when business was weak, they became larger even as the economy recovered. For decades Americans had been committed to paying in full for what their government provided. But now that commitment had given way to a policy of never paying in full for our government under any circumstances at all.

Chapter VI

THE REAGAN RECOVERY

Do not look at the jar but at what is in it;
There are new jars full of old wine, and old jars which
do not contain even new wine.

—FATHERS, IV:20

In retrospect it is clear that the 1981–82 business collapse, which raised unemployment above twelve million and idled more industrial capacity than at any time since the thirties, played a crucial role in making possible the radical break in American fiscal policy that occurred in the 1980s. It did so in the first instance simply by masking what was happening. Ever since 1959, the government had run sizable deficits during economic downturns. After it became apparent that business was weak in 1981 and becoming weaker in 1982, no one expected the new president to deliver *immediately* on his pledge of shrinking deficits.

But more important, once the new fiscal policy became clear, the wounds of the recession and concerns over the subsequent recovery confused public discussion of the economic consequences that that policy implied. While most Americans knew it was high interest rates, due to monetary policy, that had brought about the recession, they somehow feared that fiscal policy would impede the recovery. Instead of asking what effects for good or ill would ensue from a regime of persistent deficits and rising government indebtedness, they focused on whether the mounting deficit would choke off the business recovery by forcing interest rates back up as private borrowers increasingly had to compete with the government for funds.

When in time the deficit did not abort the recovery—for there was no reason that it should—supporters of the new policy seized this victory over what was never a real threat anyway to deny that the deficit either had or would have adverse consequences. And as the postrecession recovery developed into the longest running business expansion in American peacetime experience, apparently without sacrificing the reduced inflation that the recession had brought, a complacent attitude spread that lasted until the stock market crashed in 1987.

Most Americans, if asked whether economic conditions have improved in the 1980s, will point to slower inflation and lower unemployment as the decade's most visible gains. In 1980 consumer prices rose by 12 percent, and 7 percent of the labor force was unemployed. In 1987 prices rose 4 percent and unemployment was 6 percent.[1] But because the recession that slowed inflation also raised unemployment to nearly 11 percent for a while, the comparison many Americans have in mind makes the improvement look large in that respect too. Moreover, many people—including Ronald Reagan—had long argued that deficits were inflationary. Continuing low inflation, despite the expansion, therefore provided yet another reason for complacency about any harm the growing deficit might cause.

But the fear that the deficit would halt the recovery and the belief that it would necessarily bring inflation had both been invalid in the first place. So was the counterclaim that the deficit would have no other ill effects.

.   .   .

What was initially forgotten against the backdrop of the worst business downturn in fifty years is that expansionary fiscal policy is expansionary. When tax cuts increase take-home pay, people spend most of that increase on clothes, cars, furniture, appliances, movies, vacations, and the entire range of consumer goods that make up more than two thirds of what American business produces. The typical American family spends 95 percent of its after-tax income on consumer goods of one kind or another and saves just 5 percent. Although some evidence suggests that people save more out of whatever additional income they receive from one-shot tax rebates, tax cuts that are perceived to be lasting are probably the most direct way of all to expand consumer spending.

Similarly, when tax credits or faster write-offs of plant and equipment reduce the share of their profits that corporations pay to the government, their after-tax cash flows increase. Companies can then use those larger cash flows to buy inventories, invest in new equipment, modernize facilities, hire additional workers, and in general expand production. And because more than three quarters of corporate dividend payments go directly to individual stockholders, whatever part of their expanded after-tax cash flows companies devote to raising dividends mostly increases individual incomes and therefore boosts consumer spending in yet another way.*

Nor are tax cuts the whole of the story of how expansionary fiscal policy works. Most kinds of government spending also directly raise the incomes of specific employee or recipient

---

*Because most individuals who are stockholders already have high incomes, however, the resulting stimulus to consumer spending is smaller and less immediate than in the case of direct tax cuts that affect individuals throughout the income range. Only 19 percent of all Americans directly own any stock at all, and just 2 percent of Americans own some 50 percent of all the stock that individuals hold.[2]

groups. Engineers who design military aircraft, construction workers who build post offices and repave highways, computer programmers and secretaries who work in federal offices all earn more at these jobs than they would receive on the unemployment line. These government employees, as well as the employees of government contractors, can and do spend more on everyday living than if they were jobless. By hiring more workers, either on the federal payroll or through military and civilian contractors, the government directly adds to the purchasing power of some of the nation's consumers. And the same is true for still different groups when the government raises Social Security benefits, or housing allowances, or farm price supports.

The point is that the deficit is not a self-contained phenomenon that springs to life spontaneously, unconnected to whatever else the government is doing. It is no more—and, sadly for America in the 1980s, no less—than the difference between what the government spends and what it takes in. To focus only on the consequences of financing the deficit, without recognizing that the higher spending and lower taxes that gave rise to the deficit in the first place also affect business activity, and do so quite directly, is like worrying about a rifle's recoil without first looking to see where the bullet went.

Both the higher spending and lower taxes that increased the deficit from $74 billion in 1980 to $208 billion in 1983 were important spurs to business recovery. Defense spending almost doubled, from $134 billion in Carter's last year to $210 billion in Reagan's third. Construction of two new nuclear-powered aircraft carriers, two nuclear-powered attack submarines, and five warships; procurement of the F-15 jet fighter and the DIVAD division air defense gun; and stepped-up development of the B-1B and Stealth bombers and the MX missile, not only added to the Defense Department's budget but also stimulated production and created nearly 300,000 jobs at military contracting firms in 1982 alone. General Dynamics hired 7,000 new employees in Detroit just to work on its portion of the M1 tank project. Rockwell International took on more than 4,000 new people to work on its part of the B-1B bomber. Boeing, Lockheed, Raytheon, McDonnell Douglas, United Technologies and General Electric all added jobs for their shares of the new defense contracts.[3] The Defense Department itself added 56,000 new jobs in 1981, 83,000 more in 1982 and 1983, and another 116,000 in the next two years.[4] In the meanwhile, despite the highly visible cuts in nondefense activities like school lunches and the CETA training program, the total number of employees on the federal payroll declined between 1980 and 1982 by only 127,000 out of almost three million. After 1982 total federal employment again began to grow.[5]

Direct government payments in support of individuals' incomes also grew rapidly during these years. As the deepening recession raised unemployment above ten million for the first time since 1938, federal spending for programs like unemployment insurance and supplemental income benefits rose from $87 billion in 1980 to $123 billion in 1983. Over the same three years, the volume of Social Security checks sent out rose from $119 billion to $171 billion, as payments kept up with inflation, while an additional half a million Americans began receiving benefits. Because people who get unemployment compensation and Social Security benefits often have few other sources of income, they typically save even less of what they receive than the mere 5 percent average for all Americans. The surge in income-support payments during these years probably added to consumer spending on a nearly one-for-one basis.

At the same time, Kemp-Roth made sure that those Americans who were still at work had more left for themselves after paying their taxes. Receipts from individual income taxes increased from $244 billion in 1980 to $286 billion in 1981, the last federal fiscal year not affected by the tax cut. Despite the recession, which slowed income growth, without Kemp-Roth individual Americans would have paid $330 billion in income taxes in 1982 and $362 billion in 1983. Instead, three successive rate cuts over twenty-one months held individuals' tax payments to just $298 billion in 1982 and then reduced them to $289 billion in 1983 even as business began to expand again. And in 1984, despite the advancing recovery, payments of individual income taxes rose only to the same $298 billion mark they had reached two years earlier when economywide personal income was fully one sixth lower.

The 1981 tax bill also reduced business taxes. Although the Tax Equity and Fiscal Responsibility Act that Congress passed the following year curtailed much of the 1981 bill's cut in business taxes, the net reduction in the amount of tax that businesses had to pay was still substantial. Because profits declined sharply during the recession, even in the absence of any new legislation the taxes paid by corporations would have fallen from $65 billion in 1980 to $47 billion in 1983.[6] With both the 1981 and 1982 tax bills in effect, taxes on profits actually paid by U.S. corporations fell to just $37 billion that year.

More jobs in the government, more jobs in the private-sector defense industry, higher income supports for the unemployed, higher Social Security benefits for retirees, lower income taxes for individuals, lower profit taxes for corporations—the entire package added up to a massive injection of fiscal stimulus for an economy that was operating with plenty of unused resources to begin with. The American economy responded to this stimulus —and as we shall see, to the Federal Reserve's sudden easing of monetary policy in the summer of 1982—by rebounding sharply in 1983 and then continuing to advance solidly through most of the next year. By the end of 1984, just two years into the recovery, business activity overall had grown by an impressive 11 percent in real terms, and four million fewer workers were unemployed. The Reagan recovery was well under way.

And not despite the deficit but *because* of it. The increased spending and reduced taxes that ran up more than $400 billion in accumulated deficits during just the three fiscal years 1982–84 were the same increased spending and the same reduced taxes that spurred the business recovery. The fear that these actions would somehow choke off the recovery while the economy still had large amounts of idle resources was simply wrong. But understandably, especially when businesses had been folding, banks had been failing, and most workers were still either unemployed or worried about their jobs, that possibility is what most Americans thought about when they first began to grasp the new fiscal facts.

A further problem was that some critics of the new policy, who presumably understood that continued large deficits would not abort the recovery, apparently concluded that this fear might generate political support for a more responsible fiscal stance and therefore encouraged it despite its lack of foundation. In America's crisis-activated political system, it is difficult enough even under the best of circumstances to motivate an energetic response to a policy that threatens ultimately to erode our standard of living yet does so only gradually, without the immediate, tangible consequences that focus public attention. How could critics who knew that the new fiscal policy would eventually undermine productive investment, but would do so only after the recovery had restored business activity to something like full employment, attract attention to these future prospects when widespread bankruptcies and joblessness still dominated public discussion and the first priority was to nurse the business recovery? In the end, even opponents of the new policy who no doubt knew better were careful not to contradict the claim that the deficit's main threat was a near-term collapse of the nascent recovery.*

But as both the deficit and the business expansion continued, this tactic backfired. By the 1984 election campaign, the recovery had become not just a plus for Reagan but the principal basis for his continued advocacy of the new fiscal policy. In the first of the two Reagan-Mondale debates, in the very first question posed, the president was asked about the deficit. He responded by emphasizing the business recovery and specifically the role Kemp-Roth had played in bringing it about: "Already we have a recovery that has been going on for about twenty-one months, to the point that we can now call it an expansion. . . . Our tax cut, we think, was very instrumental in bringing this recovery about."[8] And, of course, he was right.

Increasingly however, the fact that the deficit did not stall the recovery came to be seen as evidence that deficits were harmless and that a fiscal policy producing outsized deficits into the indefinite future was no cause for concern. In January 1984, Treasury Secretary Donald Regan proudly unveiled a new study widely interpreted as showing—though as we shall see, it actually showed nothing of the kind—that deficits had no impact on interest rates or the dollar.[9] If deficits did not raise interest rates, as critics had feared, how could they depress

---

*Budget Director David Stockman, for example—who quickly developed second thoughts about the policy he had so aggressively helped sell to Congress in the administration's early days—told the Senate Finance Committee in March 1982 that if the deficit were to continue for three or four years at the $100 billion level (which then seemed unbelievably large), "The prospects for sustaining a permanent recovery rather than simply a temporary recovery would not be high."[7] Such statements by Stockman and others did not, of course, directly predict that the growing deficit would choke off the expansion, but they were enough to suggest as much.

investment? If they did not raise dollar exchange rates, how could they depress exports or spur imports? Besides, business investment in 1984 was not weaker but stronger than a few years earlier, as was our economy in most other respects. The Reagan recovery spoke for itself.

The distinction that the public discussion at that time missed is not just that expansionary fiscal policy is expansionary but that it is expansionary when the economy has room to expand. Reagan's expansionary policy at the outset of the 1980s worked, and the resulting deficit spurred rather than impeded the business recovery, precisely because the American economy was then in the midst of a major slump. By the end of 1982, more of our economic resources were unused than at any time since the thirties. More than twelve million workers were unemployed, including not just new entrants to the labor force but also millions with significant skill and experience. Industry overall was using only 69 percent of its capacity, a far cry from the 82 percent postwar average, including both recessions and expansions.[10] And beneath these economywide aggregates, extraordinary pockets of unemployed labor and shut-down plants were scattered throughout the country.

With this abundance of available resources, the combination of lower taxes and faster spending was bound to stimulate business and it did. Even from the perspective of investment in new plant and equipment, the most important reason for avoiding large deficits under normal conditions, expansionary fiscal policy more likely helped than hurt in the underemployed American economy of the early 1980s. Not only did the deficit not choke off the business recovery, but the lower taxes and higher government spending that stood behind it fueled the recovery. Interest rates were higher than they would have been without the deficit, but the stronger demand for goods and the increased profits resulting from expansionary tax and spending policies both encouraged and facilitated investment nonetheless.

In fact, with so much of our resources unemployed at the outset of the decade, the extraordinarily high interest rates that prevailed during these early years were not primarily due to the deficit. They were instead the product of tight monetary policy designed to halt inflation. Most interest rates reached the highest levels yet posted in American financial markets—over 16 percent on Treasury bills in May 1981 and 15 percent on ten- and twenty-year Treasury bonds in September 1981—while the budget was still Carter's and even the first of the three Kemp-Roth tax rate reductions was yet to take effect. The blame for the 1981–82 recession, and conversely the credit for the slower inflation it brought, lies with monetary policy. So does a share of the credit for the subsequent recovery, which did not begin until after monetary policy was eased.

In evaluating how our unbalanced fiscal policy has shaped our economy in the 1980s and how a new fiscal course might correct those imbalances in the future, it is essential not to lose sight of the role played by monetary policy. Fiscal policy, consisting of the entire set of tax and spending programs legislated by Congress, is one way government influences the overall economy. But there are other ways too. Chief among them by far is monetary policy, which the Federal Reserve System carries out (and which some observers say its chairman, Paul Volcker, carried out personally from 1979 until President Reagan replaced him with Alan Greenspan in 1987) under authority delegated to it by Congress. Like fiscal policy, monetary policy in the 1980s has also been different from what it had been in earlier decades. One important reason for that difference was—and is—the swollen deficit. But at the outset of the 1980s, the chief concern at the Federal Reserve was to stifle inflation.

When Congress first created the Federal Reserve System just before World War I, no one mentioned fighting inflation or so much as contemplated the active role monetary policy was subsequently to play in American economic life. The clearly stated purpose of the new central bank was to provide stability to the financial markets and thereby prevent the occasional panics that had severely disrupted business. The new institution was to achieve this end by acting as a bank for the nation's banks, lending in small ways as required to smooth out interest rate fluctuations and lending in a big way if in a crisis the financial system as a whole needed a lender of last resort.

But over time, it became apparent that the new central bank had the means to be a more active force. The Federal Reserve's staff and officials soon saw how the new system's operations affected not just banks but financial markets generally. At the same time, continued advances in communications were gradually integrating what had been mostly regional financial centers, geographically dispersed across the country, into a nationwide market. In this increasingly centralized setting, the Federal Reserve found that it could do more than just stabilize interest rates and lend to banks on the edge of failure. It could also establish financial conditions that encouraged business expansion or, if it chose, create financial stringencies that slowed business down.

The evolution of a positive monetary policy was interrupted by the spreading financial collapse after 1929. And soon afterward it was interrupted again by the Federal Reserve's World War II commitment, which lasted until 1951, to keep interest rates fixed so that citizens who had bought Treasury bonds in the war effort would not see the value of their securities fall as interest rates rose. By the mid-fifties however, active use of monetary policy to stimulate or retard business had become a recognized part of the Federal Reserve's institutional mission, fully on a par with its original charge to stabilize financial markets.

The fact that both fiscal and monetary policy influence economic conditions overall, without explicitly singling out specific industries or individual businesses, has been fundamental to our political acceptance of these two key means of government economic control. In the end, of course, tax changes and variations in government spending do have diverse effects on different businesses and different individuals, and so do fluctuations in interest rates. But at least public discussion of these policies can focus on issues of aggregate economic performance, such as whether business is expanding or contracting nationwide or how fast prices are rising or how many workers are unemployed. The different impacts that separate industry from industry, firm from firm, or individual from individual can remain comfortably implicit.

To be sure, neither American businesses nor individual Americans have ever been reticent about pushing for government policies that serve their specific private interests. And increasingly, lobbying for federal programs that will benefit their states or their cities constitutes much of the everyday workload of America's governors and mayors. But as citizens, Americans have traditionally preferred the impersonality of government actions with economywide effects that work through private markets. Actions explicitly designed to promote one industry or one city or geographical area smack too much of socialist-style central planning. They cut against the grain of a market-driven, competitive enterprise system. They also raise the specter of exploitation through political influence.* Americans instead prefer the impartiality of blunter

---

*Fears of both sorts strengthened resistance to the argument in the early 1980s that because Japan's phenomenal rise as a world competitor may have

mechanisms that rely in the first instance on market competition rather than bureaucratic discretion to distribute their uneven impact. In light of this political ethos, it is hardly surprising that fiscal and monetary policies have become, and remain, our two chief means of pursuing government economic objectives.

In the nearly four decades since the Treasury released the Federal Reserve from its wartime commitment to stabilize bond prices, and thereby freed monetary policy to serve as an independent means of economic policy, the most visible and effective role played by monetary policy has been as an occasional brake on inflation. First in 1953, and then again in 1957, 1959, 1966, 1969, and 1974, the Federal Reserve raised interest rates by preventing banks from lending as much as businesses and individuals wanted to borrow. Each time, the motive behind monetary restraint was to arrest inflation. And except for 1966, when the Vietnam War continued to spur an economy that had already built up substantial momentum, monetary restraint was in each instance the forerunner of a business downturn.

Monetary policy in the early 1980s again followed this well-established pattern. But because inflation this time was more entrenched than it had been since the end of World War II, the restraint that the Federal Reserve sought was correspondingly greater. By the 1980s, the use of tight money to fight inflation by slowing the economy was a thoroughly familiar tactic. What was new this time was the severity of the inflation and the magnitude of the necessary recession, and hence the required degree of monetary stringency. What was also new in

---

been the result of successful direction and protection provided to key industries by its Ministry of Trade and Industry, we too should have an "industrial policy."

the 1980s was the political will to sustain whatever business downturn was needed to restore stable prices.

It was this tight monetary policy, not expansionary fiscal policy, that drove interest rates to record highs in 1980 and then again in 1981. In October 1979, Volcker announced that henceforth monetary policy would follow a new path. At one level the new regime featured a redesigned set of day-to-day operating procedures intended to be more effective in preventing banks from lending and therefore creating money in amounts greater than what the Federal Reserve deemed appropriate, even if their customers wanted to do more business than that. More important, the new approach to monetary policy meant a greater resolve to reduce inflation, even if at substantial economic cost.

Interest rates jumped immediately. They continued to rise into the next spring, reaching then-record levels. In March, President Carter used the Credit Control Act of 1969 to authorize the Federal Reserve to reinforce the restrictive effects of these high interest rates with mandatory ceilings limiting how much institutions ranging from banks to department stores could lend to their customers. The Federal Reserve promptly did so. When business activity immediately slowed, the Federal Reserve removed the credit ceilings and allowed interest rates to fall. Shortly afterward, business began to recover. But it soon became clear that this hiccup in economic activity had come nowhere near stopping the inflation.

With the election over and a new president in office who had inveighed against inflation throughout the campaign, the Federal Reserve was free to return to its assault on inflation despite the costs in terms of forgone output, lost jobs, and lower incomes and profits. Everyone had always known that a steep enough economic decline that lasted long enough could squash even a double-digit inflation. What was new after 1979 and especially by early 1981, was the willingness to pursue such a course. The way was clear for yet a new round of tight monetary policy.

This time there were no credit ceilings. High interest rates were left to do all of the work. As the Federal Reserve steadily restricted the ability of banks to lend, interest rates rose past the record levels set just a year earlier. By the summer of 1981, a new business downturn had begun. It lasted until the end of 1982, after the Federal Reserve had relaxed its monetary policy and after both tax and spending policies had turned expansionary too.

The Federal Reserve abruptly shifted to an easier monetary policy in mid-1982. With no end to the recession in sight and both unemployment and business bankruptcies at levels not seen since before World War II, continued monetary restraint was becoming less and less tenable as each month passed. Perhaps even more important from the Federal Reserve's perspective, signs of increasing fragility in the financial system were everywhere. More banks failed in just the first six months of 1982 than in any entire year since the Depression. By year-end there had been more failures than in the entire decade of the fifties, with direct effects on more than two million depositors. Persisting with monetary restriction in order to halt inflation, an objective that was not even mentioned in the original Federal Reserve Act, looked increasingly likely to clash with that charter's clear instruction to maintain stability in the financial markets.

Worse still, by mid-1982 Mexico and the other large Latin American debtors had no prospect of repaying the huge amounts they had borrowed during the seventies, and in the current environment of high interest rates (and an increasingly overvalued dollar) the likelihood of their even keeping up their interest payments became more dubious almost daily. If these countries failed to make their scheduled payments, the banks that had lent to them would have to declare their debts in default. As a practical matter, most people already knew these loans were in trouble. But to acknowledge that this was so would have rendered most of America's biggest banks technically insolvent. At best, the result would be an unprecedented regulatory challenge. At worst, the Federal Reserve would fail, and by truly colossal dimensions, to achieve its long-standing primary mission of maintaining financial stability.

Faced with these unhappy prospects, Volcker and his colleagues finally concluded that enough was enough. Inflation had slowed but remained at a 4 percent annual rate. That, however, would have to do. In July the Federal Reserve shifted to an easier monetary policy, suspending the new operating procedures it had adopted almost three years earlier. Interest rates immediately plunged. In October, Volcker publicly acknowledged the change, cautiously claiming at least a temporary victory over inflation and arguing that a new priority now guided policy: "The forces are there that would push the economy toward recovery. I would think that the policy objective should be to sustain that recovery."[11] By the end of the year, rates on Treasury bills were back down to 8 percent and bond rates to 10 percent. Even more than Reagan's increasingly expansionary fiscal policy, the sharp reversal of monetary policy at midyear 1982 opened the way for the vigorous business recovery in 1983 and early 1984.

But the newly expansionary fiscal policy helped. Government spending increasingly exceeded revenues as business recovered, and an ever larger share of the resulting deficit was due not to economic weakness but to the fundamental imbalance that marked Reagan's new policy. By 1984 unemployment fell below 8 percent, but the deficit was $185 billion anyway. At 6 percent unemployment the 1984 deficit would have been $144 billion. By 1986 unemployment edged below 7 percent, but the deficit was now $221 billion. At 6 percent unemployment, the 1986 deficit would have been $204 billion.[12] As Kemp-Roth cut taxes, and military spending accelerated without offsetting restraint on nondefense programs, fiscal policy became more expansionary than at any other time since World War II.

And so the expansion, driven by both monetary and fiscal policy, continued on. Unemployment fell while inflation remained modest. But even apart from the future consequences of our mounting debts and the selling to foreigners of our assets, has this economic performance—even in the present—warranted the air of satisfaction and complacency with which most Americans viewed our new fiscal policy? Reduced inflation was the result of monetary policy, not fiscal policy, and even by 1987 the expansion had merely returned unemployment to where it stood in 1979. Moreover, generating more work for its own sake has never been a highly valued object of economic policy anyway. The point is to raise the standard of living. Increasing employment is usually an effective means to that end, but not the end itself. Our new policy has clearly built up a large debt burden for the average American family to shoulder in the future, but how much better off for it have we been, even as the expansion was occurring?

Most Americans had arrived at 1980 with the feeling that they were not, in Ronald Reagan's phrase, better off than they had been four years earlier. From 1973 on, a variety of forces had combined to reduce our productivity growth. Without productivity gains, wage increases failed to keep pace with inflation. The rise in the standard of living slowed as well. Between 1948 and 1973, per capita consumer spending had risen by an average 2.2 percent per annum after allowing for inflation. Between 1973 and 1980, the average annual gain was just 1.4 percent.[13]

Other circumstances had also changed in ways that made

this consumer spending slowdown even worse for most Americans. One reason was that in the late seventies adults were increasingly outnumbering children. There were sixteen million more Americans in 1980 than in 1973 but six million *fewer* below age sixteen. Hence even an unchanged increase in per capita spending would not have stretched as far. A second reason was that, with no growth in the real earnings of each worker, more Americans had to work merely to achieve even this reduced spending growth. In 1973, 36 percent of all married couples living in the same household included both a working husband and a working wife. By 1980 the proportion of working couples was 42 percent.[14] Not only was the standard of living rising only two thirds as fast as before, but more people than ever before were working just to maintain this diminished rate of increase. The resulting discontent was real, and the 1980 presidential election forcefully demonstrated Reagan's ability to mobilize hopes for a better future.

Even on the most favorable construction of the facts however, the party thrown by America's new fiscal policy in the 1980s has merely restored growth in per capita consumer spending to 2.2 percent per annum, the same average rate that prevailed before 1973. Fueled by Kemp-Roth, consumer spending has led America's business expansion in the 1980s. Between 1980 and 1987, consumer spending has grown almost 1 percent faster per annum than total spending in our economy. Consumer spending averaged 63.4 percent of income in the fifties, 62.6 percent in the sixties, and 62.9 percent in the seventies. Thus far in the 1980s, it has averaged 65.1 percent, with a steady rise since the new fiscal policy began. By 1987 the consumption share was up to 66.1 percent, the highest for any year since the wave of consumer spending that immediately followed World War II. By then consumer spending stood 24.7 percent above the 1980 level after allowing for inflation, although our real income had risen just 19.8 percent.

That extra bulge of 4.9 percent in consumer spending in 1987 came to $145 billion, almost enough to balance our international trade if we had cut imports by that much or exported that much more of our goods instead of consuming them at home.

Moreover, even this modest apparent improvement over the seventies in the growth of our standard of living merely reflects the fact that 1980 (unlike 1948 or 1973) was a recession year. If we step back a year to before the recession began, the *ac*celeration over the slower growth pace of the seventies turns into a slight *de*celeration. Between *1979* and 1987 the after-inflation gain in per capita consumer spending was just 1.8 percent per annum, even less than the 1.9 percent during 1973–79. Recessions aside, it is not clear that there has been any improvement in the 1980s at all, even from the limited perspective of growth in consumption.

And in addition, the changes in age structures and work patterns that made the slower per capita spending growth seem so very unsatisfactory in the seventies have also persisted during the 1980s. Between 1980 and 1987, the population expanded by another sixteen million. But that growth consisted of more than fifteen million additional people age sixteen and older and less than one million below age sixteen. In addition, the share of working-age Americans who were actually at work rose still further. By 1987, 49 percent of all married couples were working couples.

Comparisons of the 1980s to our prior economic performance, based on what we earn rather than what we consume, make the 1980s look even worse—much worse. The average earnings of production workers in American businesses outside agriculture peaked in real terms in 1972, at $366 per week in today's dollars. By 1980 two recessions had squeezed weekly earnings to $319. In 1987 the average weekly pay was just $312.

Hourly wage rates have risen modestly during the 1980s, but the continuing shrinkage of the work week has held the average worker's increase in total pay to less than what it would have taken to keep up with inflation. Moreover, the failure of workers' real earnings even to regain the 1980 level, much less that of 1972, has not been the result of a further sharp drop incurred during the 1981–82 recession. Real earnings did not fall much in the last recession, especially compared to the large declines of 1973–75 and 1980. Today's depressed level instead reflects the fact that wage growth during the expansion has been unusually weak.

This failure of real earnings to recover significantly in the 1980s has been all the more surprising, and for many individuals highly distressing, in light of the advancing age and experience of the American labor force. Now that the baby boom generation has matured, the typical worker ought to be further up the pay scale than a decade or two ago. But the average worker's weekly pay remained lower in 1987 than it had been in 1980, and it was lower still in comparison to what his counterpart with comparable age and experience used to earn. In the 1980s, moving up the age and experience scale has not meant moving up the pay scale.

With essentially zero growth in workers' earnings, how have we paid for even the modest growth in real per capita consumer spending that we have enjoyed during the Reagan recovery?

Although popular discussion often points to borrowing, in fact personal borrowing has played essentially no role in maintaining the growth of consumption, at least at the aggregate level. Individual Americans have borrowed more in the 1980s than ever before both in absolute dollars and in relation to their income, but as we have seen, for Americans in the aggregate this borrowing has financed holdings of correspondingly greater volumes of financial assets. During 1980–87 individuals borrowed more than $1.4 trillion (net of repayments) in consumer credit, home mortgages, and other forms of debt. But on the other side of their balance sheets, individuals accumulated $2 trillion of bank deposits plus another $700 billion of debt securities issued by the U.S. Treasury, by government-backed agencies like the Federal National Mortgage Association ("Fannie Mae"), and the Federal Home Loan Mortgage Corporation ("Freddie Mac"), and by corporate businesses, not to mention more risky financial assets like stocks and even nonfinancial assets like houses.[15] No doubt the "me generation" has some members, but if patterns of borrowing and investing provide any guide to who they are, they do not bulk very large among Americans overall. It is the government that is running up excess debt in the 1980s, not individual Americans borrowing on their own account.

One way we have managed to increase the growth in real consumer spending in the 1980s was simply by relying as we did in the seventies on a further increase in the number of people working. Since 1980 as during 1973–80, there has been no growth in real income per worker. But the fraction of the population that is of working age has risen as the baby boom has matured, and the fraction of working-age Americans who actually work has risen even more rapidly than before. These two developments in combination have provided for at least some modest growth in per *capita* real income, and therefore in real consumer spending, despite the absence of growth in real income per *worker.*

But the more important source of increased consumer spending gains has been Reagan's fiscal policy acting directly on family budgets. In the 1980s we enjoyed a further increase in Social Security and other forms of direct income payments that individuals and families receive from government. But unlike in the past, this increase has coincided with a decline in the taxes that individuals pay in relation to their incomes.

Government income transfers to individuals and payments by the government on their behalf—including retirement benefits, health benefits, veterans' benefits, and general welfare assistance—have grown dramatically since World War II. Although the growth of these payments has slowed somewhat in the 1980s, they have not leveled off even in relation to the growth of income from other sources. Individual tax payments also rose as a share of income during most of the postwar period. But taxes paid as a share of income reached a peak in 1981 and then declined as Kemp-Roth took effect.

In 1948 individual Americans paid 11 percent of their incomes in taxes to government at all levels—federal, state, and local—including their contributions to the Social Security System. That year the payments that these taxpayers and other Americans received back from government at all levels, including Social Security benefits, comprised 5 percent of their total income. After netting the transfers they received against the taxes they paid, all individual Americans together were paying 6 percent of their income to foot the bill for other government services like national defense at the federal level or highways at the state level or schools at the local level.

By 1973 what the government did had grown. So had what it took to pay for it. But while the percentages going in and coming out were both larger, the relationship between them was much the same as it had been a quarter-century earlier. In 1973 tax and other payments *to* government took 17 percent of individuals' income. Direct transfers to individuals *from* government provided 10.8 percent of all personal income. The balance left to pay for all other services that government provides was 6.2 percent of individuals' income, essentially no different from 1948.

And it was still no different in 1979.* By then the share of individuals' income that went for tax payments was up to 18.2 percent, while the share of income provided by direct government transfers was up to 12.4 percent. What was left to pay for other government activities was still 5.8 percent.

It was only in the 1980s under Reagan's new fiscal policy, that this long-standing relationship changed. Because of Kemp-Roth, the share of individuals' income paid in taxes of all kinds other than Social Security contributions *declined* between 1979 and 1986. After including the hike in Social Security, the total tax payments of individuals was still 18.2 percent. In the meanwhile, government transfer payments kept on rising in relation to income, reaching 13.4 percent in 1986. The balance left to pay for all other government services was down to just 4.8 percent of income, fully two percentage points below what it was on average from the fifties to the seventies.† Quite apart from how much our incomes had grown, compared to 1979 Reagan's new fiscal policy based on tax cuts without spending cuts had made an extra 1 percent of our incomes available to pay for consumer spending.

The third way in which we have financed real consumption growth without real earnings growth is by reducing our saving —in direct contradiction to what Reagan said would happen under his new policies, as we shall see. Public discussion of saving in the 1980s has been highly confused, even compared to that of other economic issues, for several reasons. One is simply the difficulty of measuring something as elusive as how much of their incomes a quarter of a billion people put away.

*Focusing on 1980 would be misleading for this purpose because of that year's recession.

†Focusing on 1987 would be misleading because of the one-shot surge in tax payments made as a result of the Tax Reform Act of 1986.

Some measures suggest that on average we have saved distinctly less since 1980, while others suggest that we have saved about as much as before. Another reason for the confusion is the difficulty in sorting out the many independent influences that, at least in principle, affect saving behavior in one direction or the other. Should saving now be rising in relation to income because more Americans are in the prime of their working careers? Or should it be falling because so many couples, after delaying as long as they could before having children, have finally entered what most families find to be a peak period of needs for larger houses and apartments, new kinds of furniture, and other major expenses? To what extent did the build-up of paper values in the 1982–87 stock market rally discourage people who own stocks from saving out of their ordinary incomes? What difference has the crash made?

While it is probably impossible to determine whether individuals' saving has or has not been below par for the 1980s as a whole, it is clear that saving did drop sharply after 1984. According to the standard "national income" saving measure, individual Americans saved 7.2 percent of their after-tax income on average from the fifties to the seventies and 6.5 percent on average during 1981–84. By this gauge, saving dropped to 4.5 percent of income in 1985, lower than in any year during the prior three and a half decades, and then fell further to 4.3 percent in 1986 and just 3.7 percent in 1987. An alternative saving measure, based on the Federal Reserve's "flow of funds" accounts, tells a different story about the early eighties but shows the same fall after 1984. It indicates that individual saving *rose* from 8.2 percent of after-tax income on average from the fifties to the seventies to 9.1 percent on average during 1981–84. But this measure too shows a sharp fall to 6.1 percent in 1985, 5.6 percent in 1986, and just 4 percent in 1987.

By either yardstick, since 1985 we have been saving 2 percent to 4 percent less of our incomes, and correspondingly consuming 2 percent to 4 percent percent more, than was typical of our prior postwar experience. Along with the higher fraction of Americans who now work and the changed relationship between what individuals pay in taxes and what they receive in cash benefits, it has also taken a lower saving rate to keep the party going.

The fact that such a high percentage of Americans are now working but we have so little to show for it in additional income or even additional spending raises still further troubling questions about how good life has been during the Reagan recovery.

Despite the decline in unemployment that has attracted so much attention since 1982, the 1980s has not been a period of especially rapid job creation by postwar American standards. By year-end 1987, after five straight years of business expansion, there were thirteen million more jobs than in 1980.[16] New job creation would have to continue for the remainder of the decade at the rate maintained since the expansion began in 1983, just to make the performance of the eighties comparable to that of the sixties. Even then it would be nothing special compared to the twenty million jobs created during the seventies.

More important, income growth also depends on how well jobs pay. And for the most part, this depends on whether jobs give workers an opportunity to add much or little value to what business produces. The failure of our overall productivity growth to post more than a soggy recovery in the 1980s suggests that job growth has not been in areas that add high value to what we produce. As a result, the basis for growth in real earnings has not materialized.

Our new fiscal policy has contributed to the slower pace of pay gains in the 1980s by depressing employment prospects in what have traditionally been our high value-added industries. As we shall see, by causing the dollar to be overvalued for half a decade, our large budget deficits have impaired America's ability to compete internationally and have therefore limited job opportunities in manufacturing, where productivity is typically highest but exposure to foreign competition is also greatest. Consequently, despite the recovery that has begun since the dollar has fallen, by year-end 1987 manufacturing payrolls remained smaller by 1.7 million workers than they were at the end of the seventies. Domestic capital formation has been weak as well. As a result, the construction industry has added fewer than 700,000 jobs since the late seventies. With opportunities sharply curtailed in these areas, new job creation in the 1980s has naturally provided less overall growth in earnings than American workers used to enjoy.

And unfortunately there has been more to it than that. New job creation in the 1980s has centered on genuinely low-paying positions to a greater extent than even the familiar shift from manufacturing to services would ordinarily imply. It is not just that the average worker today no longer earns in real terms what the average worker earned in the early seventies. Of all new year-round full-time jobs created since 1979, 36 percent have provided workers with *less than half* of what the average worker made in 1973.[17] Loss of jobs in manufacturing, where pay is typically some 30 percent more than the average for all businesses, and their replacement in the service sector, where pay is typically much less, can account for only part of this sharp erosion in pay scales.

What makes the sudden growth of extremely low-paying full-time jobs in the 1980s even worse is the increasing prevalence of part-time work. More than ever before in modern times, Americans are taking jobs that involve working less than year-round or less than the standard thirty-five to forty hours a week. Since 1979, part-time employment has grown at more than one and one half times the rate that full-time work has grown.[18] Although it is easy enough to think of circumstances in which part-time work is preferable—mothers with small children, for example, or students continuing their education —surveys show that half of the Americans who have taken these part-time jobs in the 1980s would prefer full-time work.[19] The prevalence of involuntary part-time work also suggests that to an unusually great extent the jobs created in recent years lack not just high pay but also prospects for significant advancement in the future.

These changes in the complexion of the American labor market in the 1980s threaten long-standing presumptions about the value of work and the relationship between work and one's place in society. The prospect of economic advancement is simply disappearing for many Americans. The typical worker no longer earns what his father or older brother earned at a comparable age a decade or two ago. Nor does he have the same apparent opportunity to move ahead. Since 1980, for the first time since the thirties, the fraction of American families who own their own homes has been declining. And with increasing numbers of Americans reluctantly at work only part time, the environment is hardly conducive to the development of strong labor force attachments, much less a sense of commitment to a specific employer. Economic opportunity, the traditional key to social mobility in America, is simply losing its relevance for a large and growing segment of our population.

Along with the erosion of the average worker's position and prospects, there is some evidence that the distribution of income and wealth has also become more unequal—at both the top and bottom. Americans have always accepted disparities in individual material well-being, and we have rightly felt that such inequalities provide the incentives that fuel the economic process at the individual level. Material inequalities are also a sign that the response to those incentives is vigorous, and that the system is working as it should.

But especially at the bottom end of the scale, we have also tried to prevent our least fortunate citizens from sinking much below the accepted norms of the day. Ever since the thirties, government has borne much of the responsibility for raising those at the bottom to within the acceptable range. Progress in improving the lot of those at the bottom was particularly evident in the late sixties. In 1960 more than 18 percent of all American families lived below the government's official "poverty level." By the end of the decade, the poverty roll included less than 10 percent of all families.[20]

But from this perspective too, in the 1980s we have failed even to hold the advances we achieved earlier on. Not surprisingly, given how real incomes on average have fallen since then, fewer Americans lived below the poverty level in 1973 than in any year before or since. Recession increased the poverty rate from 8.8 percent of all families that year to 9.7 percent in 1975, but by 1979 renewed economic growth had cut it almost back to the 1973 level. The more serious increase has come in the 1980s. As of 1986, despite four years of steady growth after the recession that began the decade, 10.9 percent of all families lived in poverty. Including individuals living alone, in 1986 more than thirty-two million Americans were below the poverty level. With wages as low as they now are in some jobs, the poverty roll in 1986 included not just the retired and unemployed and disabled, but also nearly three million Americans who worked full time all year long. Even more troubling, the group of Americans who now suffer the greatest percentage incidence of poverty is our children. As of 1986, one out of every five American children lived below the poverty line. The Reagan recovery has not been all that great on average, and many Americans have missed it altogether.

Our economic experience in the 1980s has not only run up costs to be paid in the future but reaffirmed the limitations in the present of an economic policy that simply raises consumption with no advance in productivity to support it. The debt we have accumulated under our new fiscal policy is real and growing. Americans in the future will have to service this debt by paying taxes and by transferring the goods they produce and the assets they own to lenders in other countries. Even so, the splurge we have enjoyed in the 1980s has been only thin stuff, and Americans are entitled to ask just what economic benefit our new fiscal policy has brought.

Chapter VII

DEFICITS, INTEREST RATES, AND THE DOLLAR

The store is open, the storekeeper extends credit, the ledger is open and
  the hand writes;
All who wish to borrow may come and borrow.
But the collectors make their continual rounds each day,
And collect their dues from man with his consent or not.

—FATHERS, III:16

As the Reagan recovery continued, the change from an economy rendered underemployed by the fight against inflation to
one increasingly using its available resources bore especially
important implications for our new fiscal policy. Expansionary
fiscal policy is expansionary only when the economy has room
to expand. After its resources are fully in use, tax cuts and
government jobs may very well inflate prices but will not increase production and real incomes, and therefore will no
longer stimulate capital formation by increasing sales and profits as they did during the expansion. The depressing side effects
that ensue from the government's continuing need to borrow
the difference between its spending and its revenues remain,
however, discouraging investment. Indeed, when there is little
or no room left for overall expansion, the effects of having to
finance the deficit are no longer a side show, as they were
during 1983 and even 1984, but the main event.

．．．

The heart of the matter is that deficits absorb saving. When more of what we save goes to finance the deficit, less is available for other activities that also depend on borrowed funds. In the United States, most businesses rely heavily on bond issues or bank loans to finance inventories, to buy new machines, and to build new facilities. Most families pay only a part of the purchase price in cash when they buy a new house (the average down payment is 25 percent), and seven of every ten new cars are purchased with loans behind them.

When the government borrows to finance its deficit, therefore, companies that want to invest in new plants or new machines and families that want to buy new houses must compete among themselves all the harder for whatever saving is left. In our market-oriented financial system, the main way both businesses and individuals conduct this competition is by paying higher interest rates. The more of our saving the deficit absorbs, the harder everyone else must compete for the rest and the higher interest rates go.

Except perhaps in time of war, no American has ever spent less or earned more out of a public-spirited desire to make the nation's overall financial ledger balance. Instead our financial system relies on incentives—chief among them the incentive provided by higher or lower interest rates—to induce people to act individually in ways that in the end render the total of saving that some put into the financial system equal to what others take out. This process is the essence of the market mechanism. Neither buyers nor sellers care whether total buy orders match total sell orders. But there is a buyer for every successful seller (and vice versa) nonetheless, just as in the financial markets there is a lender for every successful borrower.

In principle, the market incentives provided by higher or lower interest rates could maintain the balance between the saving that some individuals and businesses generate and the saving that others use, in a variety of ways. But in actual American experience, interest rates mainly affect business investment in new plant and equipment and investment by individuals in new homes. A new plant that looks like an attractive profit opportunity when a firm faces a low interest rate can be a sure loser if financing charges are higher, just as a house may be unaffordable if mortgage payments are too large for a family's income. The effects of interest rate fluctuations on business investment and on home building are often readily visible.

Other potential influences of interest rates on economic behavior are typically less important. The willingness of businesses to hold inventories is usually not very sensitive to interest rate fluctuations, and as we shall see, the willingness of individuals to save out of what they earn is remarkably immune to whether interest rates are high or low. As a result, when deficits drive up interest rates by increasing competition for saving, the effect in the first instance falls primarily on business and residential capital formation.

The specific circumstances of individuals and businesses often change sharply from one year to the next and so therefore does the relationship between their respective spending and income. But all together, American families and businesses save a surprisingly steady amount each year in relation to the country's total income. Aside from what is necessary merely to replace the plant and equipment and the houses and apartments that are wearing out—that is, after what running is necessary just to stay in place—all individuals and businesses together regularly save 7 percent to 8 percent of the total income produced in America.

The economy's overall net private saving rate does fluctuate modestly over the course of the business cycle. During business downturns it is typically somewhat lower than during periods of prosperity. But there has been no systematic tendency for the saving rate to rise or fall over time since the end of World War II. Net private saving averaged 6.9 percent of total income in the postwar forties, 7.5 percent in the fifties, 8.2 percent in the sixties (when real economic growth was unusually strong), and 8 percent in the seventies. Thus far in the 1980s, which began with the worst slump in a half century, the average has been just 5.7 percent.[1]

Even within the total of net private saving, the respective saving rates of individuals and businesses considered separately have also been steady over time. Personal saving compared to economywide total income has varied systematically over the business cycle and (until the 1980s) has shown a slight tendency to rise over time.* But on the whole the variation has been small. Personal saving averaged 4 percent of all income produced in America in the postwar forties, 4.7 percent in the fifties, 4.8 percent in the sixties, and 5.5 percent in the seventies. Thus far in the 1980s, it has averaged 3.9 percent.

Corporate saving, which accounts for a smaller share of the total, fluctuates even more sharply over the business cycle than does personal saving.† In contrast to personal saving however, corporate saving has gradually shrunk over time as a share of the economy's total income (except during the unusually strong 1960s), as the typical American corporation has relied more on debt financing, so that interest payments have grown in relation to total revenues. Corporate saving averaged 2.9

---

*Personal saving is the difference between what all individuals together earn after taxes (including pension contributions that their employers make in their behalf) and what they spend on all consumer goods—but not on houses or capital improvements to houses.

†Corporate saving—in other words retained earnings—is what is left from business corporations' profits after they meet all their operating expenses (including taxes and interest payments but not repayment of debt principal or investment in new plant and equipment or in inventories) and after they pay dividends to their shareholders.

percent of the country's total income in the postwar forties, 2.8 percent in the fifties, 3.4 percent in the sixties, and 2.4 percent in the seventies. Thus far in the 1980s—in which a sharp fall in profits due to the recession was followed by a surge in corporate debt resulting from the subsequent wave of mergers, acquisitions, leveraged buy-outs and other corporate reorganizations—corporate saving has averaged only 1.8 percent of economywide income. With personal saving and corporate saving both showing only limited variation compared to total income, and more often than not in opposite directions, the American economy's net private saving rate has therefore been even more stable than either of its two components.

If government budgets were always balanced (and if imports always matched exports), the share of America's income available to finance new investment would simply be this 7 percent to 8 percent that the private sector typically saves. But when budgets are unbalanced, what is available for net investment is the private sector's net saving *plus* any government surplus or *minus* any government deficit. Ever since World War II, government saving or dissaving has played an important role in affecting our overall balance of saving and investment. This has been especially true under Reagan's fiscal policy. In the 1980s rising federal deficits have occurred against a background of essentially no increase—indeed, a decline—in the saving of individuals and businesses. As a result the deficit has consumed most of what individuals and businesses have saved during this period.

The contrast between the 1980s and our prior experience is extraordinary in this regard. In the postwar forties, the government ran a budget surplus on average and therefore *added* to the private sector's saving. In the fifties, the government approximately balanced its budget, thereby leaving essentially all of private saving available to finance private investment. In the sixties, the budget was almost always in deficit but by only .5 percent of income on average, against an average net private saving rate of 8.2 percent. Even in the seventies, the federal deficit averaged just 1.8 percent of income, against a net private saving rate that averaged 8 percent.

The discontinuity has come in the 1980s. Despite the return to approximately full employment after the 1981–82 recession, the deficit for the decade as a whole thus far has averaged 4.2 percent of total income, against 5.7 percent for net private saving. Financing the federal government has therefore absorbed more than two thirds of all net saving by businesses and individuals. What remains to finance net investment has therefore been a mere 1.5 percent of our income: less than two cents out of every dollar, a fourth as much as in the seventies and only a fifth as much as in the sixties.

As we have seen, if the government runs a large deficit when the economy has ample unused resources, it will typically stimulate business—as Reagan's policy did after the 1981–82 recession. Whatever saving firms and individuals do out of the additional profits and incomes that they earn can then replace a part of the saving the deficit absorbs. But huge deficits have persisted long after the economy had recovered from the recession. As we have returned to approximately full employment, this further fiscal stimulus has had little or no ability to raise incomes or profits, and so there has been no additional saving. Since the middle of the decade therefore, the deficit has reduced available saving on a dollar-for-dollar basis.

The trend toward fuller funding of state and local governments' pension obligations since the mid-seventies has marginally offset this drain on our saving, but only marginally. On average during the sixties, all state and local governments combined approximately balanced their budgets. During the seventies, their combined budget was in *surplus* on average to the extent of .9 percent of our income—enough to finance about half of the federal deficit at the time.[2] On average thus far during the 1980s, state and local governments have increased their collective surplus to 1.3 percent of our income, but this modest further gain has been no match for the increase in federal dissaving. Moreover, the combined budget surplus of all state and local governments peaked in 1984 at $65 billion, or 1.7 percent of that year's income. Since then, under the pressure of reduced federal grants as well as the tax limitation movement, most states' surpluses have shrunk. By 1987 the combined surplus of all state and local governments had fallen to only $44 billion, or just 1 percent of that year's income.

Even after allowing for the state-local surplus therefore, the growth of the federal deficit in the 1980s has significantly shrunk the saving available to finance investment in new homes or in new plant and equipment. And because our net private saving rate has modestly fallen, the decline in saving available for net investment has been even sharper. In the fifties, an average 7.1 percent of all income produced in America was available to finance the country's net investment. In the sixties, the available share was 7.8 percent and in the seventies it was 7 percent. The average for the 1980s thus far is only 2.8 percent, not even three cents in every dollar, and down by well over half compared with prior decades.

With our available saving more than halved by the federal deficit, but our investment needs certainly no less than before, businesses and individuals have had to fight harder than ever for what saving has been left. *Real* interest rates—that is, interest rates compared to prospective inflation—have therefore remained historically high despite our easier monetary policy since mid-1982.

The point of interest rate fluctuations from an economic perspective is that they affect how individuals and businesses conduct their nonfinancial activities. When the government preempts the majority of the economy's saving, the resulting rise in interest rates necessarily changes enough actions by enough individuals and enough businesses that the private economy can get along with whatever saving is left over. Whether it is fewer families building new houses or fewer businesses buying new machines or building new facilities, or both, the decision to hold back stems not just from the movement of interest rates but from an increase in interest rates in relation to inflation.*

The experience of American interest rates in the 1980s, and in particular since the Federal Reserve eased monetary policy in mid-1982, has dramatically demonstrated the impact that large deficits have in raising real interest rates by increasing competition for saving. Before the 1980s, the link between deficits and interest rates had been harder to observe, much less to document conclusively. Apart from wars, deficits had been small compared to income and even fairly small compared to private saving. More important, what few large peacetime deficits there were had typically occurred either during or immediately after economic downturns, when interest rates were likely to be *lower* than usual anyway (because of both sluggish business and the resulting easy monetary policy). Especially since economics must rely on actual experience rather than laboratory experiments to draw inferences about what effects

---

Nominal interest rates—that is, interest rates *before* allowance for inflation —are also relevant for many investment decisions. For example, even if higher mortgage rates no more than match an increase in the rate at which house prices are rising, home buyers still must meet bigger monthly payments, and so the higher nominal rate alone may be reason not to buy. But by far the greater effect of interest rates on economic activity and especially on business investment comes from interest rates in relation to inflation.

what, sorting out how deficits and monetary policy and the business cycle each affected interest rates was just too difficult.

In the 1980s however, deficits have no longer been so small. And they have no longer occurred only or even primarily as a consequence of business slowdowns. The federal deficit has exceeded 4 percent of our income and two-thirds of our net private saving on average throughout the decade. And from 1984 onward, more than three fourths of each year's deficit has reflected the gap between revenues and spending that would have occurred even at full employment. As a result, the influence of deficits on real interest rates that was at best difficult to disentangle earlier on has been unusually clear.

The connection is easiest to draw for short-term interest rates, simply because of the inevitable uncertainty about how much inflation borrowers expect over long time horizons.* The real interest rate on a company's three-month commercial paper or on a three-month loan from its bank is the stated nominal interest rate minus whatever inflation it expects over just that next three months. Because inflation in America usually fluctuates in a fairly smooth way over time, with few sudden accelerations or reversals, most borrowers can usually make reasonably accurate guesses about price changes over horizons as short as just the next few months ahead. Calculating the short-term real interest rate in any year by simply

---

*The inflation that matters for borrowing and spending decisions is not the current inflation, nor inflation in the past, but the inflation that people expect in the future. Because we cannot directly measure expectations, it is difficult to know what *real* interest rate borrowers associate with any observed nominal interest rate. And because there is rarely much agreement about the future course of anything, inflation included, different borrowers may associate different real interest rates with the same nominal rate. This problem is obviously less severe for short-time horizons.

subtracting from the prevailing nominal rate whatever inflation actually occurred in that year is therefore likely to be not far off the mark, at least on average over time. In America during the 1980s, short-term real interest rates calculated in this way have clearly reflected the extraordinary monetary policy that began the decade and the extraordinary fiscal policy that followed.

During the fifties, the interest rate on commercial paper issued by corporate borrowers of recognized high credit standing averaged 2.82 percent per annum. But because the average inflation rate was 2.60 percent, the real interest rate on companies' short-term borrowing was just .22 percent.[3] Real interest rates were higher in the sixties but not by much. The average commercial paper rate was 5.02 percent and the average inflation rate 3.12 percent, for an average real interest rate of 1.90 percent. In the seventies, real interest rates were practically zero. The commercial paper rate was up to 7.63 percent on average, but by then the average inflation rate was 7.39 percent, leaving a real rate of just .24 percent on average over the entire decade. On average from the fifties to the seventies, the real interest rate was .79 percent.

By contrast, the average real interest rate on short-term business borrowing thus far in the 1980s has been 4.95 percent per annum. The nominal commercial paper rate has averaged 9.56 percent and inflation 4.61 percent. The change from the prior thirty years is startling. Not surprisingly, as we shall see, this great rise in real interest rates has strongly affected both business and individual investment.

Long-term interest rates appear to have been extraordinarily high in real terms during the 1980s too, although drawing solid conclusions in this regard is more problematic for long-term than for short-term borrowing. Even so, the limited available evidence suggests an increase of real long-term interest rates about comparable to what has happened to short-term rates.

The average nominal yield on new issues of long-term bonds by corporations with an upper-medium credit rating was 9.76 percent per annum in the seventies. Thus far in the 1980s, it has been 13.37 percent.[4] The average nominal rate on single-family home mortgages was 9.22 percent in the seventies. Thus far in the 1980s, it has been 12.26 percent.[5] No one knows how much inflation borrowers expect to see over the life of a twenty-year bond, or a thirty-year mortgage. But it is unlikely that in the 1980s, borrowers' expectations of future inflation have risen in pace with these increases of three to four percentage points in nominal interest rates, especially since the actually prevailing inflation rate has fallen.

As we have seen, these high real interest rates did not initially reflect large deficits. In 1981 when the average commercial paper rate hit a record high of 14.76 percent (the record for a single month, 16.66 percent, came in May), the overall inflation rate was 9.7 percent. The real rate was therefore about 5 percent. But the deficit for fiscal 1981 was still just $79 billion, barely 2 percent of income. And if business had been operating at full employment, the deficit would have been only $47 billion. High real interest rates in 1981 were due mostly to tight monetary policy.

When the Federal Reserve relaxed monetary policy in the summer of 1982, nominal interest rates fell from 13.79 percent for commercial paper in June to just 8.50 percent by December. But by then inflation had slowed rapidly too as a result of tight monetary policy earlier on, so that real interest rates remained high. The average commercial paper rate for all of 1982 was 11.89 percent, against inflation of 6.4 percent, so that the real interest rate was still above 5 percent. Although the deficit that year was up to $128 billion, it would have been just $53 billion if the economy had been at full employment. Again in 1982, high real interest rates were mostly a result of tight monetary policy.

But even after monetary policy eased, real interest rates still remained high. Most of the drop in nominal interest rates merely reflected the slowing of inflation rather than a decline in the real cost of borrowing. From the high in 1981 to the low in 1986, the commercial paper rate fell by about 8 percent. But over these same years inflation slowed by 7 percent.* For the previous thirty years, the real interest rate on short-term business borrowing had averaged less than 1 percent. But it was over 5 percent in 1981, over 4 percent in 1986, and nearly 4 percent in 1987. Our new fiscal policy, generating ever larger deficits even in a fully employed economy, had long since replaced tight monetary policy as the reason for high real interest rates.

And with these high real interest rates, our net investment has been smaller compared to our income than at any time since World War II. After allowing for the investment necessary just to replace what is wearing out, what businesses have spent on building and improving their plant and equipment and adding to their inventories plus what individuals have spent on building and improving their houses has come to just 4.6 percent of our income thus far in the 1980s. This tiny net investment rate, not even a nickel out of each dollar's income, is only two thirds of what it was during the prior thirty years.

High real interest rates have discouraged both business and individual investment about equally. On average from the fifties to the seventies, net business investment in plant and equipment and additions to inventories came to 4.1 percent of our income. In the 1980s, our net business investment rate has been just 2.7 percent. Our net investment in housing averaged 2.9 percent of total income during these three prior decades. In the 1980s, our net residential investment rate has been merely 1.9 percent. In both cases, net investment in the 1980s

---

*The rise in consumer prices slowed by 9 percent.

has fallen to just two thirds of what it was before our new fiscal policy began.

Even at that, the deterioration of our investment would have been substantially worse had it not been for funds coming into the country from abroad. What has enabled us to hold the decline in net investment to "only" one third, while our available saving has declined by more nearly two thirds, is a massive turnaround in America's international economic relations.

Moving saving across national boundaries is big business in both directions. Since World War II, countries around the world have progressively dismantled the legal and administrative barriers that once hindered cross-border transactions. At the same time, phenomenal advances in global communications have vastly simplified international dealings. Each year our businesses make deposits in foreign banks, our banks extend loans to foreign borrowers, and our insurance companies and pension funds buy stocks and bonds issued by foreign companies or even foreign governments. In an average year in the seventies for example, what we sent abroad in all of these ways came to $35 billion, more than a quarter of our total net saving.

At the same time, each year foreign businesses make deposits in American banks, foreign banks extend loans to American borrowers, and foreign financial institutions buy American-issued stocks and bonds. In an average year in the seventies, $30 billion moved into America from abroad in this fashion. For the foreigners who sent their saving here, no less than for the Americans who sent theirs abroad, the ability to choose among investment opportunities in other countries presumably provided better ways to achieve their financial objectives. Even if the total saving we sent abroad just matched the total saving sent here by foreigners, international transactions would still contribute to the efficiency of saving and investment by allowing both borrowers and lenders to diversify across national boundaries.

But there is no reason for the totals to match, and in most years they do not. As a result, the main importance of international financial flows for many countries stems from the *difference* between what goes out and what comes in. This difference enables an entire country to save more than it invests at home and invest the excess in claims on foreigners' future incomes, such as bonds issued by foreign companies or deposits in foreign banks. In the other direction, this difference enables a country to invest more at home than it saves and finance the excess by issuing to foreigners claims against its own future income.

The difference between saving invested abroad and investment financed with foreign saving—*net* foreign investment—is a crucial part of the economic process for many countries at key points in their history. Most newly developing countries rely heavily on net inflows of saving from abroad to finance their initial industrialization. As we shall see, America did at four crucial periods during the nineteenth century, as did Germany and Japan after World War II, and as countries across the world from Brazil to Egypt to China are doing today. By contrast, mature economies with limited natural resources sometimes rely heavily on net outflows to invest abroad the saving that they generate but cannot profitably deploy at home. Spain did so in the sixteenth century and Holland in the seventeenth. Britain especially did so from the mid-nineteenth century until World War I, as did other European countries like Germany and France until they lost their colonial empires.

In this century until the 1980s, Americans typically invested their saving abroad to a modestly greater extent than they relied on foreign saving to finance their investment at home. But except for short periods during and immediately after the two world wars, our net foreign investment was relatively small compared to our net investment at home. On average from the fifties to the seventies, net foreign investment was .3 percent of our income versus an investment rate at home of 6.9 percent. Throughout these years, our net foreign investment was just the excess of what American businesses and individuals saved over what it took to finance our investment at home—plus what it took to finance the government's deficit, which was usually small.

But in the 1980s, the deficit is no longer small, and so we have had no excess private saving to send abroad. From 1981 on, the high real interest rates caused by our scarcity of available saving have dramatically realigned the incentives influencing where savers decide to place their funds.

If real interest rates in other countries had matched those in America, there would probably have been no major shift in international investment patterns. But with the major European countries and Japan either maintaining a steady fiscal posture or moving toward fiscal conservatism just as our budget policy was tearing loose from its hinges, there was no reason for real interest rates abroad to rise in step with ours. Between the latter half of the seventies and the first half of the eighties, as our federal deficit widened from an average 1.9 percent of total income to 4.2 percent, the British deficit *narrowed* from 4.6 percent of income to 3.6 percent, and the German deficit narrowed from 2.1 percent of income to 1.9 percent. In Japan, where the saving rate is far higher than ours, the deficit varied more irregularly, but between 1980 and 1985 it narrowed from 7 percent of income to 4.9 percent.[6]

During the mid-seventies, real interest rates in other major industrial countries had consistently exceeded real interest rates here.[7] The difference was typically between two and four percentage points, on average for the major foreign economies. Even as late as mid-1980, real interest rates in foreign markets still exceeded the real interest rate here by more than 2 percent. But then the relationship switched. In November 1980 as the Federal Reserve renewed its attack on inflation, real interest rates in America moved above the foreign average for the first time since 1976. By 1982 the differential in favor of American rates was nearly 3 percent. The differential narrowed slightly in 1983, but in 1984 it climbed to over 3 percent. Only in 1985, when the Reagan administration finally abandoned its hands-off approach to the dollar and America joined four other countries in a coordinated interest rate policy, did the American-over-foreign real interest rate differential begin to shrink.

The sudden reversal of international real interest rate relationships at the outset of the 1980s powerfully affected investment decisions. The international financial system works much like any domestic financial system. No citizen of any country has ever lent or borrowed in order to make his country's overall net foreign investment hit a specific target. People decide where to invest according to the incentives that the market provides. The chief incentive motivating these decisions internationally is the relationship among different countries' real interest rates.*

The sharp rise of American real interest rates in the 1980s, due at first to antiinflationary monetary policy and then to the growing fiscal imbalance, spurred foreigners to want to send more of their saving here and Americans to want to leave more of theirs at home. But buying American stocks and bonds or making a deposit in an American bank requires American dollars. Foreign investors who want to place their funds in our

---

*When investors expect exchange rates between different countries' currencies to change, then what matters for international investment decisions is the relationship between countries' real interest rates after allowing for the gain or loss due to the movement in exchange rates.

financial markets must first exchange their marks or yen or their francs or pounds for dollars. Because the change in the relationship between American and foreign real interest rates that occurred after 1980 led foreigners to want to buy more American stocks and bonds and make more deposits in American banks, it also made them want to buy more dollars. And because foreigners can buy more dollars only when Americans are willing to sell, their efforts to buy extra dollars at first only pushed up the dollar's price in terms of the foreign currencies they were offering in exchange.

The limitations on how rapidly foreigners can accumulate dollars—or get rid of the dollars they already hold—are not widely understood, and the result has been substantial confusion about how the increasing importance of foreign investors can affect our financial markets and our economy. Ordinarily, of course, any one foreign investor can buy whatever amount of dollars he wants. Foreign exchange markets around the world have grown to the point that they can handle just about any transaction at any time of the day or night. But most of the trading of dollars in these markets ultimately amounts to one foreigner's buying dollars from another. The process often involves a long chain of transactions with countless banks and other intermediaries in between, but in most instances the chain has a foreign buyer and a foreign seller at each end. And one foreigner's buying dollars from another does not increase the total amount of dollars that both together hold, no matter what other currencies pass between them in exchange.

Foreigners *taken all together* can buy more dollars only if Americans are willing to sell them in exchange for either foreign currencies or foreign goods. There is no other source of dollars for foreigners in the aggregate to buy.

The chief reason that American businesses and individuals may want to buy foreign currencies is to invest our saving abroad. Whenever foreigners' desire to invest their saving here —that is, to increase their dollar holdings—just matches our desire to invest abroad, the market for dollars bought and sold in exchange for foreign currencies balances evenly. In the first half of the 1980s however, high American real interest rates not matched elsewhere sharply increased the desire of foreign businesses and individuals to send their saving here, with no equivalent increase (and more likely a decrease) in our eagerness to invest abroad.

The only other source of dollars for foreign investors to buy is what we pay to buy foreign goods over and above what we receive for our exports. If we always imported the same amount of goods we exported, there would be no extra dollars for foreigners to buy in order to invest in our financial markets. The dollars we sent abroad to pay for Venezuelan oil and Japanese cars would just balance the dollars coming back to pay for our lumber and computers and airplanes. But when our imports outstrip exports, what we pay to foreign sellers exceeds what we receive from foreign buyers. Foreign individuals and businesses together then can—indeed they must—accumulate these dollars by investing their saving in America to a greater extent than we invest our saving abroad.

Failure to understand this direct correspondence between the dollars we send abroad to pay for each year's excess of imports over exports and the dollars that foreigners accumulate each year has frequently led to discussion of these issues as if they were separate. In fact they are the same. Most recently for example, there has been much ill-founded talk about what would happen if foreign investors decided to "pull out" of our financial markets. But as long as we continue to import more than we export, all foreign investors together will have to continue to *increase* the amount of dollars they hold. They may *try* to sell their holdings—and in so doing drive dollar exchange

rates lower—but they can reduce their aggregate
dollars only if we run an overall import-export surp
in goods but also from services and earnings on for
Similarly, in the early years of the decade, when Ar
interest rates first rose above real interest rates abro
investors could not increase their aggregate holding
until we began to run a deficit in our internationa

In 1981 our imports, including physical goods
services like foreign hotel rooms and restaurant me
by American travellers abroad, cost $349 billion.
exports that year came to $383 billion.[8] The differe
that foreigners as a group not only were not able to i
of their saving here than we invested abroad but ha
less. Our *net* foreign investment was positive in 198
been throughout most of this century.

The irresistible force of increased desire by foreign
dollars, brought about by high American real inte
therefore collided with the immovable object of a st
ited amount of dollars available for foreigners to t
demand in excess of supply, the price of dollars rose
of yen, marks, pounds, francs, and other major c
Each foreign investor, of course, saw only that he w
dollars in a large and anonymous market, in which
anyone could have been on the other side of each tra
Each foreign investor's ability to increase his dollar
ultimately depended, however, on some other forei
tor's willingness to sell.

With the steady widening of the (now positive) di
between American and foreign real interest rates aft
the dollar rose rapidly. The dollar's average price in
nine key foreign currencies, weighted according to th
tance of each in American foreign trade, rose almost 16
between December 1980 and December 1981. And in

to many previous ups and downs in exchange rates, which had merely reflected faster or slower inflation in different countries, almost all of the dollar's higher value represented a genuine increase in its international purchasing power.

With no slackening of the real interest rate differential favoring American over foreign financial markets, the real dollar exchange rate continued to rise sharply. The dollar eventually rose from 209 against the yen in December 1980 to 260 in early 1985. Against the mark it went from 1.97 to 3.30. On average against nine major currencies, the dollar gained 13 percent in 1982, another 11 percent in 1983, and yet another 12 percent in 1984. Only after the real interest rate differential began to narrow in early 1985, as the newly choreographed policies of the major countries' central banks led our interest rates to decline more rapidly than interest rates abroad, did the average dollar exchange rate begin to fall. But by then the dollar was worth 74 percent more than in 1980, or 64 percent more after allowing for international differences in inflation.[9]

Although other factors, like America's traditional political stability or the slowing of inflation or even the loosening of attitudes toward business regulation and antitrust policies, may have played some role in stimulating foreign eagerness to invest in America—and hence to buy dollars—real interest differentials were the primary force that pushed the dollar higher during the first half of the 1980s. Throughout the late seventies when real interest rates were below those abroad, the dollar fell. When the real interest differential turned around in 1981 so did the dollar. And when the real interest differential declined sharply in 1985 and then became negative again in 1986, the dollar began its steep fall.

The American political system was no more stable in the early 1980s than it was in the late seventies, but the dollar reversed course in 1981 anyway. Inflation did not pick up in

1985 nor did regulatory and antitrust policies toughen, but the dollar reversed direction once again. The extraordinary rise of almost two thirds in our real exchange rate in the first half of the decade instead reflected the influence first of monetary and then fiscal policy, working in both cases through relative interest rates.

And as we shall see, as the dollar rose our imports surged far ahead of our exports. Our eagerness to buy Toyotas instead of Fords or Sonys instead of Zeniths depends on how much each car or each television costs, and that in turn depends on the dollar-yen exchange rate. In the other direction, foreign airlines' willingness to buy Boeing planes also depends on the dollar's exchange rate and so does the ability of American farmers to sell their wheat abroad. With the dollar high and rising, American producers could no longer compete effectively for sales in foreign markets, and increasingly they could not compete at home either. By 1983 our exports were down to $353 billion, off 8% from the level of two years earlier, while imports had risen to $359 billion despite the lingering aftermath of the recession. For the first time since World War II, and in peacetime for the first time since 1895, our total exports had failed to match our imports.

But the small net export deficit in 1983 was just the beginning. High American real interest rates kept pushing the dollar up, and so exports weakened while imports rose. And because international commercial transactions often respond only slowly to changes in exchange rates—the dollar had first risen in 1981, but its effect on our trade appeared in a major way only in 1983—our import-export gap continued to widen even after the dollar peaked in early 1985. In that year, our exports were still just $370 billion, not yet back to the 1981 level, but our imports were now $449 billion, up 29 percent over 1981. America had run an export *surplus* in every year since World War II, but by 1986 our annual export *deficit* was over $100 billion thanks to the higher dollar that resulted from the higher interest rates due to our widening fiscal deficit. Only in 1987, two years after the dollar peaked, did our import-export gap begin to stabilize.

The dollar peaked and then reversed its upward climb not only because monetary policies here and abroad had realigned international interest rates—by early 1987 real interest rates abroad were more than 1 percent *above* ours—but also because over time our growing excess of imports over exports increased the supply of dollars held abroad. Earlier on, the dollar had risen because interest rate differentials made investing in our markets more attractive, yet there was only a limited amount of dollars for foreigners to hold. With each year's growing trade deficit, however, that amount increased ever faster. Especially once real interest rates abroad began again to match ours, and then moved higher foreign investors found our markets less attractive. But with our trade in deficit, in the aggregate foreigners had to keep accumulating dollars. Their efforts to sell this continuing accumulation now began to push the dollar lower.

Meanwhile, the large and growing excess of foreign saving invested here over our saving sent abroad has enabled us to limit the decline in our net investment to "just" a third compared to the prior postwar average. As recently as 1981, the *positive* difference between what we invested abroad and the investment here that we financed with foreign saving was .3 percent of our income—the same as it had been on average over the prior three decades. But 1981 marked the end of American positive net foreign investment. In 1982 the balance was negative, though by only a tiny amount, and thereafter the gap has continued to widen.* By 1987 even with the dollar back down to 1 percent *below* the 1980 level (5 percent below after allowing for differential inflation), it was minus 3.5 percent. Without all this foreign saving, our investment would have had to decline in step with the fall in our own available saving brought about by the enormous federal deficit. So instead of declining by a third, our overall net investment rate would have shrunk by more than half.

What would have brought about that further decline in our investment, in the absence of all the foreign saving we took in, is an even higher real interest rate than actually occurred. Without the foreign saving, American businesses and individuals would have had to compete all the harder for the smaller amount of our own saving left over after the government had borrowed what it needed. Without foreign buyers for its securities, the U.S. Treasury would have had to sell all of the bonds and bills it issued to Americans. The heightened competition for an even more sharply reduced supply of saving would have driven real interest rates still higher—to whatever level was necessary to discourage enough investment in plant and equipment, or enough home building, to reduce net investment to less than 3 percent of our income, since that is all that was left of our saving after financing the government deficit.

Our new fiscal policy has steered more of our spending into consumption and less into investment in productive plant and equipment and housing than ever before in the post World War II era. This extraordinary shrinkage of America's capital formation in the 1980s is, as we have seen, highly serious in its

*Our export-import balance was still in surplus in 1982, but net foreign investment was negative. The two approximately mirror one another, but because of miscellaneous financial transactions the correspondence is never exact.

implications for our future. Without the inflow of foreign saving, the damage would have been far worse.

But as we have also seen, America's new dependence on foreign saving has come at high cost too. The positive net foreign investment that we maintained throughout the twentieth century was the mirror image of our positive balance of international trade. The turn to foreign capital *in*flows in the 1980s has reflected the wholesale loss of markets at home and abroad to foreign producers. Instead of paying for imports with exports, we now enjoy foreign goods to an extent that dwarfs our ability to sell abroad. Instead of *lending* to foreigners therefore, we now *borrow* from them. In the end, our resulting status as the world's largest debtor may be even more dangerous than a still lower investment rate would have been.

Chapter VIII

INVESTMENT, PRODUCTIVITY, AND COMPETITIVENESS

He that tilleth his ground shall have plenty of bread;
  but he that followeth after vain things shall have poverty enough.

—PROVERBS, XXVIII:19

The linkages connecting the fiscal policy we have pursued in the 1980s to the harsh realities we now face are complex. Our prospects for raising our standard of living in the future are diminished not just because the deficit has raised real interest rates but because high interest rates impede investment and low investment hinders productivity gains. America is a debtor nation not just because the deficit pushed the dollar too high for half a decade but because the overvalued dollar impaired our competitiveness. Moreover, these two problems have compounded each other in that our failure to invest adequately at home, especially in industries that can plausibly export what they produce, has further hindered our ability to take advantage of the opportunity to compete now that the dollar has fallen.

Because these links are neither simple nor automatic, much of the public discussion about what effects our fiscal policy has had and what to do about it has been confused. But because what is at stake is so serious and because the corrective actions we must now take will involve real sacrifices, it is important that Americans understand not just how different our fiscal policy has been in the present but how it has affected our future prospects.

Explaining the slowdown in America's productivity growth —and conversely, deciding how best to foster improved productivity—is one of the most perplexing problems confronting economic researchers. The difficulty should not be surprising. How productive a country is, presumably depends on many factors. Some of these, like how much it is investing or which industries are growing and which are becoming less important, are amenable to analysis at the aggregate level. Others, like the quality of management, or whether what we do invest is invested wisely, are difficult to address except at the level of individual companies.

Our overall productivity gains first began to slip after the mid-sixties. Between 1948 and 1965, average output per worker in our nonagricultural businesses had risen from $25,-900 to $38,600 in today's prices.[1] After allowing for a shortening of the average work week—in other words, taking the gain in output per *hour worked* rather than in output per employee on the job—the productivity of American workers had risen at an average rate of 2.7 percent per annum. By 1973 on the eve of the OPEC price increase, America's average output per worker (again in today's dollars) was $41,600. After allowing for a further decline in the work week, the average gain in per-hour productivity was just 1.8 percent per annum, only two-thirds as fast as before.* But it was not until after 1973 that the most serious deterioration occurred. By 1980 average

---

*Including farms, where continual technological advances have made productivity gains especially rapid, the average annual increase for all American business combined slowed from 3.2 percent during 1948–65 to 2.1 percent during 1965–73.

output per worker had fallen back to $40,900 apiece in today's dollars. Because the work week had also declined, output per *hour* had actually risen, but at less than .4 percent per annum on average (just .5 percent even including farms). As we have seen, after-inflation wage gains closely tracked productivity gains throughout this period. Not surprisingly, by 1980 flagging productivity growth had become a major public policy issue.

As in any mystery, the problem here is not too few potential perpetrators but too many. Nor is there any reason to suppose that only one of the forces impinging on American business has necessarily accounted for all or even most of our deteriorating productivity gains. Because different potential explanations for the slowdown call for differing public policy correctives, it would be more convenient if the problem did spring from a single cause—especially if it were one that could readily be addressed by legislative or administrative action. But that need not be the case.

The factor governing business productivity that bears the closest connection to fiscal policy is investment in new plant and equipment. At an intuitive level, the contribution of facilities and machines to our ability to produce outputs from labor and raw material inputs appears obvious enough. And as we shall see, the evidence roughly bears out the importance of capital investment in this context. Other industrial economies around the world that have achieved consistently faster productivity increases than ours have maintained consistently higher investment rates. For all the discussion of whether Japanese management methods (and Japanese managers) are better than ours, it is clear that Japanese industries have done much more investing in new plant and equipment than have ours. And although the correspondence is not exact, the severe productivity slowdown in this country since the early seventies has coincided with a decline in our own investment rate. But even so, the precise contribution of capital formation to productivity has proved elusive.

The alternative explanation with the greatest merit is that we have progressively shifted from producing goods, especially manufactured goods, to producing services. As we have seen, wholly apart from its bearing on productivity, the shift from manufacturing to services raises other troubling issues. Most service-sector jobs provide lower wages than the typical job producing something or building something. In 1987 the average employee in retail trade earned $179 per week compared to $406 in manufacturing and $477 in construction. The steady increase in the share of the American labor force working in service industries, from 52 percent in 1948 to over 70 percent today (more than 75 percent including the government sector), has therefore raised sensitive questions about the distribution of income.

The shift to services has also figured prominently in the debate over our deteriorating international competitiveness. Bankers, stockbrokers, and business consultants can and do market their services across national lines. But except when they cater to foreign tourists, barbers, dry cleaners, and garage mechanics do not. As the services share of our output has risen so have questions about what we will have available to export when the dollar settles at the right level. Fortunately from this perspective, the shift over time in what we *produce* has been small compared to the change in where we work. After allowing for changing prices, the services share of our total production (even including the work of government employees) rose from 40 percent in 1948 to just 47 percent in 1987.

But the reason for this contrast is that productivity growth is typically much slower in service industries. The technological breakthroughs that save so much time in manufacturing and mining, and especially in farming, are not available in many service fields. On average over the entire 1948–80 period, output per worker in the service sector rose by just 1.1 percent per annum versus 2.4 percent in manufacturing. For this reason, the increasing importance of services in our output mix also bears significantly on the overall productivity slowdown.

It is important to keep in mind that increases in what a country produces can take the form of greater *quantity* or improved *quality*. Because measuring quality changes is much harder in the service sector than in most goods-producing industries, it is possible that part of the slower productivity growth recorded there is a statistical illusion. The government's statisticians may simply do a better job of comparing color to black-and-white television sets, or graphite to wood tennis racquets, than they do when they compare the services of today's travel agents or stockbrokers to what their predecessors provided before desk-top computers gave instant information on every customer's itinerary or investment portfolio.

Most careful analyses have suggested that there is more here than just a measurement problem, however. Despite obvious exceptions like telecommunications, transportation, and public utilities, most service industries apparently do achieve productivity gains at a genuinely slower pace than what the goods-producing industries typically manage. To the extent that they do, at least part of the productivity slowdown is just the natural consequence of the changing output mix.

Even so, it is doubtful that this shift has accounted for all or even half of our productivity slowdown. Although estimates vary widely, most studies have attributed about a fourth of the slowdown to the changing composition of our output.[2] The issue is in part one of timing. The importance of service industries in our economy has been growing throughout much of the twentieth century, but the productivity slowdown first appeared after the mid-sixties and did not become severe until the mid-seventies. In addition, productivity gains *within the goods-producing sector* have also slowed. Output per hour in manufacturing, for example, grew at 2.7 percent per annum between 1950 and 1965 but then slowed to 2.5 percent during 1965–73 and then to only 1.2 percent during 1973–80. Clearly other factors, beyond the shift to services, have also been at work.

Other frequently suggested explanations for the productivity slowdown include the changing demographic composition of the labor force, the two sharp increases in oil prices during the seventies, reduced efforts by business in research and development and in technological innovation, and the burden of environmental regulation. At a different level, some observers have also pointed to repeated management failures and to poorly trained or unmotivated workers. No doubt each of these explanations has played a role to some degree. But none appears to have been as important as either insufficient capital formation or the changing output mix in accounting for what has happened to American productivity.

The basis for the changing labor force explanation is the fact that, as the postwar baby boom generation matured and went to work, the average age and on-the-job experience of American workers declined. In 1954 only 14 percent of all workers were less than twenty-five years old. By 1980 the under-twenty-five share was almost 22 percent. But although so sharp a change could plausibly have hindered business performance, its timing did not correspond closely to that of the productivity slowdown either. The increase in the share of younger workers began in 1955, fully a decade before the productivity slowdown. And it was practically over by 1973, before the more serious phase of the productivity slowdown began.

By contrast, the coincidence of timing appears at first glance to be almost exact for explanations based on higher oil prices. The more modest productivity slowdown that began in the mid-sixties was unique to America, but the sharper slowdown after 1973 was worldwide. OPEC's fourfold increase in world oil prices that year rendered obsolete many forms of energy-intensive equipment everywhere. With labor suddenly cheap compared to oil and other purchased energy sources, companies around the world had little incentive to use labor-saving equipment that consumed large amounts of fuel or electricity. But since 1980 the coincidence in timing between fluctuations in energy prices and growth in productivity either in America or elsewhere has been much looser. Most recent studies have assigned some role to energy prices in explaining America's productivity slowdown, but not a large one.[3]

Research and development efforts also seem intuitively to be essential to productivity growth. Spending on R&D by American business grew irregularly from some three fourths of 1 percent of nationwide income in the early fifties to approximately 1 percent by 1970 but then remained at about that level until it began to rise again in 1979.[4] The annual volume of patents granted to American inventors rose irregularly to a peak of fifty-eight thousand in 1966 and then declined on balance throughout the seventies.[5] Nevertheless, most of the R&D slowdown in the seventies was in government-sponsored defense projects. While there are obvious examples like solid-state radios and hand-held calculators, the broader connections between defense-related R&D and private business productivity are harder to establish. Most studies have assigned R&D efforts a significant though small role in explaining our economywide productivity slowdown.[6]

Finally, environmental regulation also gained momentum during the sixties and seventies, just as productivity gains slowed. Congress passed the initial Clean Air Act in 1963 and the Clean Water Act in 1967, and in 1970 it created both the Environmental Protection Agency and the Occupational Safety and Health Administration. In response, power plants installed stack scrubbers, chemical companies established waste disposal procedures, and construction firms bought reinforced ladders. Designing and documenting compliance also absorbed personnel that employers could have assigned to other tasks. But most of these regulations and the equipment and procedures they required were in place by the mid- to late seventies, and the share of our total investment devoted to meeting them declined steadily after 1975.[7] Most quantitative studies have assigned environmental regulation as well only a small role in explaining the productivity slowdown.[8]

That leaves business capital formation. The realization that workers are more productive when they have the tools to do the job, and that they are more productive still when they have more tools or better tools, predates written history. And ever since the industrial revolution, the use of mechanical power has increasingly supplemented or replaced purely human effort, freeing labor to be deployed in more efficient ways. From the first widespread use of the steam engine in the eighteenth century; to the advent of railroads, steel foundries, and then electricity in the nineteenth century; and trucks, bulldozers, airplanes, and finally nuclear reactors in the twentieth, production has become steadily more capital intensive. At the same time, specialized equipment, ranging from casting dies and chemical processors to computers and other electronic devices, has become basic to production in one industry after another.

Until recent years, an ever greater reliance on physical capital in the production process was a key feature of American business. Except during the decade and a half spanning the Depression and World War II, when net investment was typically negative and the average American's living standard showed almost no growth, our productive capital stock has consistently grown faster than our labor force. The rise in the amount of capital available to the average worker presumably accounted for at least some part of the rapid productivity growth that we once enjoyed.

Between 1948 and 1965, the amount of capital behind the average worker in American business outside agriculture rose from $24,300 to $34,900 in today's prices. The nation's non-residential capital stock had grown 2.4 percent per annum faster than the growth in labor input. With the maturing of the baby boom generation, together with women's increasing willingness to work outside their homes, the labor force began to grow more rapidly around the mid-sixties. But so did our stock of business capital. By 1973 the average worker had $40,200 in capital behind him. Policy actions like the investment tax credit (enacted in 1962) and liberalized depreciation write-offs (beginning in 1964), together with the influence of steadier economic growth overall, had increased business investment by enough to make capital grow 2.5 percent per annum faster than labor input: a slightly greater margin than earlier on despite the record growth in employment. The decline in productivity growth that began in the mid-sixties must have reflected other influences.

The situation since the early seventies has been different, however. The rapid expansion of the labor force has slowed, but investment still has not kept pace. By 1980 workers in nonfarm businesses had $43,100 of capital apiece (at today's prices). Our capital stock had grown since 1973 at just 1.6 percent per annum faster than labor input, only two-thirds the margin maintained in earlier years. Unlike the earlier productivity slowdown therefore, the more severe problem that appeared after 1973 did correspond to a sharp change in our use of capital versus labor.

Comparison of investment rates and productivity growth

rates across different countries for this period also suggests a close relationship between the two. Japan led the way on both counts, with 19.1 percent of national income devoted to net fixed investment of all kinds (including investment by business and government, and residential investment) and output per worker growing by 3 percent per annum on average during 1973–80. France, Germany, and Italy were highly similar, with total net fixed investment rates tightly clustered in the 9.9 percent to 10.7 percent per annum range and productivity growth rates between 1.8 percent and 2.5 percent per annum. The British fell far behind, with a 7.6 percent net investment rate and 1 percent productivity growth. America lagged all these countries, with net investment in business plant and equipment, government facilities, and housing equal to just 6.1 percent of our income and output per worker *declining* by .1 percent on average during 1973–80.[9]

Moreover, these systematic differences in countries' capital formation had not been a matter of just a few years in the mid- and late seventies. By 1980 Japan's total fixed capital stock was almost ten times what it had been in 1960. In France, Germany, and Italy the capital stock had increased during these two decades by multiples ranging from three to four. The British capital stock in 1980 was barely two and a quarter times its 1960 level. Ours did not even double over this period.[10]

On the strength of evidence like this, most studies of America's productivity slowdown have concluded that a significant part of the problem—more than a fourth and perhaps more than half—has been due to the lack of adequate business investment.[11] These estimates are plausible. They especially make sense in light of the importance of both too little and not the right kind of capital. New machines and new facilities give industry access to new technology. In some extreme cases like our steel industry, it would do little good merely to add capacity that resembled existing mills. What steel needs is modern facilities. More generally, even if capital per worker does not grow at all, merely replacing old machines and old buildings with new ones can sometimes increase productivity too. The link between capital formation and productivity, and hence the connection between our fiscal policy and the diminished prospects for our future standard of living, is real enough.

Capital formation also matters for our international competitiveness. Staying competitive necessarily means staying productive. But only a small part of international economic competition takes place in markets for standardized products, like steel and chemicals, in which price is a company's only competitive tool. Product mix and product design change rapidly in many markets. When they do, staying competitive also means being able to produce the right product, with superior design and performance, to capture an adequate market share. An economy that is investing heavily in new plant and new equipment is more likely to succeed in this competition than one that must continually retrofit old buildings and old machines to function in new ways. In some cases, like that of semiconductors, making new products is impossible without new investment. Without the necessary capital formation, we could not compete in those markets at any price or any dollar exchange rate. Similarly, without adequate investment in new capacity of the right kind, we will not be able to meet the foreign demand for our products that has already begun to appear now that the dollar has fallen.

The contribution of capital formation to both productivity and competitiveness depends of course on other factors too. The latest electronic equipment can bring new technology to bear on production only after someone has devoted enough effort to R&D to devise that new technology in the first place and to figure out how to use it efficiently. Bulldozers sidelined by higher fuel prices may remain on a contractor's lot, but they do not help erect any new buildings. And while stack scrubbers cut air pollution and reinforced banisters reduce staircase accidents, neither help labor to make more of the products that business actually sells. Adequate investment means having enough capital, of the right kind, employed in the right activities, and backed by a labor force that knows how to use it correctly and is motivated to do so. How many dollars business invests may be the most obvious factor governing an economy's capital formation, but it is certainly not the only one.

The emphasis that Reagan placed on business capital formation in his early descriptions of his economic program, therefore, made good sense. Inadequate investment during the seventies *had* contributed heavily to the slowdown in the growth of our productivity and consequently of what we earned after inflation. Devoting more of our resources to business investment would help turn the situation around. A greater investment rate would also make us more competitive in world markets. It was hard to imagine a "New Beginning for the Economy" without at its center increased investment in new plant and equipment.

But as we have seen, Reagan's new fiscal policy delivered not more capital formation but less, not faster growth in productivity but slower, and an economy that is not a stronger but a weaker competitor. High real interest rates and an overvalued dollar depressed our net business investment in the 1980s to the lowest levels since World War II despite new tax incentives. Net business investment averaged 3.3 percent of our income from the fifties to the seventies, with little variation over periods long enough to average out the business cycle. Thus far in the 1980s, it has been just 2.3 percent. After allowing for inflation, the dollar volume of net business investment declined by more than half between 1979 and the post-recession low in 1983. By 1986, after four years of expansion, we had not yet regained the 1979 level. In manufacturing, where we will especially need new capacity to take advantage of the lower dollar, investment has increased hardly at all during the expansion.

The widespread belief that business investment has been *strong* in the 1980s and especially so since the 1981–82 recession ended stems from several confusions, beginning with what "investment" means in this context. Investment means new plants or office buildings or new equipment or enlarged inventories. By contrast, many of the everyday transactions in which both businesses and individuals engage and which they typically describe as "investing" do not actually constitute investment—at least not in any sense that matters for our stock of productive capital. Most individuals who instruct their brokers to buy stock in General Motors, for example, think they have invested in GM. And from a personal perspective, they have. But unless they buy just when GM is issuing new stock, something it did last in 1955, what they have actually done is buy an investment in the company from someone else. General Motors has no more money as a result of the new shareholder's purchase. Nor is there any reason to think GM will spend more of what funds it does have on building new assembly plants or buying new casting dies, just because one person rather than another owns its stock.

Similarly, when one company buys existing facilities from another—or, as is increasingly common in the 1980s, even buys a whole other company—the press release usually says it has invested in whatever it has bought. When U.S. Steel bought Marathon Oil in 1982, most people described its purchase as investing in the oil industry. But the transfer of Marathon's stock from its previous owners to U.S. Steel built no new rigs nor drilled any new wells. The money U.S. Steel paid went to the previous shareholders, not into new investment in an economic sense. The same is true for most of the other corporate acquisitions that have been the focus of so much recent attention.

Investment, in the sense of new capital formation, means not just exchanges of ownership but the creation of new assets. That is why investment matters for productivity and competitiveness, and that is why our low and declining investment rate is a proper object of concern.

A further source of confusion about our investment performance in the 1980s has been the distortions due to the 1981–82 recession. Just as the recession initially disguised Reagan's new fiscal policy, it also led to widespread misunderstanding of how this policy affected our investment once the recession ended. Business investment was a major casualty of the fight against inflation. In 1981 our net business investment rate was still 3.2 percent. But as the recession worsened, investment dried up. In 1982 we invested only 2.1 percent of income in plant and equipment beyond what was necessary to replace depreciating assets, making that our worst year for net business investment since World War II. And although the economy overall had started to recover by 1983, that year the net investment rate sank to just 1.3 percent, barely a third of the previous postwar average. But as we have seen, all this was the result not of fiscal policy but of tight money. Machines not bought and factories not built are part of the cost we paid to slow inflation, no less than the jobs lost and the incomes and profits not earned. If anything, a more expansionary fiscal policy during these years would probably have kept investment from falling as far as it did, because it would have cushioned the recession.

Our new fiscal policy began to retard investment only after the recovery was well under way. Net business investment rose to 2.4 percent of total income in 1984 and 2.5 percent in 1985. In 1986, however, the net investment rate fell back to just 1.9 percent, a weaker performance than in any year of the postwar period except 1983. On average during the three middle years of the decade—years otherwise marked by continuous economic growth—we devoted just 2.3 percent of our income to new business capital formation. Neither the fifties nor the sixties nor even the seventies had posted an average net business investment rate below three percent. Not a single year since 1981 has yet made it as *high* as 3 percent.

The belief that business investment has been strong since the 1981–82 recession ended rests partly on the familiar statistical illusion created by growth from a small base. The total volume of business capital spending expanded by 18 percent after inflation in 1984 and another 7 percent in 1985, for the largest two-year percentage gain since World War II. And after allowing for the replacement of depreciation, net business investment almost doubled as a share of total income during the same two years, rising from 1.3 percent in 1983 to 2.5 percent in 1985. Proponents of our new fiscal policy have greeted these gains as a major achievement.

But what is missing in this familiar story is any sense of how high is up. What made the 1983–85 percentage gains in dollar volume so large, and what permitted the net investment rate to double, was the extraordinarily depressed level of investment in 1983. If the recession had been even worse and had driven investment still lower in 1982–83, the new policy's cheerleaders could then have pointed to yet greater percentage gains in 1984–85. Indeed, if the recession had been so severe as to halt net capital formation altogether, the subsequent rebound would have been infinite in percentage terms.

We should never confuse getting up off the basement floor with scaling new heights. In 1983 we hit the low point of our net business investment since World War II. Since then, compared to our average postwar performance, we have not even reached the middle of the ladder.

Yet another source of confusion has been the difference

between net and gross investment. Net investment, of course, is not all the investment there is. A firm's total capital spending also includes what it spends to replace the plant and equipment that wears out. Whether gross investment, including replacement, is a useful guide to an economy's performance is a question no one has yet answered. No firm expands its production capacity merely by replacing machines and facilities as they depreciate. It can do that only by undertaking investment beyond what is necessary to match its genuine depreciation (which typically differs from the write-offs it claims for tax purposes). As a result, net investment is certainly the superior guide.

But when production technologies change, the new machines that a company buys are usually not identical to the ones they replace. Electronic programming takes the place of manual control, compact designs replace units that take up more space, better motors use energy more efficiently, and calibrations become finer. New buildings are not like old ones either. They economize on space, conserve energy, and sometimes provide more efficient working conditions. In many cases, therefore, businesses *can* increase production capacity merely by replacing old facilities with new ones.

For well over a century, American business has had enough plant and equipment in place that more than half of its capital spending has gone just to replace existing facilities as they have worn out. And over time, our stock of plant and equipment has grown ever larger in relation to our income. In 1945 American business had 54 cents' worth of productive capital for every dollar of the country's income; by 1980 it had $1.03. As a result, the pace at which our capital has worn out has also grown in relation to income.

In addition, ever since the mid-1930s, changing technologies have led business to add equipment more rapidly than plants and office buildings. In 1935, 22 percent of America's total business capital stock consisted of equipment. By 1980 equipment accounted for 48 percent of the total. Because machines wear out faster than buildings, this shift in the composition of our capital stock has raised the need for investment for replacement purposes still further.

With the steady growth in depreciation, *gross* capital spending by business has generally risen as a share of our income ever since World War II. Gross investment in plant and equipment rose from 9.6 percent of our income on average in the fifties to 9.9 percent in the sixties and 10.8 percent in the seventies. Thus far in the 1980s, the average has been 10.9 percent. The reason is that with more capital than ever and more of it consisting of equipment, depreciation on average has also risen to a record share of our income. *Gross* investment has therefore edged higher despite low net investment. Defenders of our new fiscal policy have hailed this too as a significant achievement. But a record high rate of depreciation is nothing new compared with prior trends, and a record low net investment rate is certainly no achievement.

More important, a closer look at the 1980s also gives a very different picture. Because net investment virtually stopped in the wake of the 1981–82 recession, our capital stock is now falling in relation to our income. In 1982 we had $1.06 of business capital for every dollar of our income but by 1987 it was just 91 cents. As a result, depreciation of existing plant and equipment has been *declining* in relation to our income since 1982. Although our gross business investment rate has been slightly higher on average during the 1980s as a whole than it was in the seventies, it peaked in 1981—before Reagan's new policy even took effect. By 1987 gross business investment was back down to 9.9 percent of our income, the smallest share since 1964.

. . .

Finally, it is also important to remember that business investment in plant and equipment is not the only form of investment that can help make a country more productive and therefore more competitive. Government investment in roads, bridges, airports, port facilities, and other kinds of infrastructure also has a direct bearing on how easy or difficult it is, and also how cheap or how costly, for many companies to do business. So does education at all levels, ranging from basic literacy skills to advanced research training. Broadly construed, productive capital formation includes all these aspects of investment in both physical and human assets. There is substantial evidence that each has played a significant role in advancing America's productivity throughout the twentieth century.

If our net business investment rate had fallen in the 1980s because we were financing extensive new infrastructure projects or because we were applying ourselves to reeducating our labor force to meet the needs of the modern work place, there might be little cause for concern. Indeed many observers of our productivity slowdown have suggested diverting massive amounts of money and effort into just such activities. In light of the rapid advance of electronically run and computer-controlled production technologies, the case for either retraining today's workers or at least educating tomorrow's along new lines has attracted particularly wide attention.

But America in the 1980s is not investing in infrastructure or in education any more than in business capital formation in the conventional sense. After World War II, the share of federal spending devoted to physical investment outside the defense establishment—interstate highways, airports and harbors, office buildings, research laboratories, weather stations, information transfer facilities—rose quickly to 6.9 percent in 1952. It then declined during most of the fifties but rose again in the early sixties to a peak of 4.4 percent in 1965. It has been declining ever since. On average during the seventies, the government devoted only 1.5 percent of its spending to civilian investment applications. Thus far in the 1980s, the average investment share has fallen to 1.2 percent, the lowest since World War II. The deficit in the 1980s has certainly not been due to any burst of government capital formation.[12]

The decline has been even more substantial at the state and local level, where more of what government spends has traditionally gone for investment purposes than at the federal level. In the fifties, when the baby boom led cities to add more classrooms, and most communities were building hospitals and sewer systems too, an average 31 percent of what state and local governments spent went into capital investments. That share held at 29 percent on average in the sixties but then dropped to 17 percent in the seventies. Thus far in the 1980s, it has been just 13 percent.[13]

As a result, growth in our stock of government-owned capital (apart from military installations) has slowed even more dramatically than growth in our stock of business capital. Measured at today's prices, our stock of business plant and equipment has grown at 2.5 percent per annum thus far during the 1980s in contrast to 3.8 percent from the fifties to the seventies. Our stock of government-owned capital (again in today's prices) grew by 3.5 percent per annum during those three decades but has slowed to just .9 percent since 1980.[14]

Education too has received a shrinking share of our resources in the 1980s. Spending on elementary and secondary education, where demographics are more of a determining influence than at the college level, rose from 2.9 percent of the nation's total income on average in the fifties to 4.2 percent in the sixties and then edged up to 4.4 percent in the seventies. It has fallen back to 4 percent thus far during the 1980s. In the wake of Sputnik, spending on higher education more than doubled as a share of our total income, from just 1.1 percent on average in the fifties to 2.3 percent in the sixties. Investment in "human capital" through higher education then rose to 2.6 percent of our income during the seventies, and it has remained at that level thus far during the 1980s.[15]

In the 1980s we have been cheating our future in all these respects—not just in business capital formation but in government infrastructure and education too. The weakness in business investment has had a counterpart in strength in other areas of the nation's capital formation, broadly defined. It is part of a broader failure to invest in America's future through capital formation in any of its major dimensions. While demographics and changing government priorities have played significant roles in the slowdown of investment in infrastructure and education, the weakness of business investment has been chiefly a product of America's new fiscal policy.

And as our earlier experience had suggested, without adequate capital formation we have also failed to restore our productivity growth. At first it looked as if capital formation might not matter so much for productivity growth this time. As almost always happens in the initial phase of business expansions, after the 1981–82 recession many companies were able to raise output without recalling employees they had laid off or even significantly raising the hours of those still on the job. Productivity for the nonfarm business sector overall jumped by 3.3 percent in 1983 and then continued to rise at a 2.5 percent per annum rate in the first half of 1984. These gains were almost up to average for the first year and a half of prior postwar expansions. They raised hope in some quarters that notwithstanding the absence of significant capital formation, the more important side of the American economy's "New Beginning" had arrived.

Those hopes were disappointed. In the latter half of 1984,

not yet two years into the recovery, productivity growth stopped altogether. Productivity then began to grow again, but at rates well below our average performance for the postwar period overall, not to mention the higher rate typical of business expansions. The increase was just 1.2 percent in 1985, 1.6 percent in 1986, and only .8 percent in 1987. On average since 1980, our productivity growth has been just 1.3 percent per annum.* Only in manufacturing has there been a superior performance. Since 1982 productivity in manufacturing has posted a stronger gain than in any prior business recovery since World War II. Even including the two recession years, the average annual rise in manufacturing productivity growth between 1980 and 1987 was 4.1 percent, well above the postwar average. But these hefty gains have sprung less from expanded production than from the failure ever to recall the workers dismissed in the recession. In 1979, 21 million Americans worked in manufacturing. At the low point in 1983, only 18.4 million were left. By year-end 1987, five full years of economic expansion had generated less than one million jobs to replace the 2.6 million that had disappeared during the recession.

The virtual absence of improvement in productivity growth outside manufacturing and the dependence of gains in manufacturing on job reduction rather than expanded output would be disappointing under any circumstances. They are especially so because several of the factors that were at least potentially behind the productivity slowdown in earlier years have been reversed during the 1980s. Changing demographics have reduced the under-twenty-five age group from 22 percent of all employees on the job in 1980 to 17 percent in 1987. Between

---

*And because 1980 was a recession year while 1987 was a year of mature expansion, the underlying gain due to factors other than the business cycle has been even less. On average since 1979 productivity growth has been 1.1 percent per annum.

1973 and 1980, wholesale energy prices had risen more than twice as fast as finished goods prices, but by 1987 energy prices were 22 percent *lower* than in 1980 while finished goods prices were 15 percent higher.[16] Business R&D spending grew more than twice as fast as economywide income between 1980 and 1987. The share of gross business capital spending used to meet environmental regulations has fallen from 4.6 percent on average during the seventies to 3.6 percent thus far during the 1980s.

Each of these developments should have boosted productivity. But without any increase in capital formation of any kind —instead with a *lower* net business investment rate than in any prior period since World War II—none of these reversals, nor even all in combination, proved sufficient to turn our productivity growth around.

And as we have seen, without productivity growth there has been no improvement in the average worker's wage even since the recession ended. Except in manufacturing, where productivity did rise, wage gains have barely kept pace with inflation. For all of business outside agriculture, wage gains outpaced inflation by 1.6 percent in the first year of the recovery and then lost ground on average during the next four years. For the first time since World War II, America has had a major business expansion with no significant real increase in hourly pay scales. For the 1980s overall, including the two recession years and the five subsequent years of steady expansion, the average gain in real hourly wages has been less than one tenth of 1 percent per annum. The links connecting deficits to interest rates, interest rates to investment, investment to productivity, and productivity to the standard of living have been as strong in the 1980s as ever before. What is different is our new fiscal policy.

Chapter IX

BECOMING A DEBTOR NATION

So then, brethren, we are debtors.

—ROMANS, VIII:12

The connection between our new fiscal policy and our new status as the world's largest debtor is just as direct as that between our fiscal policy and the diminished prospects for improvement in our standard of living. As the deficit grew even as we neared full employment, borrowing from abroad became essential to maintain even our much reduced rate of business and residential investment. By the middle of the decade, foreign saving had become almost as important as our own in financing the joint requirements of the deficit and our domestic capital formation. In 1986 our total reliance on foreign saving was $144 billion, roughly two thirds of that year's federal deficit and nearly twice the net investment in plant and equipment by American business. In 1987 both the deficit and our domestic investment were smaller, but our reliance on foreign saving increased to $157 billion. As we have seen however, the privilege of drawing on foreign countries' saving has come at a high cost.

As with the other abrupt changes that our new fiscal policy has brought, it is easy to lose sight of how recent this remarkable transformation has been. Reagan was correct in pointing out when he took office that American producers were no longer able to hold their own markets at home against foreign competition in automobiles and steel and some other products as well. But on an overall basis, our international economic relations were fully in balance as recently as the beginning of this decade.

In 1980 American businesses sold abroad $224 billion of all kinds of merchandise, including industrial machinery, computers, airplanes, chemicals, coal, wheat and other grains, soybeans, and even some automobiles. At the same time, we purchased from abroad $250 billion worth of merchandise, including especially oil and petroleum products ($79 billion worth), but also steel, cars, electronic equipment, household appliances, coffee, wines, and the vast array of everyday consumer goods that have become a part of each American family's life.

Although we had a deficit in our merchandise trade in 1980, our international economic relations were in balance because we owned more assets abroad than foreigners owned here. That year we earned $73 billion of income on assets like stocks, bonds, bank deposits, and even whole companies in other countries, while foreigners earned only $42 billion on their American assets.* The difference more than covered our merchandise trade deficit. Even after allowing for other international payments like purchases of airline tickets and other travel services, or pension payments to retirees living abroad, or money sent to relatives abroad, our balance on all current transactions (that is, all payments other than investment flows) still showed a surplus in 1980—as it had throughout the postwar era, at least

---

*In addition, we earned another $13 billion from transactions like payments of royalties and fees for technology that we had licensed for use abroad, while foreigners earned only $5 billion from us in this way.

on average over periods long enough to even out the business cycle.

The collapse of our international competitiveness during the first half of the 1980s was spectacular in both speed and extent. One industry after another, laboring under an increasingly overvalued dollar, withered before the force of foreign competition—cars, motorcycles, bicycles, steel, textiles, shoes, electronic equipment, televisions and radios, cameras, personal computers, toasters, telephones, lawnmowers, pianos. The list of industries that suffered severely from foreign competition reads like the chamber of commerce directory. And in the markets for some newer products, like videocassette recorders, we did not become a producer at all. Since early 1985, the dollar has fallen sharply, but by 1988 our trade had only begun to recover. There is no guarantee that the market shares lost by American firms at home and abroad, or the jobs lost by American workers in industries exposed to ruinous international competition when the dollar was so sharply overvalued, will readily return. Moreover, with the dollar so much cheaper, we must pay more for the foreign goods we buy, so that the improvement in our trade deficit *measured in dollars* has lagged still further behind what modest improvement has taken place in actual volumes of exports and imports.

Foreign producers selling in our markets were quick to take advantage of the huge currency swing during the first half of the decade. The dollar prices of foreign goods that trade in highly competitive markets (like basic metals and agricultural products) fell as the dollar rose, so that large price differentials developed in favor of foreign producers. For intermediate goods used as inputs in manufacturing for example, dollar prices of goods made abroad *fell* by 20 percent on average between year-end 1980 and early 1985, while prices of goods made in America *rose* by 12 percent.[1]

By contrast, foreign manufacturers of finished products used the rising dollar both to expand market share and to fatten profit margins. Prices of finished manufactured goods made in America rose by 16 percent over these years, while prices of comparable foreign-made goods sold here rose by just 6 percent. The resulting price differential gave foreign producers a competitive advantage, and with their dollar prices worth 80 percent more in terms of their home currencies than before, they were also able to take out more profit on their sales.

As a result, by 1987 we imported $410 billion of merchandise but exported just $251 billion. Moreover, our imports rose even as the average price of oil (our greatest single import) fell from almost $31 a barrel in 1980 to $17 in 1987. The combination of sharply lower prices and slightly lower volume (due to continuing conservation) cut our oil import bill from $79 billion in 1980 to $42 billion in 1987. Without the weak oil market our 1987 trade deficit would have been even larger.*

Aside from oil, the collapse of our foreign trade in the 1980s has been practically all-pervasive, affecting both agriculture and industry. The decline in farmers' incomes during these years and the drop in the price of farmland would have been much less severe if farm exports had merely held steady at their 1981 levels. So would the plague of debt defaults and bankruptcies that have faced banks and other lenders in most of the farm states and that have even forced a piecemeal bail-out of the federally sponsored Farm Credit System. Only now that the dollar has fallen has the farm economy begun to improve.

Our industrial exports have suffered on a much larger scale even if in less dramatic proportions. Exports of industrial supplies—coal, paper, textiles, chemicals—had more than doubled during the late seventies, but they shrank after 1980. So did sales of industrial machinery like electrical generators, broad-

---

*In 1986 when the average price was only $15 per barrel and our imports were somewhat smaller, our oil import bill was just $34 billion.

casting and telephone equipment, construction machinery, and tractors. If computer sales had not *risen* by $11 billion between 1980 and 1987, the decline in our machinery exports would have been that much greater. Even airplanes, one of America's pioneering developments at home and once a mainstay of our competitiveness abroad, suffered shrinking sales for several years.

These abrupt reversals in our ability to sell manufactured goods abroad occurred in step with foreign producers' newfound ability to crack our markets. Automobile imports had more than doubled between 1975 and 1980 as foreign auto makers raised their share of our market from 18 percent to 27 percent of all new cars sold.[2] Despite the "voluntary" restraints on auto imports from Japan from 1981 on, by 1987 new car imports had more than doubled yet again.* Imports of electrical machinery more than doubled between 1980 and 1987. Imports of household electric appliances—radios, television sets, VCRs, stereo equipment, toasters, air conditioners—more than trebled. Even high-tech manufactures, once practically America's exclusive franchise and increasingly the source of optimistic expectations, came under growing competition. Foreign makers flooded the market with low-priced clones of IBM's personal computers and peripherals and then introduced new improvements like lap-top machines. Imports of computers and other office-type equipment increased sevenfold between 1980 and 1987. Imports of scientific instruments

---

*Worse yet, restrictions on how many cars Japanese producers can sell in America have led them to change their competitive strategies to emphasize selling more expensive cars and thereby eat into what was always the more profitable end of the market for the American auto companies. In addition, the form of these restrictions, with a separate quota for each firm, in effect eliminates the incentive for Japanese producers to compete among one another for U.S. sales.

and other professional equipment more than trebled. Only in 1987, with the dollar back below its 1980 level, did our import-export gap begin to stabilize.

Just how important has the dollar, and behind it our new fiscal policy, been to all this?

It would be naïve to suppose that the entire erosion of America's international competitiveness during the 1980s has been simply a matter of an overvalued currency in the first half of the decade and therefore entirely a product of our fiscal and monetary policies. Other influences have also been important. Some of the additional forces at work, like slower growth of productivity than other countries have achieved or diminished ability to make new products that require investment in specialized equipment or facilities, have also stemmed at least in part from our new fiscal policy. But other factors have had little to do with America's fiscal policy one way or the other. For example, the "green revolution," which has transformed countries like India into food exporters and even made Bangladesh self-sufficient in food on an overall basis, helped shrink our agricultural surplus from $29 billion in 1980 to just $6 billion in 1986.[3] The restrictive trading practices that bar our exports from some foreign markets may also have stiffened in the 1980s, although there is little direct evidence that they have.

Because of the many factors involved, it would also be naïve to think that only a cheaper dollar can restore America's competitiveness, so that there is nothing else to be done now that the dollar has fallen. Continuing negotiations to remove other countries' trade restrictions, selective but tough import restraints against persistent violators, policies to prevent developing countries' debt problems from destroying their ability to import, and even steady pressure on European countries to end their decade-long economic stagnation (which one would think they should want to do anyway) can all make a contribution.

So can efforts at the individual company level to design better products and to make them and market them more efficiently. So can efforts by employers and by government to train our labor force to work more effectively with changing technologies.

But it would be even more foolish to pretend that the overvalued dollar played no role in what has happened to American competitiveness or to suppose that a different fiscal policy, which had allowed the dollar to remain appropriately valued and had also facilitated new business investment, would not have made an important difference.

Apportioning the blame for our trade collapse is as complex as accounting for our productivity slowdown. In both cases, the immediate difficulty is not a lack of plausible explanations but an overabundance. As in the case of productivity, each potential explanation for the trade imbalance corresponds to a corrective course of action that has attracted its own constituency in the resulting debate over what to do.

But no alternative explanation can match the compelling coincidence of both timing and magnitude linking the surge in our imports and weakness of our exports to the dollar's rise. The most familiar alternative explanation is our slower average rate of productivity growth compared to other major industrialized countries. Our failure to achieve satisfactory productivity growth is crucially important to our prospects for raising our standard of living, as we have seen, but the connection to our ability to compete in international trade is less clear-cut. The most immediate problem with this idea is that it fails to explain why our long-term disadvantage in productivity growth has only so recently and so suddenly caused such an enormous loss of competitiveness. Our competitors' productivity gains have outstripped ours since well before the mid-sixties and long before 1973 when our productivity slowdown became acute. Moreover, in manufacturing, where our trade losses have been greatest, the productivity growth advantage in favor of our competitors *narrowed* after 1973 and has almost disappeared since 1980.* Judged on the basis of timing, these changes in relative productivity performance seem an unlikely cause of the sudden collapse of our manufacturing trade balance in the 1980s.

Even apart from questions of timing and magnitude, however, the link between productivity growth and international competitiveness is far from clear. There is no one-for-one tie between productivity growth and the rise or fall of production costs to business, since costs also depend on the prices of inputs like energy and basic materials. More important, productivity gains reduce production costs only to the extent that producers do not pay them out as higher wages. Individual firms may regard wages as set independently of productivity for a short time, but over longer periods labor is unlikely to let employers apply all gains from higher productivity to lowering costs and none to raising wages.

As we have seen, in America trends in real wages have closely tracked trends in productivity growth over most of the postwar period. In Europe and Japan, real wages have displayed less

---

*From 1950 until 1973 the average growth of output per hour in American manufacturing was 2.7 percent per annum versus 9.9 percent in Japan, 6.5 percent in Germany, and 5.1 percent elsewhere in Western Europe. During 1973–80 our average manufacturing productivity growth slowed to 1.2 percent per annum, but Japan's average gain fell to 5.7 percent, Germany's to 3.7 percent, and that of other Western European countries to 3.3 percent. During 1980–85—just the period when the dollar rose so rapidly—our average manufacturing productivity growth quickened to 4.1 percent per annum while Japan's recovered only to 5.9 percent, Germany's slowed further to 3.5 percent and that of other Western European countries recovered to 4.6 percent. (In 1986 our manufacturing productivity growth *exceeded* that of Japan, Germany, and most other Western European countries.)[4]

sensitivity to changes in productivity gains. If anything, this difference between American and foreign labor markets ought to have helped rather than hindered our competitiveness. Between 1950 and 1973, when the gap in productivity growth rates was fairly wide, real hourly wages in American manufacturing rose by 2.4 percent per annum versus 6.9 percent in Japan and 7.1 percent in Germany. During 1973–80 as the productivity growth gap narrowed so did the gap in real wage growth. Since 1980 the productivity growth gap has narrowed still further versus Japan and disappeared altogether versus Germany, but both countries' real wages have continued to grow more rapidly than ours. Between 1980 and 1985, as the dollar was rising, our real wage gains in manufacturing averaged just .4 percent per annum versus 1.9 percent in Japan and 1.6 percent in Germany.[5] Here again, the changes in cost relationships that occurred during this period appear unlikely to have accounted for the sudden, sharp deterioration in our competitiveness.

The crucial point is that even that part of a firm's productivity growth that is left over to reduce its production costs after it pays higher wages still does not guarantee it any advantage in international competition. What matters is production costs as the firm's potential customers see them—that is, on a comparable foreign currency basis—not just costs measured in each producer's own currency. When an airline compares the dollar price of a Boeing 757 to the price of an Airbus A-340 in French francs, the comparison hinges crucially on the dollar-franc exchange rate. Americans shopping for new cars neither know nor care about the price of Toyotas in yen. What matters is the Toyota's price in dollars, compared to the dollar prices of American and other cars. Holding production cost increases to a much slower pace than what producers elsewhere can manage will not help a firm's competitiveness if its own country's currency rises enough to cancel out the advantage it achieves. Only after allowing for exchange rates, in addition to comparisons of productivity growth and real wages, is the picture complete. And only then does the experience of international cost comparisons correspond at all closely to our loss of competitiveness.

Until 1980 American manufacturers enjoyed a growing *advantage* over competitors abroad in that our production costs rose more slowly than foreign producers' costs, after repricing both in terms of a common currency. During 1950–73, our firms paid out wage increases modestly in excess of their productivity gains, so that their labor costs per unit of production rose on average by 2.5 percent per annum. After allowing for the falling dollar-yen exchange rate, Japanese manufacturers' unit labor costs *priced in dollars* rose on average by 3.6 percent per annum during this period. Similarly, after allowing for the falling dollar-mark exchange rate, German manufacturers' unit labor costs *priced in dollars* rose on average by 5.3 percent per annum. At least on the basis of cost, our manufacturing industries had a clear, if modest, advantage throughout this period of gradual dollar decline.

During the remainder of the seventies, as the dollar fell further our manufacturers continued to enjoy that advantage over European industry, while they approximately maintained their cost relationships versus Japan. As inflation picked up while productivity growth faltered, American manufacturers' unit labor costs rose by 8.5 percent per annum during 1973–80 versus 8.6 percent for Japanese firms' costs and 11.2 percent for German firms' costs, with both priced in dollars.

During the 1980s, as we have seen, our manufacturers succeeded both in boosting their productivity growth (mostly by reducing payrolls) and in holding down wage gains. In most industries they have done so to an extent that is fully comparable to what their competitors in other countries have achieved.

But instead of declining by 3 percent to 4 percent per year to make up for the gradual erosion of our technological advantage, as it had throughout much of the postwar period, the dollar rose sharply during the first half of the decade. In the end, the rising dollar entirely overwhelmed our success in advancing productivity and holding down wages. Our average increase in manufacturing unit labor costs during 1980–85 was 1.7 percent per annum, not all that different from other countries' cost increases priced in their own currencies. But after allowing for the sharp rise in the dollar, other countries' costs *declined* in every case: by 2.2 percent per annum in Japan, 7.3 percent in Germany, and 7.2 percent in other European countries.

Accumulated over just five years, this combination of rising costs in America and declining costs abroad *in dollar terms* shifted our relative costs by 21 percent versus Japan, 54 percent versus Germany, and 53 percent versus other European countries. It is little wonder that these countries' manufacturers had ample room to hold their price increases below ours yet still enjoy higher profits. Now that the dollar has fallen, these cost comparisons have turned around, and with the usual lag, our trade has begun to do so as well. But along the way the role of the overvalued dollar was clear enough.

In contrast to our situation relative to Japan and Western Europe, our flood of imports from Asia's newly industrializing countries does appear to have been more a matter of cost differentials than currency values. Taiwan, Korea, Hong Kong, and Singapore boosted their collective sales to America from $18 billion in 1980 to $58 billion in 1987. During the same period our exports to these countries barely increased at all. At first glance, this swing does not seem to have resulted from changes in exchange rates. During the first half of the 1980s both Taiwan and Singapore simply tied their currencies to the dollar for all practical purposes, allowing them to rise or fall with the dollar. And although both the Korean won and the Hong Kong dollar fell against the American dollar, in both cases what movement occurred mostly reflected faster inflation in those countries rather than a change in real exchange rates.

In large part because of their aggressive exploitation of technologies developed by other countries, these four exporters have achieved productivity growth rates far superior not only to ours but also to Europe's and Japan's. And because workers earn so little there by our standards, even large percentage increases in wages still leave labor costs far below ours, Europe's or Japan's. Translated into dollars, the average total compensation rate for manufacturing workers, including fringe benefits, was less than $2.50 per hour in 1987 in each of these four countries. Ours was over $13. Here if nowhere else, our competitiveness seems genuinely caught in a scissors of slower productivity growth at home and increased vulnerability to competition from low-wage production abroad. Although these four countries accounted for less than a fourth of the decline in our overall trade position between 1980 and 1987, they present a serious problem nonetheless. Extrapolated into the future, their success raises fundamental questions about our ability to live so much better than citizens of low-wage countries, when they too can take advantage of whatever new technology we (and other rich, industrialized countries) develop.

Even for trade with the four Asian "tigers," however, exchange rate movements are far from irrelevant. Part of the reason that their labor costs have remained so low compared to costs elsewhere is that they have not allowed their currencies to *rise* as they have steadily bolstered their productivity and competitiveness. Our problem here is not that the dollar rose when it should not have, as was the case versus Japan and Europe, but that the dollar on an inflation-adjusted basis should have *declined* against each of these four countries' currencies and did not. Moreover, since 1985 these countries have allowed their currencies to appreciate against the dollar by only small amounts compared to what has happened to the yen and most European currencies. Hong Kong has held its dollar fixed against ours during this period, and by year-end 1987 the upward movements of the other three currencies— measured against 1984–85 peak exchange rates—were just 13 percent for Korea, 27 percent for Taiwan, and 10 percent for Singapore. Even in the case of the four tigers, the overvalued dollar has been at least a significant part of the problem.

Still other potential explanations for our loss of competitiveness in the 1980s inevitably lead to similar questions. Like productivity differentials and wage differentials, the relevant influences at work have typically not changed enough to account for the startling collapse since 1980. Restrictive trading practices, for example, no doubt do hinder American exporters from selling a variety of products in many countries around the world. Removal of such barriers would of course help. But there is no reason to believe that these restrictions have dramatically increased during the 1980s.*

Moreover, most other potential explanations either work through productivity or wage differentials in the first place or could just as well have been neutralized by an appropriate change in the dollar—just as the effects of productivity differentials and wage differentials were offset throughout the post-war period until the 1980s. The recent American fascination with Japanese business skills, for example, is an interesting cultural and social phenomenon in its own right. Presumably there is much to learn. But from a competitiveness standpoint, what matters is whether superior management techniques have enabled Japanese firms to achieve higher productivity. As we

---

*Now that a fourth of our nonoil imports are subject to official nontariff trade barriers, it is also less clear that other countries systematically employ more "unfair" trading practices than we do.

have seen, the difference between Japan's productivity growth and ours has been narrowing for some time.

Similarly, the failure of Germany and other European countries to stimulate their economies, despite a decade of what Americans have increasingly come to call "Eurosclerosis," no doubt has held back our exports. Twenty years ago a major challenge was to explain why our unemployment was permanently greater than that of most Western European countries. During the sixties, the average unemployment rate was just .6 percent in Germany, 1.7 percent in France, and 2.8 percent in Britain. Today even after these countries have sent many of their foreign "guest workers" back home, their unemployment rates are all higher than ours, and in some countries much higher. The Japanese unemployment rate remains low by American standards (just 2.8 percent in 1987) but stands at a historic high point for Japan.[6]

A major thrust of American economic diplomacy in recent years has therefore been to urge these countries to expand their sluggish economies. If their own economic expansion had been faster, they would have bought more from us even with an overvalued dollar. But a less overvalued dollar would also have led them to buy more from us. Now that the dollar has fallen, the main reason for urging these countries to grow faster is to prevent the threat of a global economic contraction if the higher price of foreign goods leads us to reduce our imports.

However much these and other influences may have aggravated the situation, it is difficult to escape the conclusion that our competitiveness problem is primarily a product of the overvalued dollar and therefore ultimately of our new fiscal policy. Because of the dollar's remarkable rise in the first half of the decade, more of the cost of that policy has fallen on our international sector and less on our domestic capital formation than most analysts of Reagan's policy predicted at the outset.

Now that the dollar has fallen sharply lower, the cost will shift back toward depressing our capital investment.

But even if the lower dollar soon restores the equilibrium in our international payments that we enjoyed for so many years until the 1980s, the legacy of debt from our decade of huge trade imbalances financed by capital inflows will remain. As we have seen, the ultimate consequences of this debt that we owe abroad will probably prove the most damaging of all the changes resulting from our new fiscal policy. It is important, therefore, to place our new status as a debtor nation in some perspective if we are to appreciate fully the new realities with which our policies must now deal.

Like any newly developing country, America began its economic life as a borrower. Debts owed by Americans to foreign lenders probably started to accumulate as soon as the first permanent European settlers stepped ashore at Saint Augustine in 1565.* As the flood of Spanish, English, and French colonists arrived, their accumulating debt to lenders wherever they had come from grew. Even so, because the livelihood they developed here was predominantly agricultural, based on land and human labor and perhaps some animal power but not much physical capital, what they had to borrow to establish themselves was typically small. By the time the United States became an independent country, its entire net debt to foreigners was only $70 million.[7]

The real surge of American foreign borrowing came during the nineteenth century beginning with the wave of investment in canals and railroads in the 1830s.[8] The Erie Canal, completed in 1825, was the first major American project built with

---

*If the Vikings did settle "Vinland" in the eleventh century, they too probably owed at least some amounts to their relatives and backers at home.

significant foreign financing. Its commercial success stimulated interest at home in digging more canals, while its financial success encouraged foreign investors to put up the money.* By the mid-1840s, Americans had built some 3,400 miles of canals, and had financed almost half the cost abroad. In addition, between 1830 and 1840 the number of railroad miles in operation in America increased from just 23 to more than 2,800. Railroads too required capital that Americans did not have. Roughly a fourth of the proceeds that the states raised from bonds in the 1820s and 1830s—almost as great a fraction as went into canals—went into railroad construction, as states (and later on, cities) competed to attract the new rail lines. Foreign investors, primarily in London, bought a majority of these bonds. Overall the resulting net inflow of foreign capital amounted to 1.9 percent of the new nation's annual income on average during 1831–39.[9]

By the time this first wave of borrowing from abroad ended, America's net foreign debt came to approximately $300 million, equal to about 20 percent of a year's income. Economic depression here and the fears of foreign investors after a rash of defaults by states that had issued bonds halted the flow of funds from abroad after 1839.† Net foreign indebtedness fell. By the mid-1840s however, the business climate had recovered, and the states began to pay interest once again.

A second, smaller wave of foreign borrowing developed in the 1850s. By then railroads had supplanted canals as the main form of transportation attracting heavy investment. Rail construction reached 3,400 miles of new track laid *per year* by

*New York State paid a premium to redeem before maturity the $7 million of bonds it had issued to pay for the canal.
†Florida and Mississippi formally repudiated their debts and seven other states stopped paying interest—events we do not often recall as we try to collect from today's developing country debtors.[10]

1854. In addition, the investment boom of the 1850s financed the beginnings of our manufacturing industries. Even so, in part because of gold from the new fields in California, the *net* capital inflow was just .6 percent of total income on average during 1850–59. By 1860 the net foreign debt was still less than $400 million, or not quite 10 percent of what was by then a year's income—about the same as our foreign debt ratio today.

The remaining two waves of American reliance on foreign lending, in the years just after the Civil War and again in the 1880s and into the early 1890s, were far larger in dollar terms. But America had expanded, so that only the foreign borrowing of the late 1860s and early 1870s exceeded that of the 1830s in relation to the country's income.

Railroads and steel dominated America's investment in the immediate post Civil War period. The Union Pacific and the Southern Pacific completed the first transcontinental rail link in 1869, and by the early 1870s rail construction regained the peak mileage last seen in the 1850s. Cities and counties financed most of this boom, but after 1870 the railroads also borrowed directly both here and in London. In the meanwhile, the new Bessemer process for decarbonizing iron had made steel rails more economical than iron. Alexander Holley was putting up Bessemer plants in America as early as 1865, and Andrew Carnegie began to convert the Pittsburgh iron works to steel making in 1872. Soon steel was taking the place of iron not only for rails but for bridges, locomotives, and rolling stock.

After another interruption due to worldwide financial panic in 1873 and spreading economic contraction for a half decade thereafter, American investment gathered renewed vigor in the 1880s. Railroads and steel were important factors again as the nation's rail mileage doubled again to 182,000 miles by 1890. The new industrial era also saw countless factories spring up to produce machinery, clocks, hardware, gas stoves, pipes, bicycles, and textiles. By the time renewed panic and recession set in in 1893, manufacturing output had also doubled from 1880. At the same time, cities spent heavily to install gas lighting and fresh water systems.

From the end of the Civil War to the close of the nineteenth century, Americans put more resources into investment in relation to their income than at any time before or since. The share of income devoted to all investment—in transportation and communication facilities, in business plant and equipment, in basic fixtures for cities and towns, and in housing for a growing population—rose from 14 percent to 16 percent before the Civil War to 17 percent to 20 percent for the remainder of the century.[11] As in the 1830s and again in the 1850s, a principal source of financing for all this was borrowing from abroad. In addition, as in the 1850s, exports of gold and now silver too helped pay for part of it.

Net borrowing from abroad during 1866–73 averaged 2.2 percent of total income. By the end of 1873, America's accumulated net foreign debt was $1.8 billion, or about 25 percent of a year's income. This level, about comparable to Brazil's *net* foreign indebtedness today—and what ours will be if it takes until the mid-1990s to balance our trade—turned out to be the historical peak. The final wave of foreign borrowing was smaller than in the 1830s or the post Civil War period, averaging just 1.1 percent of income during 1882–93. By 1893 the accumulated net foreign debt had risen to $3.2 billion, but that was less than 25 percent of a year's income.

After the early 1890s, much of the country's rail and telegraph network and also much of the cities' basic social capital were in place. So were the makings of the nation's new industrial base. Just as important, once the recession of the mid-1890s ended, incomes were higher and therefore so was available saving. America had outgrown its need for foreign capital. Net international debt peaked at $3.3 billion in 1896. From then on, Americans were investing more of their saving abroad than the amounts of foreign saving they took in. Apart from World War II and a few other scattered years, they continued to do so until 1982.

Two decades proved sufficient to eliminate the net foreign debt altogether. The last year in which Americans owed more abroad than foreigners owed them was 1914. America's foreign lending surged to new record volumes as World War I began in Europe in August of that year. Early in 1915, America became a net creditor.

For the next six and a half decades, Americans continued to be net lenders to the rest of the world in almost every year. As they did so, their overall net foreign asset position steadily grew. By 1940 Americans held $34 billion of assets abroad versus only $14 billion of foreign-owned assets here. By 1970 the gap in America's favor had widened to $166 billion versus $107 billion. By year-end 1981, Americans held $720 billion of assets abroad versus foreign-owned assets here of just $579 billion.

But 1981 was the last time we were net suppliers of saving to other countries. That year's $141 billion net asset position marked the high point of America's status as a net creditor country.

The reversal of our international financial position since then has been just as spectacular as the decline in competitiveness that lay behind it. Just three years under our new fiscal policy, through 1984, was sufficient to dissipate the entire net foreign asset position that three generations of Americans had accumulated since 1914, while in just the next three years, through 1987, we have accumulated the world's largest net foreign *debt* for the next generation of Americans to service. And because the improvement in our trade flows has lagged behind the dollar's fall (as it always does), the next three years, through 1990, are certain to increase our foreign debt still further. But even after the cheaper dollar finally brings our foreign trade into balance, whether that occurs by 1990 or later, the debt we owe to foreigners will remain. So will our obligation to service it.

Our net foreign asset position first began to slip in 1982, the same year the federal deficit first exceeded $100 billion. But the deterioration in 1982 was only $4 billion, and as we have seen, that year's deficit was due more to economic weakness than to expansionary fiscal policy. The more serious erosion followed in 1983 and 1984, as the deficit widened further despite the advancing business recovery. Between year-end 1981 and year-end 1984, our foreign holdings grew to $896 billion while foreign assets here grew to $892 billion. Moreover, almost half of our foreign assets in 1984 consisted of loans by American banks to foreign borrowers, and approximately half of those were to developing countries whose ability to pay was dubious at best.

America officially became a net debtor country again in the first weeks of 1985. By the end of the year, foreign assets in America exceeded Americans' foreign assets by $112 billion, almost as much as the difference going the other way had been just three years earlier. Our *net* foreign borrowing in just one year had exceeded the entire outstanding *gross* foreign debt of Mexico or Brazil—or any other country for that matter. In 1986 the pace quickened further. By year-end our net foreign debt was $264 billion, more than the gross debt outstanding of Mexico, Brazil, and Argentina combined. By the end of 1987, our net foreign debt was presumably near $400 billion, even if we count all of our banks' foreign loans at a hundred cents on the dollar despite the fact that these loans traded in the market at prices like fifty-three cents for Mexico, forty-seven cents for Argentina, thirty-nine cents for Brazil, and twenty-eight cents for Nigeria.[12]

Not surprisingly, attempts to dismiss our increasing net foreign debt as the result of special circumstances or even as a statistical illusion have now become commonplace. But on careful inspection these arguments lack merit. For example, until the market crashed in October 1987, one popular view attributed much of the turnaround in our financial position to the sharp rise of stock prices from mid-1982 on. But despite the increased interest of stock market investors in diversification across national lines, stocks still account for only a small share of foreign investors' American holdings. Between year-end 1981 and year-end 1986, foreign holdings of American assets grew from $579 billion to $1.3 trillion, but the increase in foreign ownership of American stocks during this period, *including* the rise in market prices, was from $64 billion to only $167 billion. Foreign holdings of other kinds of assets increased much more, and not because of price changes but because our trade gap increasingly gave foreigners the dollars with which to buy these assets. During the same period, foreign deposits in American banks rose from $192 billion to $476 billion, foreign holdings of U.S. Treasury securities and American corporate bonds rose from $154 billion to $415, and direct foreign holdings of American business firms and real estate rose from $109 billion to $209 billion. Even if stock prices had remained at their 1982 level, our international financial position would have deteriorated almost as much as it did.

Similarly, while it is always possible to downplay these developments by pointing to the thorny problems that inevitably plague any attempt to measure who owns what and what it is all worth, it is unlikely that even a perfectly accurate set of accounts would make our position look better. For example, valuing our gold stocks at the market price, rather than at $42.22 per ounce as in the official accounts, would add about $100 billion to America's assets. Also on the plus side, valuing both Americans' and foreigners' direct holdings of businesses and real estate at current market values would increase both sides of the balance sheet, but on net it would result in another

sizable shift in our favor. As we have seen, our recorded holdings of direct investments abroad still exceed foreigners' holdings here (by $260 billion to $209 billion as of year-end 1986).
And because foreigners have acquired most of their investments more recently than we acquired ours, marking both to
current prices would boost our holdings by more on average.

A fully accurate set of accounts would also reflect some
minuses for the American position, however. The true value of
American banks' outstanding claims on developing countries is
presumably well below the more than $200 billion that the
banks still showed on their books at year-end 1986. Even more
important, the U.S. international payments accounts consistently fail to balance by an amount indicating more than $25
billion *per year* of net investment in America by foreigners that
simply goes unrecorded. Allowing for the accumulation of this
unrecorded net inflow over just the last decade would swamp
any plausible statistical adjustments in our favor. On balance,
the official estimates—a net debt position of $264 billion at
year-end 1986 and much more in 1987—are probably about on
the mark.

As we have seen, our change from a creditor to a debtor will
profoundly affect how Americans live in the future, for hereafter an increasing share of our income will go abroad in the
form of interest on what we owe. In 1980 we could afford our
$26 billion excess of merchandise imports over merchandise
exports, because we earned more on our foreign holdings than
foreign investors earned on their American holdings. But that
advantage depended on our owning more assets abroad than
foreigners owned here. Our new fiscal policy has long since
dissipated the differential in ownership, and by now our surplus
of income earned from foreign assets is almost gone. The
surplus peaked at $34 billion in 1981, the same year our net

investment position peaked. By 1987, it was just $14 billion. At the same time, the fact that we have borrowed in order to consume—in contrast to the nineteenth century when we borrowed to invest—means that the income we have available to pay foreigners what they are earning here is diminished.

Indeed, the true balance of our international investment income is probably worse than even the shrunken surplus remaining in 1987 implies. One reason is that the reported income from our foreign assets includes the interest credited by American banks on their loans to developing countries. In many cases these countries "pay interest" on their loans only by borrowing it. Our banks are able to report interest earnings only by arranging for the extension of yet more loans to the same borrowers. These elaborate reschedulings allow the banks to avoid the regulatory difficulties that they would face if they officially admitted the condition of their loan portfolios. But they provide no income that we can use to pay for what we buy abroad.

Another reason that our reported foreign investment earnings now overstate what we actually earn abroad is that the decline in the dollar since early 1985 makes the income we earn in foreign currencies look larger in terms of dollars. For example, buying German government bonds bearing a 7 percent interest rate in late 1984 would actually have provided an American holder with interest payments representing a return of 8.6% in 1985, 10.9 percent in 1986, and 13.3 percent in 1987, because in each successive year the same amount of marks translated into a larger number of dollars. These higher gains are illusory, however, because the same number of marks buys no more German-made goods than it did before.

Despite these overstatements, our genuine net income earned from foreign assets still has not disappeared as fast as our net foreign asset position vanished. Many American holdings abroad do deliver greater rates of return than what foreign investors earn on their holdings here. The difference may be partly a reward for making more astute investments, but it is also the reward for taking more risk. For example, as of year-end 1984 the respective totals of American assets abroad and foreign assets in the United States were almost identical. But our direct holdings in foreign businesses and real estate amounted to $211 billion, while foreign direct investments here came to only $165 billion.* Because this kind of investment is typically more risky than average, it usually yields higher than average returns. By contrast, foreign holdings of safe (and therefore lower yielding) U.S. Treasury securities amounted to $201 billion in 1984 versus only $62 billion of American investors' holdings of debt securities issued by all foreign governments and private debtors combined.

But our investment income surplus is dwindling, and as our net foreign debt position worsens, in its place we will soon have an investment income *deficit* that will progressively widen. That is why we will no longer be able to import more than we export, except by borrowing more from abroad than ever—as long as foreigners continue to accept dollars in payment for their goods and reinvest them in our assets. Once we have an investment income deficit, our only alternative to borrowing ever more and selling off ever more of our assets will be to import less than we export. But reducing our imports so that they fall below our exports will sharply cut our standard of living at home and threaten prosperity abroad. And increasing our exports so that they exceed our imports will require not just skill and determination but investment in new capacity on a scale far beyond the diminished capital formation permitted by our new fiscal policy in the 1980s.

*And as we have seen, these historic-cost values presumably understated the direct investment gap in our favor.

Chapter X

ROOTS OF REAGANOMICS

The way of a fool is straight in his own eyes:
But be that is wise hearkeneth unto counsel.

—PROVERBS, XII:15

How did we get into this mess? While there may have been
some element of deceit on the part of those who designed our
new fiscal policy, and there was certainly some self-deception
by Americans who supported it, nevertheless there was a story
—a coherent set of economic arguments—behind it. These
arguments turned out to be wrong, and by now most Americans have seen that. But as we now face the hard choices
necessary to change course, it is essential that we understand
not just that these ideas proved wrong but why that was so.
Otherwise the same wishful thinking may, and probably will,
continue to stand in the way of a sensible new set of policies
for the future.

If the postwar period to 1980 had been the era of "tax and
spend"—which in a very real sense it was—and if Americans
wanted a change, where did the new direction lie? Ronald
Reagan's message in 1980 was that taxes were not just high but
too high and that a "New Beginning for the Economy" should
itself begin with lower taxes.

But making lower taxes the main focus of the new economic

policy left open what that meant for national defense, Social Security benefits, Medicare and Medicaid, and all the other government activities that these taxes paid for. Reagan ruled out from the start any cuts whatever in Social Security, by far the largest nondefense program. Nor would there be any cuts in Medicare or veterans' benefits. Reagan knew that Americans wanted lower taxes, but also that they were not interested in losing the benefits to which they had become accustomed and to which they now felt entitled. And he also promoted accelerated defense spending on a scale not seen since Vietnam. As we have seen, enacting all of Reagan's proposals—including the cuts he proposed in nondefense programs, as well as the full defense build-up for which he asked—would have rearranged the composition of federal spending, but it would not substantially have changed the total.

The real challenge Reagan faced in 1980 was therefore to overcome the traditional American reluctance to leave the country's bills to the next generation. His answer, which has continued to dominate discussion of tax policies throughout the 1980s, was to emphasize—and in the end to magnify beyond all plausibility—the effect of taxes in dulling Americans' incentives to undertake economically worthwhile activities: The average factory worker is in the 21 percent marginal tax bracket? According to Reagan's theory, cutting his tax rate to 16 percent will let him keep so much more of each dollar he earns that he will work extra hours or even look for a higher-paying job. The typical savings account pays 6 percent interest, or only 3 percent for a taxpayer in the 50 percent bracket? According to Reagan's theory, cutting his tax rate to 30 percent will increase the after-tax yield by enough that he will save more and spend less. The projected return on a new steel rolling mill is too low to warrant going ahead after allowing for investment tax incentives as well as the 46 percent corporate tax rate? According to the theory, cutting the tax rate to 36 percent will raise the return enough to make it worthwhile for some steelmakers to undertake the project.

Taxes, after all, really do affect incentives. And when taxes are as large in relation to incomes and profits as in postwar America, it is always possible that some effects of taxes on incentives may be large as well. Reagan's central economic assumption was that these incentive effects were very large indeed. That assumption provided the link that made lower taxes consistent with the basic morality that had traditionally guided Americans' public choices. With lower taxes, people would work harder and save more, businesses would invest more, and individual Americans would start more new businesses. Lower taxes, in other words, supported one basic American value after another—in addition to being in themselves most agreeable. And, of course, the emphasis on incentive effects solved the problem of how to pay the cost of all that government does.

Each of these incentive effects was familiar enough, at least in principle. What was new in 1980 was the magnitude Reagan claimed for them. Even in versions that were less extreme than the view Reagan advanced during the 1980 presidential election campaign, "supply-side" economics argued that these incentive effects would be far larger than anyone had supposed before. Even if some spending cuts were still necessary to balance the budget after all, they would therefore be small. There was certainly no need to cut core government programs like Social Security and Medicare or to hold back on a major defense build-up.

The instantly popular idea of supply-side economics severed tax *rates* from their consequences for tax *revenues,* and hence for government spending as well. It therefore put reduced federal taxes at the same level on the public agenda as the taxpayers' revolt in states where demographic changes and the completion of major building projects had sharply eased spending requirements.* In neither case did proponents of lower taxes have to face the question of what government services to eliminate, what benefit programs to slash, which offices to close, which employees to fire. Nor did tax cuts therefore mean unbalanced budgets with debt accumulating to be shouldered by the next generation—the prospect that Americans had so overwhelmingly rejected in Kennedy's day. The deficit in 1980 was a sign of Carter's failed policies. By cutting taxes, Reagan would balance the budget by 1983.

Reagan put the case as directly as possible in the chief economic policy address of his 1980 campaign, delivered in Chicago that October: "We can do it. We must do it. We must do all three together: balance the budget, cut tax rates, and build our defenses."[2] And in the television address he gave as president the next summer to urge the public to support Kemp-Roth on the eve of the crucial votes in Congress, he predicted that if taxes were cut, "Starting next year, the deficits will get smaller until in just a few years the budget can be balanced. And we hope we can begin whittling at that almost $1 trillion debt that hangs over the future of our children."[3] What could be better?

But the novel idea that substantially cutting tax rates would not reduce tax revenues, or at least not by much, turned out —predictably—to be wrong. So did several other key assumptions that provided the economic underpinnings of Reagan's fiscal policy.

Economics, or at least the aspects of the subject that matter

*For example, in 1978, before voters approved Proposition 13, California's revenues exceeded expenditures by $4.7 billion.[1]

for public policy, involves both theoretical issues and factual ones. That is part of the reason that making good economic policy is often so difficult. Merely looking at "the facts" without any conceptual framework to organize them and judge which are more relevant than others is of little use. There are simply too many facts to look at. At the same time, merely pointing out what is theoretically possible, without any evidence to indicate which possibilities are more likely than others to describe reality, is not much help either. Too many potential outcomes are possible, depending upon the prevailing circumstances, and too often these different possibilities squarely contradict one another.

The distinction between what is possible and what is likely somehow got lost in the public discussion of tax rates and tax revenues in 1980. The idea that lower tax rates *can* produce higher revenues under some circumstances is different from the claim that lower tax rates *will* produce higher revenues under the specific conditions prevailing in a particular country at a particular time. The first is a matter of what is possible somewhere and sometime. The second is a matter of what is actually likely to happen in a real place and time.

The idea that lower tax rates *can* lead to higher tax revenues under some conditions is not controversial. It is also not new. More than two hundred years ago, Adam Smith explained the point succinctly enough in *The Wealth of Nations:* "High taxes, sometimes by diminishing the consumption of the taxed commodities, and sometimes by encouraging smuggling, frequently afford a smaller revenue to government than what might be drawn from more moderate taxes."*[4]

---

*Smith's discussion throughout makes clear that he understood the principles at issue in the supply-side argument. Later in the same chapter, for example, he wrote of a tax that ". . . it may obstruct the industry of the

Because Smith wrote before the day of income taxes, he stated this basic idea as it applied to excises and tariffs. But the same reasoning holds for income taxes too. If the tax on income earned from working rises enough, some people may work less. And if enough people do so, the government will collect less revenue from its income tax despite the higher tax per dollar of wages earned.* Reagan's reasoning was a straightforward application of Smith's logic. If under some conditions a *rise* in tax rates will produce smaller revenues, then under those conditions *lower* tax rates will deliver larger revenues.

The logic was impeccable. But as usual in economics, logic alone is only half the story. Establishing that some outcome is possible does not necessarily make it likely. Pointing out that lower tax rates can produce higher revenues *if* enough people work more is not the same as showing that they will do so under the actually prevailing conditions. That is a matter not just of theory but of fact as well.

We have now run the necessary experiment to find out whether lower tax rates actually produce higher revenues under the circumstances of modern-day America. They do not. As we have seen, in the wake of the largest tax cut in the nation's history, mostly consisting of an across-the-board reduction of marginal tax rates on individuals' incomes, there is no evidence

---

people, and discourage them from applying to certain branches of business which might give maintenance and employment to great multitudes."[5]

*Smith's one-liner also gave a second reason, and it too applies to an income tax. If the tax rises high enough, especially in a country like America that relies heavily on voluntary compliance with the tax code, some people may stop reporting what they earn. And if enough people do so, the government will again collect less revenue. This prospect too has been disappointed, however, since the Internal Revenue Service estimate of taxes due but not received has risen from $81 billion in 1981 to $103 billion in 1986 despite lower tax rates.

of a surge of work effort anywhere near as large as what would have been necessary even to keep revenues rising along their previous growth path, much less increase them above it. Instead, the tax cut reduced federal revenues and by large amounts. It simply did not have the effect advertised for it.

But even before the Kemp-Roth experiment began, was it ever plausible to believe the theoretical possibility that lower tax rates would produce higher revenues might correspond to the practical reality of modern-day America and our income tax?

The revenue generated by a tax depends on both the tax rate and the volume of the taxed activity. For a fixed tax structure, more income earned obviously means more revenues, and for a fixed amount of income earned, higher tax rates also mean more revenues. The reason that under some conditions higher tax rates can reduce revenues is that they may discourage work effort, as the supply-side argument emphasized. If they do, the resulting revenue will be the product of the higher tax rates applied to smaller incomes. But merely knowing that people will work less at higher tax rates is not sufficient to say whether revenues will rise or fall. It is also necessary to know *how much less* they will work. The question is essentially quantitative, not subject to resolution on the basis of logic alone.

With an income tax of 100 percent, of course, no one would work at any job he would not also be willing to do as an unpaid volunteer. But American income tax rates are nowhere near such a theoretical maximum, nor were they in 1980. The average federal taxpayer that year was in the 21 percent marginal tax bracket.[6] The *maximum* rate paid on income earned from wages and salaries was 50 percent.* Social Security took

---

*The maximum rate on income from other sources like interest and dividend payments, levied above the $215,000 line for married couples, was 70 percent.

another 6% of incomes up to $25,900 but nothing thereafter. Including Social Security and state and local taxes, the average taxpayer in 1980 paid approximately thirty cents on each extra dollar of income earned.*

It is also important to distinguish an *across-the-board* cut in income tax rates, like under Kemp-Roth, from more specific tax changes that affect narrower activities. In a country as large as America, an across-the-board change in federal income tax rates is one of the most broadly applicable tax actions imaginable. People cannot avoid it by buying one product rather than another or by working at one job rather than another or even by living in one state rather than another. Apart from leaving the country or just not declaring their income, people can avoid the federal income tax only by working less.

By contrast, some evidence suggests that the reduction in the maximum tax payable on capital gains, from 49 percent (a 35 percent statutory maximum, raised even higher by the effect of provisions like the "alternative minimum" tax) to 28 percent in 1979 and then just 20 percent in 1981, may actually have *increased* the amount of taxes individuals paid on income from capital gains.[9] With the lower tax rate, people became less

---

*With a top bracket of 50 percent at the federal level alone, extra labor income earned by some individuals would clearly have been taxed more heavily. But many taxpayers faced overall marginal rates below 30 percent. At the federal level, for example, where the average taxpayer was in the 21 percent bracket, more than a fourth of all returns were in the 16 percent bracket or below. And many people earned too little income to pay any tax at all. The 6 percent Social Security tax would have applied to an extra dollar earned by the great majority of taxpayers, since only one out of eight tax returns filed for 1980 (even including joint returns covering two incomes) reported income above the $25,900 ceiling.[7] The marginal income tax rate levied at the state level obviously varied widely, but the average appears to have been 3 percent to 4 percent.[8]

reluctant to sell assets when their prices rose above what they had paid to buy them. But such specific, narrowly based changes constituted only a small part of the 1981 tax bill, and the additional revenues from greater capital gains were small in any case. Taxes paid by individuals on capital gains rose from $9 billion in 1978 to an average $12 billion per year in 1979–80 and an average $18 billion during 1981–85.[10] Whatever part of this increase was due to the lower tax rate (rather than the post-1982 stock market rally for example) was tiny compared to roughly $300 billion per year of individual income taxes. The heart of Kemp-Roth—and the part Reagan emphasized so forcefully both before the 1980 election and after—was the one-fourth across-the-board cut in individual income tax rates.

Just how strong would the incentive effect of lower tax rates on work effort have to be in order to make revenues rise, or even stay the same, in response to such a change? And was there ever any reason to believe that the effect might actually be that powerful?

With an overall "tax wedge" of 30 percent, representing the marginal tax that government at all levels levied directly against individuals' labor income in 1980, on average for all Americans, changes in tax rates translate into changes in *after-tax* pay rates that are less than one half as large in percentage terms. Cutting the federal component by fully a third, from 21 percent down to 14 percent, would have reduced the *overall* marginal tax rate from 30 percent to roughly 23 percent, or by about one fourth.* Doing so would therefore have raised the take-home share of an extra hour's gross pay from 70 cents on the dollar to 77 cents—for example, from $4.66 an hour to

---

*The correspondence is not exact because state income taxes are deductible at the federal level.

$5.13 for the average employee in nonagricultural businesses in 1980. With a beginning marginal tax rate of 30 percent, therefore, cutting the tax rate by one fourth corresponds to increasing the take-home pay for extra work by only about one tenth.

By contrast, cutting tax rates by one fourth will reduce revenues by one fourth if nobody works any harder and earns any more income as a result. If revenues are to remain unchanged, therefore, there must be on average roughly a one-fourth increase in work effort.

Comparing the one-tenth average increase in after-tax pay rates to the one-fourth average increase in work effort that is necessary to keep revenues from shrinking provides a rough indication of how strong the response of work effort to after-tax wage rates would have to be for Reagan's theory to be true. For lower tax rates not to reduce revenues, the percentage increase in work effort that higher after-tax wage rates elicited would have to be *two and a half times* as great as the percentage increase in after-tax wage rates itself. And for lower tax rates to *increase* revenues as Reagan predicted, the percentage increase in work effort would have to be *more than two and a half times* the increase in after-tax wage rates.*

A response of this magnitude is wildly at variance with the available evidence on Americans' work patterns, including the studies available before 1980. How much people change their work effort in response to wage changes depends on their occupation, age, sex, family situation, and other individual characteristics. On average for all Americans however, the

---

*This relationship is only approximate, for several reasons, but it appears to be a fairly good estimate nonetheless. Most detailed studies have concluded that for a cut in tax rates not to lower revenues, the percentage increase in work effort must be two to two and a half times as large as the percentage increase in after-tax pay rates.

overwhelming majority of evidence suggests that the actual response of work effort to higher after-tax wage rates is not even a tenth as strong as it would have to be for lower tax rates not to reduce revenues.

The evidence is clear that most of the response of Americans' work effort to wages reflects the large number of women who at any time must decide whether to take jobs outside their homes. The higher the wage the more women do so. Even for women however, this response falls far short of what would be needed to keep revenues from falling as tax rates go down. Most studies have suggested an average percentage response of women's work effort somewhere between one fifth as large as the percentage change in after-tax pay rates and nine tenths as large—far short of the required two and a half.[11]

By contrast, because most working-age men already have jobs, their ability to work more is limited. Some can decide to defer retirement. Others can leave school earlier. But for most men, the opportunity to increase work effort is limited to working longer hours or looking for a new job. Moreover, in many occupations individual employees have little ability to set their own hours. It is therefore plausible to expect men's work patterns on average to exhibit substantially less variation in response to wages than women's.

In fact, most studies have shown either that men's average work effort does not respond at all to changes in after-tax pay rates or that it actually *declines* slightly on average.[12] Although it seems more natural to think that higher pay encourages more work effort, there is no reason that that must be so. Some people—for example, married workers who provide the sole or primary source of support for their families—may have in mind a specific target level of income that they feel obliged to earn. For them, higher after-tax pay rates *reduce* the number of hours they must work to meet their income goals. No doubt some men do work more in response to higher wages, but the evidence suggests that more respond by working less. As a result, the average work effort for all men tends to *decline* slightly as after-tax wage rates rise.

The average response of work effort to after-tax wage rates for the labor force as a whole reflects a combination of the modest positive response by women and the zero or even slightly negative response of men. Most studies suggest that on balance the overall response is positive but small. When after-tax wage rates rise, work effort rises too, but only by one tenth or possibly one fifth as much in percentage terms. The response is at best an order of magnitude weaker than it would have to be for lower tax rates to increase tax revenues.

Our experience under Kemp-Roth gives no reason to doubt the consensus of these earlier estimates. The unprecedented surge in economic activity that the Reagan administration insistently predicted simply never materialized. Nor did the flood of tax revenues that would have accompanied it.

The 1981 fiscal year was the last before Kemp-Roth took effect. The first fiscal year in which the final Kemp-Roth rate structure was fully in effect was 1984. During this period, business underwent first a severe recession and then a rapid recovery. With inflation however, nominal incomes rose each year. By 1984 total personal income was $3 trillion versus $2.5 trillion in 1981.[13] But federal revenues from individual income taxes barely increased at all. Individual income tax payments rose from $286 billion in 1981 to $298 billion in 1982, then fell to $289 billion in 1983, and then rose again to $298 billion in 1984.

The Commerce Department subsequently estimated that if the old tax rates had still been in effect—and, importantly, if everyone had earned the same income—Americans in 1984 would have paid $110 billion more in individual income taxes.[14] The immediate effect of Kemp-Roth was therefore to reduce that year's income tax payments by somewhat more than one fourth compared to what the old tax rates would have delivered at the same level of income. With tax rates cut by almost one fourth and several additional incentive measures also included in the 1981 tax bill, a reduction in revenues of about this magnitude *for a given income level* is what should be expected.

But this kind of calculation makes no allowance for the effect of lower tax rates in encouraging people to work—the aspect of Kemp-Roth on which Reagan had placed such great hope. It also makes no allowance for the usual effect of lower taxes in stimulating consumer spending and thereby increasing incomes more broadly, when the economy is below full employment. Because of both these effects, one on supply and the other on demand, incomes were probably higher in 1984 than they would otherwise have been. And therefore, the $110 billion of additional tax that people would have paid under the old rates *if their incomes had been unchanged* overstates the net reduction in revenues.

The crucial question from the perspective of Reagan's emphasis on supply-side incentives is how much more Americans worked because tax rates were lower. Given the evidence on the relationship between work effort and after-tax wage rates for both men and women, to assume that there was no response at all is extreme. But to assume that whatever increase in work effort occurred was large enough to offset the full $110 billion of revenue loss at a given income would be not just extreme but absurd.* On the basis of studies measuring the response of work effort to after-tax wage rates, even a highly favorable

---

*It would imply that, except for the supply-side effect of lower marginal tax rates, even *nominal* incomes in 1984 would have been far below what they had been in 1981 despite the expansionary demand effects of both the tax cut and the easier monetary policy.

estimate of the supply-side effect of Kemp-Roth on 1984 revenues is more likely about $13 billion.

As we have seen, the 1981 tax bill also raised incomes by stimulating *demand*, and that effect in 1984 was probably worth much more in revenues than the supply-side effect. Most estimates of the short-run expansionary effect of tax cuts on spending during recessions or their immediate aftermath suggest that the resulting higher incomes compensate for between one sixth and one third of the amount by which revenues would shrink if nobody spent any more or earned any more. For 1984 these estimates imply $18 to $37 billion of extra revenues. After allowing as well for as much as $13 billion of extra revenues from the supply-side effect on work effort, the net effect of Kemp-Roth in 1984 was to reduce income tax revenues by $60 to $79 billion—hardly trivial.

Moreover, in the absence of so much stimulus to demand from lower taxes, the Federal Reserve would probably have eased monetary policy further, perhaps substantially further. Throughout this period, Volcker was explicit that overly expansionary fiscal policy was a major bar to an easier monetary policy.* To the extent that a smaller tax cut would have meant an easier monetary policy, $18 to $37 billion *over*states the

---

*In presenting the Federal Reserve's monetary policy strategy for 1984 to Congress in February of that year for example, Volcker explained how the extraordinarily expansionary fiscal policy had constrained the extent to which he and his colleagues were willing to ease monetary policy: "In approaching our own operational decisions, the actual and prospective size of the budget deficit inevitably complicates the environment within which we work. By feeding consumer purchasing power, by heightening skepticism about our ability to control the money supply and contain inflation, by claiming a disproportionate share of available funds, and by increasing our dependence on foreign capital, monetary policy must carry more of the burden of maintaining stability and its flexibility, to some degree, is constrained."[15]

most likely 1984 revenue gain due to the expansionary effect of lower taxes on spending, and therefore $60 to $79 billion *under*states the net reduction in 1984 income tax revenues that resulted from Kemp-Roth.

The experience thereafter supports even stronger conclusions. Total personal income rose to $3.5 trillion in fiscal 1986. With no further declines in tax rates, revenues from individual income taxes rose to $349 billion. But if the old, higher tax rates had still been in effect in 1986—and again if everyone had earned the same amount of income—individual income tax revenues that year would have been $154 billion higher.[16] While work effort may have been modestly greater in 1986 because of lower tax rates, it is implausible to suppose it was much greater. A reasonable estimate, based on studies of the response of work effort to after-tax wage rates, is that whatever extra work effort lower tax rates may have stimulated accounted for at best $16 billion in additional income tax revenues in 1986.

More important, by as long after the recession's end as 1986, estimates of a tax cut's demand-side effects that would be appropriate if the economy had ample unused resources are less helpful than for 1984. By the beginning of fiscal 1986 unemployment was 7 percent and falling, and there was little further room for lower taxes to raise income by stimulating spending. In addition, the Federal Reserve would surely not have maintained the same monetary policy throughout 1982–86, regardless of whether the largest tax cut in history had occurred. As we have seen, the business expansion during these years was not especially rapid compared to previous expansions. What was different was the relationship between fiscal and monetary policies. It is much more plausible to suppose that by 1986 business activity would have been approaching full employment with or without the tax cut, because without Kemp-Roth the Federal Reserve would have pursued an easier monetary policy. Real interest rates and real exchange rates would have been lower, and there would have been less consumer spending, more investment, fewer imports, and more exports. But overall business activity would probably have been nearing full employment at about the same rate by then.

Apart from perhaps as much as $16 billion in added revenue produced by extra work effort, by 1986 there was little or nothing else to offset the revenues lost through lower tax rates. The net reduction in income tax revenues in 1986 as a result of Kemp-Roth was probably almost $140 billion: no small sum, even compared to that year's record $221 billion deficit. Tantalizing as it was, Reagan's claim that lower tax rates would enlarge tax revenues never had substance. The evidence available in 1980 flatly contradicted it. Now the evidence from the much more dramatic Kemp-Roth experiment has done so far more directly.

Once it became clear that lower tax rates meant smaller revenues after all, two additional mistaken assumptions provided still further economic rationales for ignoring what our new fiscal policy implied. Both concerned questions of how and why people save.

Deficits are a problem because they absorb saving that would otherwise be available to finance investment. If we had saved more, even the outsized Reagan deficits need not have posed a problem. In Japan, for example, the central government's deficit during the last decade has averaged 6 percent of total income versus 3 percent in America. At the same time, the Japanese have devoted an average 11 percent of their income to net business and residential capital formation versus only 5 percent here. Because their average net private saving rate is an astonishing 16 percent, they can easily afford a larger central government deficit than ours and more investment too.[17] If only we saved more, so could we. As America's deficit grew to unprecedented levels, therefore, the debate over our new fiscal policy increasingly focused not simply on the deficit but on the amount of private saving available to finance it.

A low saving rate, and with it a low investment rate, had characterized America since long before the 1980s. After World War II, economists who feared a return of stagnation as in the thirties initially welcomed the low saving rate as essential to fuel the successful transition from wartime mobilization to peacetime prosperity. But fears of "underconsumption" faded over time, and our persistent failure to match the productivity gains achieved by other industrialized economies made increased saving a widely accepted public policy objective well before Reagan's deficits gave it new urgency.

Once that happened, supply-side thinkers had no lack of ideas on why America's low saving rate might now rise. These arguments did not directly address the likely size of the deficit. But they were important for Reagan's new policy because they implied that even large deficits would not be a problem.

The most important of these ideas was that how much people save depends on what return they can earn, after inflation and after taxes, on their assets. The logic that motivated Kemp-Roth held that lower marginal tax rates would encourage people not only to work harder but also to save more. As President Reagan said in the first set of economic proposals he submitted to Congress, "As taxpayers move into higher brackets, incentives to work, save, and invest are reduced since each addition to income yields less after taxes than before. . . . Personal tax reductions will allow people to keep more of what they earn, providing increased incentives for work and savings."[18] With lower tax rates returns on stocks or bonds or bank deposits would be greater, even if interest rates and dividend yields on a before-tax basis remained unchanged. In 1980, for example, the average individual recipient of interest income had paid federal tax on it at a marginal rate of 36 percent. Kemp-Roth would reduce that to 28 percent.

Moreover, because our tax system (including under Kemp-Roth) has never distinguished real from nominal interest rates, lower interest rates and lower inflation rates together would raise the ultimate return to savers by still more. The before-tax interest rate on intermediate-maturity U.S. Treasury notes, for example, was 7.66 percent on average during the seventies. After paying tax at a marginal rate that varied between a low of 31 percent in 1972 and a high of 36 percent in 1980, the average individual earning interest had been left with a 5.08 percent per annum return. After also allowing for average inflation of 7.4 percent per annum, the same individual's *real* after-tax return had been *minus* 2.33 percent on average during the seventies. Even apart from lower tax rates, reduced inflation under Reagan would also raise real after-tax returns.

Hope for achieving a higher saving rate also rested on a few more specific provisions of the 1981 tax bill designed expressly to increase saving incentives. The most important of these was to allow most individuals to save up to $2,000 apiece each year completely free of tax in Individual Retirement Accounts. Most employees not already covered by company-sponsored pensions had been able to save via IRAs since 1974, but the 1981 tax bill opened this opportunity to all workers and, in smaller amounts, to their spouses. It also increased the amount that self-employed individuals could set aside on a tax-free basis through Keogh accounts (named for Congressman Eugene Keogh of New York, who had sponsored the original 1962 legislation) and the amount that business executives could contribute out of their own salaries to special tax-free pension plans that their companies could set up in their behalf. Finally the

1981 tax bill also cut to 20 percent the maximum tax rate on capital gains.* Each of these actions further reduced the tax paid on the income earned from saving, beyond the effect already to be achieved by lower tax rates across the board.

The idea that the resulting higher after-tax real returns would stimulate additional saving, and thereby enable the country to finance additional investment, was central to Reagan's new fiscal policy well before its advocates realized (or at least before they admitted) what it implied for the deficit. This idea became far more important once the new budget realities were apparent. With no change in the saving rate, the growing deficit would force America either to reduce capital formation or to borrow from abroad by running a trade deficit, or both. But with a high enough saving rate, we could afford the enlarged government deficit plus *increased* investment, and all without a trade deficit. The presumed positive response of saving to higher after-tax returns became critical once it was clear that the supposed positive response of revenues to lower marginal tax rates was not working.

But the anticipated higher saving never materialized either. As we have seen, the slowing of inflation by tight money soon brought *before-tax* real interest rates to record levels. Then, as federal borrowing continued to rise while private saving did not, real interest rates on a before-tax basis remained high

---

*Capital gains had received favorable tax treatment in the United States ever since 1922. Especially since a large part of the price increase on any asset held for a long time was likely to reflect economywide inflation, perhaps without any change in the asset's real value, some concession in taxing capital gains was only fair. Indeed, one study based on detailed tax return data for 1973 showed that inflation had accounted for more than 100 percent of the capital gains on which Americans paid tax that year. In other words, after allowing for inflation, the typical "gain" was really a loss.[19]

despite monetary easing. Along the way, Kemp-Roth lowered the relevant marginal tax rates as it was supposed to. The average marginal tax rate that individuals paid on interest income fell from a peak of 38 percent in 1981 to 30 percent in 1983 and then remained at that level. The average marginal rate that individuals paid on dividends fell from 49 percent in 1981 to 37 percent in 1984 and rose only to 38 percent in 1985 and 39 percent in 1986.[20] Meanwhile, the newly expanded IRA and Keogh provisions sheltered billions of dollars of interest and dividend income from taxes altogether.

In the end, the combination of reduced tax rates, slower inflation, and higher real interest rates on a before-tax basis raised after-tax real returns by far more than what proponents of lower marginal tax rates and other saving incentives had repeatedly said would be sufficient to generate significantly greater saving. Yet as we have seen, we certainly saved no more than in earlier years, and by most measures we saved less. What went wrong?

The idea that higher returns spur people to save more is plausible enough, but it is equally possible—odd as it may seem at first—that higher returns *depress* saving. It is true that when money market mutual funds initially offered small savers a significantly higher return than they could get on passbook accounts at banks that people rushed to put their money in. And whenever a bank raises its interest rates much above what others are paying, the public response is quickly visible. But affecting the *form* in which people save is not the same as affecting the *total amount* that they save. The fact that people respond sharply to higher returns in allocating their saving says nothing about how higher returns will affect *how much* they save. Shifting money from a bank account to a money market mutual fund (or into stocks and bonds) merely rearranges an unchanged total amount of saving. Saving *in total* increases only if someone earns more without spending more or earns the same as before but spends less.

The familiar presumption that a higher return will increase saving comes from supposing that savers start by asking how much some specific amount put aside today will be worth in the future. The higher the return after inflation and after taxes, the more each dollar saved today can buy in the future and—presumably—the more people will want to save now in order to be able to spend later on.

But people may also approach saving from the opposite direction—that is, by asking how much they need to save today in order to provide for some specific amount of spending in the future. And if they pose the question in this way, a *higher* return on the assets they hold means that they have to save *less* to achieve the same objective.* If people approach saving in this way therefore, higher returns mean saving not more but less. Moreover, this negative effect of higher returns on saving is even stronger if the purpose of saving is to provide a steady income rather than just to build up a lump sum in the bank, simply because with a higher return it takes a smaller nest egg to generate the same amount of income each year.†

---

*With an after-tax real return of *minus* 2.33 percent, the average for U.S. Treasury notes during the seventies, building up $10,000 over ten years (after allowing for taxes and inflation) requires setting aside $1,136 each year. With a return of *plus* 3.02 percent, the average for Treasury notes during the years Kemp-Roth was in effect, saving only $846 each year will accomplish the same purpose.

†For example, a couple may first be sufficiently free of family responsibilities to begin saving for their retirement at age fifty. If the goal of their saving program is to build up enough by age sixty-five to provide a $1,000 per year supplement to Social Security and company-sponsored pensions, they must first figure how large an amount that will take at sixty-five and next determine how much to put aside each year until then in order to accumulate that

Which way do higher after-tax returns actually affect saving? No doubt some people approach saving by asking (consciously or not) how much a specific amount put aside now will buy later on, while others think about how much to put aside now to build up a specific nest egg or finance a specific flow of future income. Most people probably do some combination of the two. Which effect predominates?

The only way to know is to look at the evidence from actual experience, but the available evidence provides little basis for judgment. While some studies done before the 1980s indicated a fairly strong positive effect of after-tax real returns on savings, others detected no measurable effect at all, and a few even suggested a negative effect.[21] Prior experience therefore did not flatly contradict Reagan's prediction that his policy would stimulate saving in the way that it contradicted his prediction that lower tax rates would so stimulate work effort as to produce higher revenues. But it did not provide much support for predicting a higher saving rate either. At best that was an optimistic presumption, a hope to hold out in the absence of clear-cut evidence one way or the other.

Since then, we have witnessed a massive test of that optimistic presumption, and there has been no evidence to support it. Despite persistently higher returns available to savers after taxes and after inflation, our net private saving rate has been no greater than before, and since the middle of the decade it has been well below previous levels. Saving in America does not appear to be very sensitive to asset returns in either direction.

---

amount. With an after-tax real interest rate of *minus* 2.33 percent, the necessary amount at age sixty-five (adjusted for inflation) is $26,900, and accumulating that amount requires saving $2,101 each year. With a return of *plus* 3.02 percent, the necessary amount at age sixty-five is only $15,800, and building up that smaller amount requires annual saving of just $851.

Apparently the two opposite effects of higher returns on saving roughly balance each other for the economy overall.

Indeed, this conclusion is about what a conservative reading of the evidence on saving and asset returns would have concluded in 1980. As we have seen, neither the total of net private saving nor the division of that total between individuals' saving and that of business had shown much variation since World War II. And although the relevant experience before that was clouded by the Great Depression and the two world wars, there is at least some ground for thinking that a rough stability of saving in relation to income has persisted since well before the twentieth century.

At the very least, the stability of our net private saving rate before the 1980s should have warned anyone who wanted to rely as heavily on the prospect of higher saving as the new fiscal policy's proponents did. Just to finance the new deficits and the same net investment rate as in the past, without having to borrow from abroad, would have required our net private saving rate to rise from the 8 percent postwar average to 12 percent. Financing the larger deficits and *increased* capital formation would have taken still more saving. Nothing in the prior record warranted confidence that higher returns would increase saving at all. Even with record-high real interest rates and lower marginal tax rates, counting on our saving 12 percent of our income or even more was optimistic in the extreme.

Another mistake made by some of the new policy's advocates, once the deficit began to grow, was to suppose that the very knowledge of the government's borrowing would itself spur additional saving. This idea rested on the principle that deficits do not preclude the need for taxes but merely defer them from the present into the future. If someone understands that government borrowing means less taxes today but more taxes later on, he may save more so that he will be able to afford the increase in taxes when it comes. If everyone behaved this way, the additional saving would be just enough to finance the deficit, so that it would not raise real interest rates and therefore would not impair our capital formation or our international competitiveness.

Once the reality of record-sized government deficits was clear, the idea that they might directly raise saving on anything approaching a dollar-for-dollar basis assumed great potential importance. The challenge facing the new fiscal policy's proponents then was not to talk up how much the new policy would help capital formation and competitiveness but to talk down how much damage it would do. Under these changed circumstances, the notion that deficits somehow did not matter constituted the very essence of optimism: so much so that President Reagan, notwithstanding his consistent denunciation of government deficits, eventually came to embrace this idea as the basis for claiming that mounting deficits, even at full employment, had nothing to do with high real interest rates—and therefore nothing to do with any of America's other resulting problems.

Back when the deficit was Carter's, Reagan had been clear that the government's borrowing absorbed saving and therefore raised interest rates. In his first televised address in 1981, the new president explained the connection plainly enough: "Government has only two ways of getting money other than raising taxes. It can go into the money markets and borrow, competing with its own citizens and driving up interest rates, which it has done, or it can print money, and it's done that."[22]

Once the deficits were Reagan's, however, matters seemed less sure. The Treasury Department's January 1984 study argued that government deficits might not raise interest rates after all, depending on how private savers responded. After listing no less than eight uncertain factors "that exert crucial influence on the outcome," the report weakly concluded, "There is no conclusive empirical evidence to support firmly the contending analyses."[23]

And by that fall's election campaign, when the contrast between record deficits and Reagan's earlier predictions of a balanced budget became a major issue, the President concluded that the issue was clear after all. Only now what was clear was the opposite of what he had claimed four years earlier. In his first debate with Mondale, the president simply said, "The connection has been made between the deficit and the interest rates. There is no connection."[24]

But the idea that government borrowing directly stimulates private saving has received no more support from our experience in the 1980s than the idea that higher asset returns do so. Faced with peacetime government borrowing on a whole new scale, people simply did not behave the way supply-side theorists had predicted.

In the end, both assumptions that the new policy's supporters had made about why our saving might rise and thereby neutralize the larger deficit proved wrong. Moreover, there is no single element of our saving that has been especially weak, uniquely holding down what otherwise would have been a much higher total. As we have seen, personal saving and business saving have contributed about equally to the overall decline in net private saving in the 1980s.

The failure of *personal* saving to rise merits particular attention not just because personal saving typically represents about two thirds of overall net private saving but because so much of the supply-side thinking that predicted higher saving focused on incentives at the individual level. But a more detailed examination shows no sign that even personal saving would have risen if only one or two specific forces had not dragged it down.

For example, one widely discussed theory on why personal saving has declined as a share of income in the 1980s is that corporations have put less money into the pension funds they sponsor.*[25] Most companies promise each employee a specific income after retirement (often some percentage, depending on how long he has been with the company, of his average earnings during his last five working years). As real interest rates have risen in recent years, companies have needed to put aside less each year in order to provide for these promised benefits. These reduced pension contributions are an example of how higher asset returns depress saving whenever its motivation is to provide a specific income in the future. Moreover, because the typical corporation invests about half of its pension fund in stocks, many companies were able to cut back pension contributions still further as rising stock prices after 1982 increased the value of the assets already in their funds. Indeed, companies whose pension funds had increased the most were able to recapture part of these funds for ordinary corporate purposes —that is, in effect, to make *negative* pension contributions— and some companies were even forced to do so by the tax laws prohibiting excess funding of pension obligations.

But the slowdown in corporate pension contributions that began in 1984 has accounted for only a small part of the decline in personal saving. Saving done directly by individuals on their own behalf has also been below par. The common national-income measure of personal saving *adjusted to remove all pension contributions by employers* shows that individuals' direct

*The government treats these funds as a part of individuals' holdings, so that reduced pension contributions by employers would make personal saving appear smaller even if individuals on their own saved no less than before.

saving had already declined from 4.3 percent of after-tax income on average from the fifties to the seventies to 2.6 percent during 1981–83—when employers' pension contributions were still *rising* rapidly.[26] During 1984–87, as employers' pension contributions leveled off, individuals' direct saving has fallen to just .9 percent of after-tax income. The alternative flow-of-funds saving measure, which paints a somewhat healthier picture for the 1980s overall, confirms that the slowdown in employers' pension contributions can account for only a small part of the decline in overall personal saving.*

Other factors have also probably contributed to the decline in personal saving, but even so there is still no basis for concluding that saving would have been abnormally *high* in their absence. Demographic changes may have played some role, for example, as the maturing of the baby boom generation enlarged the share of the population who typically save less (or even *dis*save) because of the financial burdens of setting up a household and starting a family. But the overall age structure has changed only slowly, and it began to do so well before the 1980s. Moreover, evidence on which age groups save more and which save less is often contradictory in any case.[27] At best, age-based differences in saving behavior are too small to have reduced saving by much.

Still another factor that probably played some role in depressing personal saving is the 1982–87 stock market rally. Between year-end 1981 and year-end 1986, rising stock prices added more than $1 trillion to the value of individuals' portfolios. Most studies show that every $100 of additional stock

*After subtracting all pension contributions by employers, this measure indicates that individuals' direct saving was 5.4 percent of after-tax income on average before the 1980s. During 1981–83 it fell to 5 percent. During 1984–87 it fell to 2.5 percent.

market wealth held by individuals increases annual consumer spending by as much as $5.[28] Rising stock prices may therefore have increased consumer spending, and depressed saving, by amounts growing from as much as $6 billion in 1983 to as much as $52 billion in 1987 before the market crashed. There is reason to be skeptical of such estimates, in that stock ownership is heavily concentrated among a small percentage of Americans who typically have high incomes anyway. But even taking these estimates at face value, the additional saving that people would have done in the absence of rising stock market values would have increased personal saving during 1983–87 by just .6 percent in relation to total income: less than half of the 1.6 percent shortfall from the average of prior decades.

Ironically, the one glimmer of hope for increased personal saving from the experience of the 1980s has now been extinguished by the so-called Tax Reform Act of 1986. Although there was never any sign that saving was responding to the across-the-board increase in after-tax returns and certainly none that saving was responding to government borrowing directly, some evidence suggests that the more specifically targeted saving incentives included in the 1981 tax bill may have had a modest effect. The increased availability of Individual Retirement Accounts in particular attracted an enormous response. By 1986 some thirty-five million Americans had IRAs, with a total value of $262 billion. New contributions to IRAs in 1986 alone totaled $45 billion compared to total personal saving that year of just $131 billion.[29]

The crucial question is how much of that was additional saving that people would not have done if they had not had access to IRAs. One negative factor in this regard is that most IRA owners are in middle- or upper-income brackets and therefore can probably afford to do a significant amount of saving in any case. Evidence from questionnaires and detailed financial surveys, however, suggests that a significant part of the saving done via IRAs—as much as half according to one study—represented additional new saving.[30]

But the political fixation with lower marginal tax rates on an across-the-board basis prevailed in 1986 no less than in 1981. And part of the price we paid to buy still lower marginal tax rates was the elimination of a variety of targeted saving incentives, including the broad availability of IRAs (and the favored treatment of capital gains). Workers already covered by company-sponsored pension plans can no longer contribute to IRAs tax free or even partially tax free unless their incomes fall below cut-offs that exclude more than half of those who contributed before. Whatever progress IRAs were making toward increasing our saving is now mostly history.

Even with IRAs however, the prospect of significantly raising our saving rate was never real in the first place—certainly not to the extent necessary to finance the new deficits. Indeed, the long-run stability of our private saving in relation to income not only should have cast doubt on the two principal lines of thinking about why saving would increase in the 1980s but should also call into question prospects for a higher saving rate held forth along other lines. The saving rate was apparently about 8 percent before World War I, when there was no income tax, and (ironically until the last few years when tax rates went back *down*) it has been about 8 percent through the high-tax decades of the post World War II period. Why should lower tax rates make a difference? The saving rate was about 8 percent before there was any Social Security System, and it has been about 8 percent since Social Security became the economic centerpiece of most families' retirement. Why should different benefit formulas or eligibility rules matter? The saving rate was about 8 percent before most individuals had much access to credit markets, and it has been about 8 percent since most Americans have carried pockets full of plastic credit cards. Why should changes in consumer borrowing arrangements affect matters?

This line of questioning still leaves open the puzzle of why our net private saving rate seems so anchored at this level. Why is our saving rate 8 percent while Japan's is more typically 16 percent (although it has been falling in recent years) and Germany's is 12 percent? Are there no systematic factors that can explain these cross-country differences? And whatever the explanation may be, is there no way to exploit it in order to save more?

The only honest answer is that no one knows. The basis of cross-country differences in saving behavior probably lies in a complex web encompassing not just government policies but also private institutions and deeply rooted cultural factors too. Even the intellectual challenge of unraveling these connections, much less exploiting the answers to achieve specific public policy objectives, seems far off at best.

Finally, a fourth mistake made by the thinkers behind Reagan's fiscal policy was to assume that even if individuals somehow resisted incentives to increase their saving, businesses would increase theirs as higher profits and more generous tax breaks enhanced cash flows. With more cash in hand, companies could afford to undertake more investment even without turning to the credit market for additional funds. And because of other elements of Reagan's overall economic policy—lower taxes, slower inflation, and reduced regulation—they would find new investments sufficiently profitable to want to use these enlarged cash flows for capital spending, not just to pay out more dividends to shareholders.

The Economic Recovery Tax Act of 1981 increased both the incentive and the ability of businesses to invest, primarily by introducing a new, more generous depreciation system allowing them to write off their existing plant and equipment more rapidly.* Any new investment that a company was considering would be more profitable than before, at least after taxes, because of the increased ability it would now provide for reducing the company's tax payments. The *statutory* tax rate on corporate profits before any deductions remained unchanged at 46 percent. But the new depreciation system lowered the average *effective* marginal tax rate on profits earned from new investment from 32 percent in 1980 to just 18 percent in 1981.[31] In addition, because the company would pay less in taxes, it would now have more of its before-tax earnings left over to finance its capital spending program. Even after allowing for the restrictions imposed in 1982, the 1981 tax bill reduced corporations' tax payments by an average $15 billion *per year* from 1982 until 1986 (after which the 1986 Tax Reform Act changed the system altogether).[32]

Finally, cutting the maximum tax rate on capital gains to 20 percent further strengthened both the incentive to invest and the ability to finance investment, especially for new business ventures. The motivation for cutting the capital gains tax was not just to make stock ownership in general more attractive, but also—and especially—to encourage entrepreneurs to start new businesses and venture capital investors to back them.

*The legislation also introduced other business tax breaks, including more liberal rules governing the use of lease transactions to transfer tax credits and depreciation deductions from firms that were entitled to them but could not use them (because they would have paid no taxes anyway) to other firms that could take full advantage of them. But after the public outcry when profitable firms like General Electric, Boeing, and Pepsico took advantage of the new rules to end up paying no tax in 1981, the 1982 tax legislation withdrew them.

But these hopes too have been disappointed. As we have seen, despite the increased incentives for companies to invest what funds they have, and the increase in corporate cash flows from more generous tax breaks, we have put less of our income into net business investment than we did on average in the fifties or the sixties or the seventies. Worse yet, the 1986 tax reform has now eliminated not just the new investment incentives put in place in 1981 but also others, like the 10 percent investment tax credit and the advantaged treatment of capital gains, that had a much longer history. As a result, prospects for a sustained revival of capital formation in the future look dimmer too.

What went wrong? Although the anticipated resurgence of business profitability in response to slower inflation and reduced regulation never happened, with more generous tax breaks, business corporations' *after-tax* cash flows have represented a larger share of our total income than at any time since World War II. After-tax corporate cash flows averaged 7.5 percent of total income in the fifties and 8.2 percent in both the sixties and the seventies. Thus far during the 1980s the average has been 8.7 percent. And in addition to the growth of their internally generated funds, corporations have also borrowed record amounts. New funds available for investment by corporations in nonfinancial lines of business alone, including their after-tax internal cash flows as well as their borrowing, have averaged 11.8 percent of America's total income during the 1980s compared to 8.7 percent in the fifties, 10.1 percent in the sixties, and 10.5 percent in the seventies.[33]

But increasing what business has available to invest is not the same thing as increasing what business actually invests. Despite record internal cash flows and record borrowing too, business has used an unusually large part of these funds for purposes other than productive new investment. Companies have increasingly distributed their cash flows outside the corporate sector, mostly through payments made to individual and institutional shareholders during the phenomenal wave of corporate reorganizations and recapitalizations that has swept over corporate America in the 1980s.

Stock repurchases, leveraged buy-outs, and other acquisitions all represent the use of a corporation's funds (whether generated internally or borrowed in the credit market) for purposes other than investment in new plant and equipment. No new refineries were built because Chevron spent $13 billion to buy Gulf. Nor did GE's $6 billion purchase of RCA put up any new electronics factories, nor Burroughs' $4 billion acquisition of Sperry put any new computer plants in place.[34] In each case, the money went to the acquired company's previous shareholders. The same is true when a corporation buys in its own stock. The $730 million that GM paid to Ross Perot and his group to buy back their stock built no new auto plants, nor will the billions of dollars GM will pay to whichever of its other shareholders accept its offer to buy back an additional 20 percent of its stock by 1990.[35] In each of these kinds of transaction, the money leaves the corporate sector altogether.* According to plan, our new fiscal policy did increase the funds business had available to finance new investment, but business simply had other plans for how to spend them.

Moreover, the few isolated strengths that business investment has shown do not appear to have resulted from Reagan's

---

*Even if the shareholder whose stock is bought out immediately reinvests the proceeds in some other company's stock, his doing so only amounts to buying the new "investment" from some other shareholder who is selling it. In the absence of new stock issues by at least some companies, the only way the corporate sector as a whole can get the money back is to earn it in profits over time (without paying it back out as dividends) or to borrow it.

new policy in any direct way. The single item that has dominated the growth of capital spending in America in the 1980s has been computers. Between 1982 and 1987, business purchases of computers and related office equipment almost quadrupled, even after allowing for inflation. By contrast, investment in new structures was smaller in 1986 than at the recession's bottom, as was investment in many other kinds of equipment. Purchases of computers made up less than a tenth of businesses' investment in durable goods in 1982, but they accounted for 60 percent of the growth that occurred between then and 1987.[36]

The strength of computers in the postrecession recovery is consistent with our ongoing shift away from goods-producing industries toward services. Retailers have put in "smart cash registers" to monitor inventories, banks and insurance companies have provided computer work stations for ever more of their employees, and airlines and other transportation industries have done the same. Overall, capital spending by companies in service industries grew by 47 percent between 1982 and 1986 versus only 1 percent in manufacturing.[37] Even within manufacturing, part of what companies have spent has gone into computers and related office equipment rather than production facilities. No one can yet say whether this emphasis on computers will result in greater productivity gains or better competitiveness than would have resulted from such alternative investments as conventional or high-tech manufacturing facilities.

What does seem clear is that this burst of computer investment has not been a result of the new tax legislation. The 1981 tax bill shortened the time over which businesses could write off computers and similar office equipment from seven years to five and thereby made such investments more attractive on an after-tax basis. But the 1982 tax bill disallowed the timing formulas that most businesses had previously used to speed up the rate at which they claimed depreciation within whatever was the allowable time period. This change made investment less attractive. The 1982 bill also required companies to subtract half of their 10 percent investment tax credit from the price of any kind of equipment in order to establish the basis on which to claim depreciation. This change too made investment less attractive. The net effect of these three changes, one favorable and two unfavorable, was significantly adverse for investment in computer equipment. Yet computers have shown by far the most vigorous expansion of any aspect of business investment.

Another item that contributed to the rapid growth of business capital spending during 1983 and 1984, albeit on a much smaller scale than computers, was purchases of automobiles. Here, however, the situation is less clear. Investment in automobiles became more attractive as a result of the various accounting changes introduced by the 1981 and 1982 tax bills. But much of the increase in business car purchases in recent years appears to have amounted to no more than an ongoing change toward leasing instead of direct ownership as the preferred way of acquiring cars for personal use. When a family buys a new car, the government's statisticians consider the purchase a part of consumer spending; but if the same family leases the car and a service company owns it, they treat the company's purchase as part of business investment. Whether people own or lease their cars makes no difference to how much or how efficiently American business can produce. The brief surge in business purchases of automobiles during 1983 and 1984 may or may not have resulted from the favorable balance of new tax incentives and disincentives. But to the extent that it merely facilitated the leasing of cars for personal use rather than increasing business use of cars for deliveries or sales or service visits, it did not add to our productivity or competitiveness.

The single aspect of business investment to which advocates of our new fiscal policy have pointed most often in trying to show that Reagan's new incentives worked is venture capital. But on close inspection this too has been a disappointment. Despite lower tax rates on income in general and the new 20% maximum tax rate on capital gains, the growth of venture capital has made only a small contribution to our overall business investment. And there are good reasons to think that what venture capital growth has occurred has had little to do with lower tax rates anyway.

At least in percentage terms, the amount of financing put into new start-ups during the 1980s has risen dramatically from what it was before 1979 when the top tax rate on capital gains dropped from 49 percent to 28 percent. Venture capital financing has increased in every year since then. By 1986 the total amount of venture financing disbursed by individuals and institutions together was more than five times what it was in 1978, and the volume of new venture commitments made in 1986 was more than seven times the 1978 level.[38]

But here too, it is important to recognize the meaning of a large growth rate arising from a small base. Because the amount of venture capital financing was so tiny before, even after this increase it still constitutes only a small fraction of business capital formation. In 1978 the total of venture capital disbursements was just $600 *million* compared to $82 billion of net business investment. By 1986 venture capital disbursements had grown to almost $3 billion out of a net investment total of $81 billion. The growth of more than $2 billion in venture capital during this period was welcome, to be sure. But it is hard to assign it a major role, even in the context of no growth at all in net business capital formation on an economywide basis.

In addition, the fact that so much of this growth in venture capital has come from investors that are exempt from taxes altogether casts serious doubt on the notion that lower tax rates had much to do with it. The GM and GE pension funds, the Howard Hughes Medical Foundation, and Harvard University have all become major venture capital investors in the 1980s. None of them is subject to federal income tax. In 1978 individuals provided 32 percent of what venture capital financing there was, and other taxable investors put up another 44 percent. By 1986 individuals provided just 12 percent, and other taxable investors 33 percent. Tax-exempt institutions—pension funds, foundations, universities, and other endowments—provided more than half of the money.

It is always possible that the importance of venture capital is greater than the modest dollar volume implies, if new businesses provide a crucial catalyst for the introduction of advanced production technologies. But there is little basis for thinking of the 1980s as an especially fertile period for business start-ups. The number of new businesses incorporated each year rose by only 3.7 percent per annum between 1980 and 1987 and by only 3.9 percent even since the recession ended in 1982, compared to 6 percent on average from the fifties through the seventies.[39] Moreover, the pattern of growth in new business incorporations within those prior decades casts doubt on the link between new start-ups and either overall business expansion or advances in business productivity. By most measures the sixties was a boom period, yet the annual growth of new business incorporations in the sixties was just 3.8 percent versus 7 percent in the fifties. In the seventies, when real economic growth slowed and productivity gains dried up almost altogether, the annual growth of new business incorporations rose to 7.3 percent. Even if the large percentage growth of venture capital financing in the 1980s had brought an increase in the rate at which Americans have started new firms

—which it did not—the connection to superior business performance would remain tenuous nonetheless.

Lower tax rates would increase revenues. Higher real returns after taxes, and even the mere fact of government borrowing, would substantially raise saving. Business would automatically invest larger cash flows in new plant and equipment. No one who read the available evidence cautiously in 1980 would have put faith in any of these mistaken ideas. Still less would a conservative reading support them now.

But Americans were in no mood for caution after the inflation, high oil prices, and repeated business downturns of the seventies. In choosing a new fiscal policy, the country gambled on hope instead of acting on careful analysis. That gamble has failed, and the contradictions between its underlying assumptions and economic reality are now apparent. What remains uncertain is whether we are ready to abandon those wishful assumptions and choose an alternative policy.

Chapter XI

HARD CHOICES

If not now, when?

—FATHERS, I:14

America needs a new economic policy, a policy that is based on realistic assumptions about our economy's strengths and about how taxes and government spending affect them, and that at the same time faces the new realities of excess debt and underinvestment left from the Reagan years.

The central requirement, if we are not merely to continue on our current path toward fiscal instability, is a combination of tax and spending policies that will once again allow our federal debt to grow less rapidly than our income—and without higher inflation. As we have seen, a sensible course is to bring taxes and spending sufficiently into line for the ratio of debt to income to decline at about half the pace at which it has risen since 1980. Doing so will mean reducing the deficit (apart from the intentional surplus for Social Security) to approximately $60 billion per year on average during 1989–96: better than $100 billion less per year than current levels. A shift of this magnitude toward less expansionary fiscal policy will not only permit an easier monetary policy, but indeed will require one if the transition is not to cause a business downturn that will vitiate, at least for some time, much of what we can expect to accomplish by adopting a new policy in the first place.

Reagan's first fiscal priority when he took office was to lower tax rates. That was easy. It took just six months for Congress to pass the Economic Recovery Tax Act packaging the Kemp-Roth across-the-board cut in personal income tax rates with a smaller collection of saving incentives for individuals and tax breaks for business. Once that was done, Reagan's fiscal agenda turned to cutting various nondefense programs—though not the largest of all, Social Security—while at the same time increasing military spending.

Reagan the candidate had repeatedly denied that spending programs that actually mattered to the American public would have to be cut, much less canceled, in order to balance the budget in the wake of Kemp-Roth. Spending cuts would be limited to the elimination of "waste, fraud, and abuse," together with superfluous programs that nobody cared about anyway. That Reagan as president promptly launched a major broad-based assault on so much of what the federal government does outside the defense sphere—job training, trade adjustment assistance, mass transit, aid to education, unemployment insurance—was a sign of how short-lived the presumption that lower tax rates would bring higher tax revenues proved to be. The search for a consensus in favor of reduced government spending to match our post-Kemp-Roth revenue trajectory has dominated America's fiscal agenda ever since.

As this search has continued, the government has implemented economies throughout large parts of its nondefense activities. The after-inflation growth of spending for all nondefense programs other than interest on the national debt has slowed to .5 percent per annum on average in the 1980s compared to 1.7 percent in the fifties, 7.2 percent in the sixties, and

6.9 percent in the seventies. But this effort has not met its basic objective as the deficit has continued to exceed pre-1980s levels by a wide margin.

President Reagan has blamed this failure mainly on Congressional Democrats unwilling to support his proposed nondefense spending cuts. Members of Congress, including especially Democrats but also some Republicans, have instead blamed the failure on the president's persistent large *increases* in military spending. Both views are right. Both are also wrong.

It is true that Congress has resisted many of Reagan's proposals to cut or cancel nondefense spending programs. But it is also true that these proposals have often amounted to far less than the elaborate public relations effort surrounding them has suggested, while Congressional resistance has come from Republicans as well as Democrats. In the end, the administration's own commitment to restraining nondefense spending has been questionable at best. Republicans controlled the Senate from Reagan's first day in office until January 1987. And despite repeated threats, in his first seven years in office Reagan vetoed only seven spending bills out of nearly a hundred that Congress passed.*

On the defense side of the budget, American military spending did more than double between 1980 and 1987. But the outgoing Carter administration's budget proposals had also called for a major acceleration of defense spending during the first half of the 1980s. And especially during the early Reagan years, when most of the big increases took place, few members

---

*As Stockman later put it, "There is another irony of the Reagan Revolution. In the crucible of political challenge and under the gun of massive budget deficits, the GOP politicians were forced to examine its programs and the premises time after time. . . . They decided when all was said and done to ratify the American welfare state as it had evolved by 1980."[1]

of Congress of either party provided much real opposition. For example, the 18 percent increase in defense spending in 1982 was the decade's largest. When the House passed the defense appropriations bill for that fiscal year in November 1981, only 61 congressmen (fifty-four Democrats and seven Republicans) voted no. When the Senate passed the bill in December, only five senators (four Democrats and just one Republican) were opposed.

In total, the six sets of budget proposals that Reagan submitted for 1982 through 1987 called for $4 trillion in federal spending for all nondefense activities. Compared to what the government was already slated to spend under existing legislation, the sum of each year's proposed nondefense spending cuts came to $226 billion—no small sum, and enough to have mattered importantly for the deficits and debt that the government actually incurred during these years. But some of the supposed proposals for cuts were fictitious from the start, and many others were merely formal gestures with little support from any quarter. As early as its first month in office, the new administration identified a list of programs—including small ones like Head Start, Summer Youth Jobs, and school lunches for children of low-income families, as well as big ones like Social Security, Medicare, veterans' benefits, and Supplemental Security Income—to be specifically exempted from any cuts whatsoever.

As a result, the administration's initial plan for balancing the budget by 1984 identified $44 billion out of $123 billion in proposed cuts for that year as "Additional savings to be proposed."[2] In the budget it submitted for 1983, $20 billion out of $43 billion in proposed cuts for that year consisted of a lengthy list of "Management Initiatives," headed by the perennial "Prevention of Fraud, Waste, and Abuse."[3] As the years have passed since then, the administration's proposals for "spending cuts" have increasingly avoided genuine reductions in spending programs in favor of sales of government-owned assets like the Teapot Dome and Elk Hills petroleum reserves, or increased "user fees" for government-provided services like national parks and the Coast Guard.* Meanwhile, both the administration and congressional Republicans have backed increases in some nondefense spending programs—for example, income supports for farmers, which rose from $7 billion in 1980 to $31 billion in 1987. In the end, what the government actually spent on all nondefense programs for fiscal years 1982–87 exceeded the administration's requests by a total of $191 billion over six years.

At the same time, Congress successfully resisted at least part of Reagan's proposal for increased military spending. For these same six years, the cost of the administration's proposed defense program added up to $1.5 trillion. The government actually spent $101 billion less. Some of this saving came from congressional refusal to go along at full strength with specific big-ticket items like the MX missile, the B-1B bomber and the M1 tank. The remainder simply reflected a steadily less generous attitude toward military budgeting across the board.

As a result, what the government has spent each year on all defense and nondefense programs combined has been remarkably close to what Reagan requested. On average for the six

*The government's accountants treat the proceeds of asset sales and user fees as "negative expenditures" rather than revenues. Regardless of whether the results of asset sales appear as increased revenues or lower spending, however, they make no contribution to reducing the drain on private saving due to financing the deficit. From this perspective it makes no difference whether the government absorbs saving by selling Treasury bonds or by selling securities giving the owner an equity interest in Conrail. Shifting government assets to private ownership may be a good idea in some cases, but not for reasons that bear on why large deficits at full employment are harmful.

fiscal years 1982 through 1987, total annual expenditures for all purposes other than paying interest on the national debt exceeded the administration's annual proposals by just $15 billion. The largest single overage, $42 billion, was in 1983. (The president vetoed just one spending bill in that budget cycle.) In both 1984 and 1985, however, total noninterest spending actually fell short of the administration's request. As we have seen, the $1.1 trillion deficit for these six years arose not from spending more than Reagan asked but from the failure of revenues to meet the administration's projections.

America's post-Kemp-Roth fiscal agenda was bound to fail. The quest for a consensus centered on sharply lower spending in relation to our income has been based largely on myths and misperceptions, spread by a rhetoric that is uninformed at best and sometimes deliberately misleading. When the greatest part of the budget pays for our defense and for the livelihood of retirees, it is pointless to pretend that public spending is an embarrassment consisting only of welfare and waste. Nor is it constructive to talk about "spending" as if military hardware were donated free of charge, or Defense Department employees served as unpaid volunteers. It also makes no sense to pursue a policy that expands the national debt and also raises real interest rates and then to complain that government spending *including interest* is higher compared to our income than it used to be.

As a result of these distortions, the increasingly urgent public discussion of our fiscal problem has mostly missed the point. In response to surveys, fully half of the American public responds that the single most important reason for the deficit is waste and fraud, and about a fifth points to the increase in military spending. Business and financial executives single out military spending in first place, followed by spending on social programs for the poor and disadvantaged (as opposed to broad-based programs like Social Security and Medicare). Despite interest payments of $139 billion in 1987, compared to a deficit of $150 billion, neither the general public nor the executive group thinks interest on the national debt has much to do with the deficit. Few people ever mention taxes.[4]

Most federal spending in fact finances activities like defense and Social Security that the great majority of Americans overwhelmingly support. Moreover, the parts add up to a total that we can well afford if we want it. To seek a consensus in favor of significantly lower spending, on the strength of the deceptive claim that much of our current spending pays for activities that nobody wants, is bound to be futile. If we continue to delude ourselves in this way, searching for a consensus that is not there while ignoring the real source of our fiscal imbalance and excluding other ways to address it, the damage from our current policy will only accumulate further.

In 1987 the federal government spent $1,005 billion. Of that, 73 percent went for defense, Social Security, Medicare and Medicaid, and interest on the national debt. Defense alone (not including veterans' benefits) cost $282 billion. Social Security benefits came to $207 billion. Medicare and Medicaid together cost $103 billion. And the interest on the national debt (net of interest received by the government) was $139 billion. The entire remainder of the budget—federal law enforcement, the courts, our embassies abroad, the immigration authority, tax collection, highway construction, the space program, the national parks, disaster relief, public health, public housing, veterans' benefits, federal civilian and military retirement pensions, child nutrition, all aid to education, all farm supports, all welfare payments, all aid to state and local governments, all foreign aid, the entire cost of paying federal employees' salaries and administering all federal programs—accounted for only 27 percent of the budget.

In 1980 the split was different. That year the government spent $591 billion, of which just 59 percent went for defense, Social Security, Medicare and Medicaid, and interest. One reason for the change since then has been the growth in defense spending, from 23 percent of the total to 28 percent. Another reason has been the rise in interest payments, from 9 percent of the total to 14 percent. Medicare and Medicaid have also climbed, from 8 percent to 10 percent. Among these core programs, only Social Security benefits have shown no growth in relation to the total, remaining at about 20% of federal spending thus far throughout the decade.

The fact that the rest of the budget has not kept pace with these five core spending programs shows that the emphasis on reduced federal spending in the 1980s achieved some successes. Spending for all other programs increased by only one seventh between 1980 and 1987. During those same years, spending on the five core programs more than doubled. As a result, the share of federal spending devoted to all government activities other than these five dropped from 41 percent in 1980 to just 27 percent in 1987.

Nevertheless, the budget cutting farce in which both Congress and the Reagan administration participated just after the stock market crashed in 1987 dramatically illustrated how hard it is to identify additional acceptable spending cuts, beginning from this level. Working under extraordinary public attention generated by the crash—and in principle, with, as the president put it, "everything on the table" except Social Security —the bipartisan group of negotiators arrived at a plan that supposedly reduced the deficit by $30 billion in 1988, and more than that in 1989.

On close inspection, however, the measures upon which

they agreed represented at best half that amount of genuine deficit reduction. Asset sales were to contribute $5.8 billion, new user fees $1 billion, supposedly increased taxes $9 billion, better IRS enforcement of the current tax laws $1.6 billion, and reduced interest costs $1.2 billion. Supposed cuts in spending, even including those that amounted to mere accounting changes, came to just $11.6 billion. By contrast, if the negotiators had done nothing, the recently revised Gramm-Rudman-Hollings legislation would automatically have cut $11.5 billion from 1988 defense spending and another $11.5 billion from nondefense programs. In the end, the highly publicized bipartisan process showed only that Congress and the president could easily avoid the spending cuts that Gramm-Rudman supposedly mandated.

Even so, it would be foolish to pretend that the search for ways to cut government spending, which has now dominated our fiscal agenda for the better part of a decade, has exhausted all conceivable avenues for limiting expenditures either within the core spending programs or elsewhere. No doubt the government is still providing some services that are not worth what they cost and perhaps even some that benefit no one other than the employees paid to provide them. There are serious questions about how much defense is enough, how generously to support retirees, and what responsibilities families should shoulder on their own when someone becomes ill. To whatever extent it is possible to achieve public agreement, further cuts in spending should make up part of the more than $100 billion per year of deficit reduction that we need to return to a stable fiscal trajectory.

Within the defense budget, for example, analysis of various options by the Congressional Budget Office showed that canceling procurement of the F-15 fighter aircraft would save $900 million per year, not replacing the Trident I submarine-launched missile with the Trident II would save $200 million per year, and retiring the *Coral Sea* and *Midway* aircraft carriers ahead of schedule would save $600 million per year in each case on average over the next five years. Similarly, reduced funding for military research and development would save $300 million per year, cutting the number of active-duty personnel back to the 1982 level would save $800 million per year, and limiting the upcoming military pay raise to 2 percent would save $1.1 billion, again over the next five years.[5] Whether any of these specific potential spending cuts is a good idea depends on a variety of issues including many too complex to admit readily of public debate. But as reflection on these few examples makes clear, the idea that defense is not a budget question, and that we must simply spend what is necessary, does not square with the difficulty and ambiguity of determining what is necessary.

The core areas other than defense likewise present potential spending cuts. Limiting each year's cost-of-living increase in Social Security benefits to two thirds of the rise in consumer prices, instead of the entire rise, would probably save $10 billion per year, on average over the next five years. Increasing the monthly Medicare premium from the scheduled $26.80 to $32.10, so that premiums would cover 30 percent of costs instead of 25 percent, would save $3.7 billion per year. Increasing the annual deductible from $75 to $200 would save another $2.4 billion per year. The emotion that many Americans (including President Reagan) display at even the mention of less generous Social Security benefits warns that these are difficult issues generating much anxiety. But here too the notion that they are not also in part budget questions is simply false. Among the government's five core spending activities, only interest is not a real target for cost cutting.

Outside these core areas potential spending cuts are even

easier to think of. Among more prosaic possibilities, we could save $800 million per year by eliminating federal support for sewage treatment plants, $900 million per year by limiting federal spending on airports and air traffic control to the revenue received from aviation excise taxes, $300 million per year by eliminating the Export-Import Bank's direct loan program, and another $300 million per year by eliminating federal support for agricultural research and extension activities—in each case on average over the next five years. Among more highly visible programs, eliminating farm price supports would save $15 billion per year, ending the food stamp program would save $12 billion per year, canceling all foreign aid for purposes of international development and humanitarian assistance would save $5 billion per year, eliminating community development grants would save $2.1 billion per year, eliminating all federal aid for elementary and secondary education other than for students with special needs would save $900 million per year, ending funding for the Legal Services Corporation would save $300 million per year, and canceling the space station would save $400 million per year. Limiting federal civilian pay raises to 2 percent would save $4 billion per year, and eliminating fifty thousand federal civilian jobs would save $500 million per year, again on average over the next five years.

The relevant question, however, is not whether it is possible to identify further potential reductions in nondefense spending or economies in defense spending. There is no lack of possibilities. The very notion of "discretionary" programs misrepresents the character of everything else that the government does. In principle, every dollar in the entire budget, except the interest on the national debt, is cancelable by act of Congress and approval of the president.

The question at issue is instead whether we actually want to implement these potential cuts. The standard rhetoric of public discussion in the 1980s repeatedly asserts that we do. But the *experience* of the 1980s—including the actions both of President Reagan and of the Congress, and within Congress, including the actions of both Democrats and Republicans— shows that we do not. We can all identify plenty of govern- ment programs that are of no interest to us individually. But the great bulk of the government's spending pays for activities that the overwhelming majority of Americans support. The makings of a consensus for major reductions simply are not there.

Between 1980 and 1987, we more than doubled our expendi- tures for national defense, increasing military spending from 5 percent to 6.4 percent of total income. We did so because most Americans wanted to. Proposals for specific new military pro- grams are often debated, sometimes on their substantive merits (as in the case of "Star Wars"), sometimes for reasons of cost. And complaints about the military's legendary inefficiency— $7,622 for a coffee pot, $435 for a claw hammer, and $792 for a doormat, not to mention the repeated scandals of large-scale procurement contracted on a cost-plus basis—have become commonplace.[6] But there is little public sentiment for a major reduction in defense spending. Public opinion surveys consis- tently show widespread support for strengthening America's defense capabilities even when doing so is expensive and even if paying for it requires additional taxes.

Social Security benefits almost doubled between 1980 and 1987, although as a share of our income they rose only from 4.4 percent to 4.7 percent. This growth reflected the increasing number of retired Americans in the population, not more gen- erous benefits compared to income for each retiree.* By 1987,

---

*It is ironic that the indexing of benefits to inflation, beginning in 1973— recently the focus of most of the criticism of Social Security—was originally

twenty-six million Americans received Social Security benefits on account of their own prior contributions, and an additional twelve million received benefit checks each month in their capacity as spouses and minor children. Beyond this huge group, tens of millions of other Americans who do not directly receive Social Security benefits are the spouses or grown children of people who do.

Social Security like defense, therefore enjoys enormous public support. Our visible progress of recent decades in eliminating poverty among the retired elderly population has attracted overwhelming approval. Despite occasional expressions of nostalgia for the "extended family" that was more typical in previous generations, there is essentially no public support for withdrawing the material means that allow so many of today's Americans to live on their own rather than in their grown children's homes.* Despite individual retirees whose benefits are grossly out of line with their contributions when they worked, there is essentially no support for returning to a world in which large numbers of elderly Americans with no children to rely on had to live in conditions that today's society deems not just physically intolerable but humiliating and degrading. As our retired population continues to grow, the cost of maintaining these achievements will only rise.

A large part of the growth of federal Medicare and Medicaid payments, from 1.7 percent of our income in 1980 to 2.3 percent in 1987, has similarly reflected the demographics of an aging population. By 1987, thirty-one million Americans were insured by Medicare, and another twenty-two million received

---

a proposal (by Republicans) for *limiting* benefit increases to *no more than* the rate of inflation.[7]

*Almost 60 percent of Americans aged sixty-five and older have annual income less than $10,000, and more than three fourths of what income they do receive comes from Social Security.

benefits under Medicaid.[8] At the same time, our accepted standard level of medical care is rising and so is the cost of providing it. Criticisms of the insurance system that finances our health care—including the private coverage most working Americans have, as well as that provided under Medicare and Medicaid—are in many cases valid.* Some proposed reforms are sensible. But there is no public sentiment for returning to a world in which large numbers of elderly Americans simply went without the medical care that their working-age children received essentially free of charge or in which low-income Americans of all ages failed to receive care that most others expected as a matter of course. Just as almost every adult American either receives Social Security benefits or has a parent who does or at least expects to do so himself in the future, almost everyone who does not now have Medicare coverage either has an insured parent or expects to be insured himself in time.

Beyond defense, Social Security, and Medicare and Medicaid, support for specific federal programs is a patchwork. Almost every American drives or rides on interstate highways. Most have attended schools that receive federal education subsidies or either have or expect to have children attending such schools. Most recognize a direct personal benefit from federal law enforcement. The great majority exhibit a strong interest in the space program. By contrast, only those who live on farms can ever expect any direct personal benefit from farm price supports. Fewer still expect ever to take advantage of federal job training programs or to live in a community that receives federal disaster relief. Federal activities like the na-

---

*The system overinsures for ordinary medical needs, encouraging overuse. It underinsures for the especially severe yet long-lasting illnesses that are catastrophic for some individuals and their families.[9]

tional parks and the student loan program stand somewhere in the middle.

But despite these lower levels of direct involvement on an individual basis, Americans as a political body are only slightly less reluctant to see large reductions in government spending for farm supports, or student loans, or national parks—or, for that matter, for highways, or elementary and secondary school subsidies, or the space program—than for defense, or Social Security, or Medicare and Medicaid. Moreover, with the pre-school population now rising again, and with the work force increasingly in need of the more sophisticated skills that competitive production technologies now require, our educational needs will only grow. Nor can we continue indefinitely to neglect our highways and our ports while more and more of our bridges deteriorate to the point that they fail to meet basic safety standards.

Exclusively focusing our fiscal agenda on the search for cuts in such areas throughout the 1980s has amounted to a large-scale experiment to discover whether or not Americans, expressing our preferences through the established mechanisms of our representative democracy, want to reduce our government's activity to a level consistent with its post-Kemp-Roth revenues. The answer is that we do not.

And there is nothing inherently wrong with that answer. Devoting 6 percent of our income to defense and another 3 percent to other services provided directly by the federal government is a decision that citizens of the world's most persistently successful economy ought to be free to make. So is redistributing 11 percent of our income among one another through Social Security, Medicare and Medicaid, and other transfer programs. America remains a strong and affluent country, well able to afford its current level of government if that is what its citizens choose. Compared to most other major industrialized countries, what stands out about America is not how large our government sector is but how small. The total government share of economic activity in America in 1987, including the federal level as well as state and local governments, even including interest on all government debt, was 35 percent. Comparable government shares in European countries are 48 percent in Germany, 46 percent in Britain, and 50 percent in France. Only in Japan, where the corresponding share is typically 29 percent to 30 percent (although it has fallen slightly as the huge trade surplus has increased Japan's total income) is the government any smaller compared to the economy.[10]

The experiment aimed at discovering whether we want significantly less of what our government spends money to provide has gone on long enough. For it to dominate our fiscal agenda becomes steadily more costly. It is increasingly clear that Americans want the level of government activity that we have and that we can afford that level. The question now should be how to pay for it.

Our experience since the 1980 election has shown that it is futile to base our fiscal policy on the expectation of eliminating more than $100 billion per annum in federal spending in addition to the cuts we have already made. That would represent more than a third of the entire 1987 defense budget. Or almost half of all Social Security benefits. Or more than all of Medicare and Medicaid combined. Or more than a third of the entire remainder of what the federal government does, other than paying interest on the national debt. A major part of this $100 billion or more per year—realistically about two-thirds of it—will have to consist of higher taxes.

The federal tax code, like government spending, does not

lack for potential opportunities to reduce the deficit by several billions of dollars here and another few billions there. In the face of Reagan's opposition to outright tax increases clearly recognizable for what they are, for the last half decade Congress has limited itself to concentrating on what it and the administration have euphemistically described as "revenue enhancement." The Deficit Reduction Act of 1984 increased revenues by an average $15 billion per year in the 1985 and 1986 fiscal years by putting together a variety of mostly nickel-and-dime measures like delaying the scheduled elimination of the 3 percent telephone excise tax, canceling the $100 per person net interest exclusion from individual income tax liability, and increasing the period over which businesses could depreciate real property from fifteen to eighteen years. The bipartisan compromise, reached after the October 1987 stock market crash, raised revenues for the 1988 fiscal year by $9 billion through such measures as accelerated corporate tax payments and yet another delay in eliminating the telephone excise.

These actions already taken have hardly exhausted the possible avenues for small-scale revenue increases. Among the more visible options, a $5 per barrel oil-import fee would raise $8 billion per year and a twelve cent per gallon increase in the motor fuel tax would raise $11 billion per year. Doubling the sixteen cent per pack tax on cigarettes would raise another $3 billion per year. Increasing the whiskey tax from $12.50 per proof gallon to $15 and also increasing the tax on beer and wine on an alcohol-equivalent basis would raise $5 billion per year. Taxing 30 percent of the capital gains realized from sales of homes would raise another $5 billion per year.[11]

Other familiar possibilities would affect mostly higher-income taxpayers. Taxing capital gains at death would raise $4 billion per year. Repealing percentage depletion and expensing of intangible drilling and exploration costs by the oil and gas industry would raise $2 billion per year. Reducing the deductible fraction of business entertainment expense from 80 percent to 50 percent would raise $4 billion per year. Limiting the deductibility of state and local taxes to amounts in excess of 1 percent of the taxpayer's adjusted gross income would save another $4 billion per year. The list's potential length and variety are limited only by finite imagination and exhaustible patience.

But just as it is futile to base our fiscal policy on spending cuts alone, it is implausible to expect to reduce the deficit by more than $100 billion simply by closing "loopholes" on the revenue side. Vigorous efforts along both lines are entirely appropriate, indeed essential. But pretending that either or even both together can fully serve the purpose is a sure way to repeat the costly errors of the past seven years.

America needs a tax increase, not a miscellaneous grab bag of petty nuisances "rounded up" from among "the usual suspects," nor a series of disguised revenue increases hidden where the average citizen can never find what he nevertheless has to pay. And we certainly do not want an increase in taxation through inflating away the outstanding debt, the most subtle hidden tax of all. We need a tax increase up front, plainly in view, comprehensible to everyone. Americans want the services that the government provides. We can afford to pay for them. It is time to do so.

A tax increase of $50 to $75 billion per year is a major act of economic policy even in a $5 trillion economy. As we have seen, an increase of that magnitude can have a significant impact on both the total and the composition of our economic activity. At the aggregate level therefore, a significant easing of monetary policy will be necessary to prevent so large a tax increase from causing a recession. Indeed, a rebalanced fiscal-monetary mix—with higher taxes, reduced government spending, and lower interest rates—is precisely what we need in order to substitute capital formation for consumption and exports for imports.

Some taxes, of course, are better suited to promoting the nation's economic well-being than others. Just as it will be counterproductive to cut spending by reducing still further our investment in our basic infrastructure or by failing to educate tomorrow's labor force, to raise taxes in ways that discourage investment in new plant and equipment will miss the point. So will raising taxes that discourage exports. So will raising taxes that discourage saving and encourage individuals to consume still more of their incomes. Especially for a tax increase of the magnitude we need, the kind of tax increase we choose is hardly a trivial matter.

The so-called Tax Reform Act of 1986 is a case in point. By 1986 few people still took seriously the notion that cutting marginal tax rates on personal incomes would have any other effect than reducing revenues on an almost proportional basis. Yet the political appeal of low marginal rates prevailed nonetheless. The 1986 legislation recouped some of the resulting revenue loss by curtailing a variety of deductions and credits that taxpayers had been able to exploit under the previous tax code—including potentially useful incentives like the deduction for IRA contributions and the favored treatment of capital gains, as well as economically worthless shelters and tax dodges.* But as experience under Kemp-Roth had proven, major across-the-board cuts in marginal tax rates were bound to mean large amounts of lost revenues. Official estimates

---

*It limited the revenue loss still further by delaying the full implementation of the new rates until 1988.

placed the likely net revenue loss from individual income tax payments at approximately $120 billion over the five years 1987–91.[12]

In its scramble to recoup these revenues too, so as to render the tax bill "revenue neutral," the Reagan administration proposed and Congress agreed to increase substantially the taxes paid by business. The 1986 tax bill did so in part by cutting back still further on depreciation allowances. Much more important in terms of the amount of revenues involved, it also eliminated the investment tax credit that companies had received in most years since 1962, whenever they purchased new equipment. Although corporations received a reduction from 46 percent to 34 percent in the statutory tax rate on their reported profits, the projected net effect was to raise corporate taxes during 1987–91 by the same $120 billion lost through smaller payments by individuals.

In an ironic contrast to the emphasis on "supply-side" incentives, this particular combination of changes in corporate taxation not only reduced most companies' incentive to invest but did so by even more than the projected five-year $120 billion increase in tax payments suggests. All corporations earning profits will get the advantage of the 34 percent marginal tax rate, whether they are making new investments or not. By contrast, the changes in depreciation schedules will apply only to newly purchased assets, and loss of the investment tax credit will affect only those companies that are buying new equipment. More detailed studies show that the resulting $120 billion net increase in corporate tax payments during 1987–91 will actually represent the combination of a *reduction* of $70 billion in taxes on income earned from business capital that was already in place as of 1986, and an *increase* of $190 billion in taxes on income earned from subsequent investments in new capital.[13]

Moreover, because the investment tax credit never applied to plants or office buildings anyway, most of the disincentive effect of this five-year $190 billion tax increase will fall on investment in new equipment. On average for all types of equipment, a plausible estimate is that the 1986 legislation raised the effective tax rate applicable to income from new business investment by some twenty percentage points. For example, under the old law the effective tax rate on investment in industrial equipment was about 10 percent after taking account of all relevant credits and allowances. Under the new law it is 32 percent. For investment in computers, the effective tax rate rose from 17 percent to 43 percent. For research equipment the rate rose from 23 percent to 43 percent and for scientific instruments from 11 percent to 36 percent.[14] It is hard to imagine a "tax reform" more likely to blunt our efforts to compete in technologically oriented industries.

From a purely economic perspective, the single best way to raise the revenue we need would probably be an entirely new tax, one on spending for personal consumption. By taxing what people spend, not what they earn, a consumption tax would avoid even the apparently small effect that income taxes have on individuals' work effort. And by excluding from tax that part of their incomes that people save, a consumption tax would not discourage saving—that is, if personal saving is actually sensitive to such influences (which the Individual Retirement Account experience suggests but other evidence does not).

Although many people fear a consumption tax on the grounds that it might fall disproportionately on low- and middle-income families (which typically spend most of what they make), a consumption tax need not be regressive in this way. A well-designed combination of tax rate structure and family exemptions can easily make a consumption tax just as progressive as America's income tax. If spending of $2,500 per person is exempt from the tax altogether, the remaining amount of consumption to which the tax would apply is so large that with a 2.25 percent tax rate it would raise approximately $75 billion per year in additional revenue on average during 1989–96. With the same $2,500 per person exemption, a progressive rate structure ranging from 1 percent to 4 percent would do the same.

A close relative of the consumption tax, sharing most of its virtues and perhaps more acceptable politically, is the value-added tax (in different variants sometimes called a business transfer tax or even a national sales tax). The VAT is essentially a sales tax paid on all purchases made by domestic final users of goods or services. Companies that pay the VAT on goods that they buy as inputs to their business get refunds. So does anyone who buys goods for export. In the end therefore, the VAT amounts approximately to a consumption tax. Many other industrialized countries rely on a VAT as a major component of their revenue systems, and critics of our tax system often point to the use of the VAT abroad as a major competitive advantage for foreign producers.

Like a consumption tax, a VAT would not discourage work effort or investment or personal saving. Also like a consumption tax, it need not fall disproportionately on low-income families. With a well-designed set of exemptions or refundable credits or both, a VAT can also be as progressive as desired. And because it is merely a form of sales tax, a VAT would be easier to administer than a consumption tax. A 6 percent VAT with all food, housing, and medical care specifically exempted would raise approximately $75 billion per year. Without the exemptions, a 3 percent VAT would do the same.

But the lengthy debate that culminated in passage of the 1986 Tax Reform Act has already considered the structure of the nation's tax system on a comprehensive basis, and Americans may now be unwilling to accept an entirely new tax: a pity since most specific "reforms" actually adopted in the 1986 law were counterproductive from the standpoint of capital formation and competitiveness. More important, the entire effort missed the chance to reorient our tax structure toward a more consumption-based system. Introducing a consumption tax or even a VAT would still be economically sensible. But if Americans at the end of the 1980s want to consider the structure of their tax system as a settled issue for the foreseeable future, we have earned the right to do so. Where, then, can we raise another $60 to $75 billion per year to pay for what we expect our government to provide?

The crucial step that launched our new fiscal policy at the outset of the 1980s was the Kemp-Roth tax cut. The three-part, across-the-board cut reduced personal income tax payments by $387 billion from 1982 through 1986 and by $110 billion in 1986 alone, compared to what the government would otherwise have received.*[15] If other measures like a consumption tax or a VAT prove politically unacceptable, then the best way to right our fiscal policy—the way most likely to promote public understanding and thereby command public support— is to admit that with Kemp-Roth we cut taxes too much, and fix our mistake.

Such an honest approach means a sharp departure from the rhetoric that has dominated our fiscal agenda for the past decade—though certainly no departure from the objectives. A realistic assessment is that across-the-board cuts in individual income tax rates have had an almost negligible effect on work

*Other provisions of the 1981 tax bill, including especially the indexing of the tax brackets beginning in January 1985, reduced individuals' income tax payments by another $110 billion during fiscal 1982–86 ($44 billion in 1986).

effort and none at all on saving, and that investment and productivity growth have suffered already and will continue to do so without adequate revenues to pay the government's bills. It is time to advance beyond rhetoric that appeals to worthwhile objectives but advocates ineffective, indeed counterproductive, measures to achieve them. When there is no evidence that even large across-the-board cuts in personal tax rates have done anything more than finance high consumption, it is foolish to go on pretending that any increase in tax rates at all would only stifle incentives.

As of 1988, our new tax system taxes what is left of personal incomes after subtracting all exemptions and deductions, at 15 percent for the first $17,850 ($29,750 for joint returns), and 28 percent above that level.* The new system also provides a $2,000 per person exemption and a standard deduction of $5,000 per family for those who do not itemize deductible expenses. A family of four with $28,000 of total income (the 1987 average after allowing for inflation) will therefore have *taxable* income of $15,000 after claiming its four personal exemptions and the standard deduction. Its tax due will be 15 percent of that amount, or $2,250.

Simply raising the new system's two benchmark rates from 15 percent to 18 percent and from 28 percent to 31 percent, while maintaining all other features of the new tax code as they are now, would raise approximately $75 billion per year in additional revenues. Although this three-percentage-point increase would raise a large amount of additional revenue in the aggregate, its impact on most individuals and families would be modest. Nor is there evidence to suggest that a difference of

---

*A 33 percent rate is in effect for incomes between $43,150 and $89,560 (between $71,900 and $149,250 for joint returns) so as to eliminate the advantage of the 15 percent bracket for upper-income taxpayers.

three percentage points in marginal tax rates significantly affects economic incentives. At the personal level, the same family of four, earning the nationwide average income and claiming only its four personal exemptions and the standard deduction, would end up paying $2,700 in federal tax instead of $2,250. A comparable family earning only half the average income would pay $180 instead of $150. A family earning twice the average income would pay $9,462 instead of $8,172.

More complicated schemes could of course make the resulting impact more progressive (or less) by reworking the new rate structure instead of simply changing by equal amounts the two key rates put in place under the 1986 tax reform. Raising the rate that is now 15 percent to 17 percent (or even just 16 percent) instead of 18 percent would mean raising the rate that is now 28 percent, higher than 31 percent. Adjusting the personal exemption or the minimum standard deduction could serve much the same purpose. Many options are possible. But however it is spread across the income range, a tax rise of three percentage points is sufficient to do the job.

Nobody enjoys paying taxes, and nobody who pays taxes enjoys paying more. But once we accept the sorry fact that Reagan's promise of a free lunch was empty, an extra $450 for the average family—or $1,290 for families with twice the average income and only $30 for those with half the average—is not an excessive price to pay if we want to continue to receive what our government now provides. It is certainly small enough compared to the consequences—economic, social, political, and international—of continuing indefinitely along the unbalanced fiscal path set in the 1980s.

At the same time, we must also be careful not to correct our fiscal policy in a way that unduly raises the costs of the transition and thereby only compounds, at least for some time, the damage that Reagan's fiscal policy has already done. As we have seen, the experience of 1960 and 1969–70 warns that abruptly reducing the deficit by as much as 3 percent of income can, along with tight monetary policy, push the economy into recession.

That risk is probably greater now than it was then. One reason is that the borrowing our businesses have done during the 1980s has stretched their balance sheets and raised their interest payments to a record share of their earnings even in a strong economy. Another is that lower stock prices may at least temporarily depress consumer spending. Yet another is that, although the falling dollar will help stimulate our economy and thereby offset our turn to tighter fiscal policy, to the extent that lower American imports will harm the already-depressed European economies, a cheaper dollar presents risks as well as opportunities. We must take care, therefore, to avoid either creating or worsening a recession.

Phasing in the necessary tax increase and the accompanying spending cuts over two years, or possibly even three, is one way to minimize this risk. If an increase in personal income tax rates is to be a major part of the solution to our fiscal imbalance, raising the tax rates to 16.5 percent and 29.5 percent in 1989 and then 18 percent and 31 percent (or whatever combination we choose) in 1990, will ease the transition and allow more time for other factors—including the stimulus from the cheaper dollar—to have an offsetting effect. That way, greater American exports can make up for much of the slower growth of American consumption, and countries abroad will have more time to offset the impact of our slower consumption growth on their export sales.

The most important part of our effort to cushion the potentially recessionary effects of higher taxes and reduced government spending, however, will be an easier monetary policy.

Even in 1960 and 1969–70, as we have also seen, what pushed the economy into recession was the combination of tight fiscal policy and tight monetary policy. If instead we now combine the shift to less expansionary fiscal policy with an *easier* monetary policy, we shall greatly increase our prospects for avoiding a repetition of those two experiences—which, given today's more fragile international economic environment, would probably be more severe this time.

The Federal Reserve, therefore, should not merely allow interest rates to come down as the burden of federal deficit financing shrinks but should actively lower interest rates beyond levels that market developments would reach in any case. Especially if the cheaper dollar narrows our trade deficit at about the same pace that increased taxes and reduced spending narrow the federal budget deficit, interest rates may fall little if at all without active downward pressure from monetary policy. The reduction in government borrowing to be financed would then simply be offset by the smaller net inflow of foreign saving to finance it. But the Federal Reserve should push interest rates lower anyway, providing banks with adequate reserves to be able to lend in sufficient volume to allow interest rates to fall. Great care will also be necessary, of course, to avoid pushing easier monetary policy to the point at which inflation becomes all but inevitable. But while our fiscal transition is in progress, if it is on the scale of what we need, the greater risk is that business will falter, perhaps seriously.

Finally, in step with our change in fiscal policy, we should also redouble our efforts to persuade our trading partners, especially the West Europeans, to stimulate their own economies. Although the merits of such a policy shift have long been apparent in some countries, our unwillingness to abandon what they have rightly seen as an irresponsible economic policy in America has blocked international cooperation along these lines. We can only hope that the increased urgency of the situation, together with our finally correcting our fiscal-monetary policy mix, will now elicit an appropriately stimulative response abroad.

Only if we firmly and credibly commit ourselves to a new fiscal policy can any of these mechanisms work, however. We cannot expect foreign governments to adopt expansionary policies in response to vague promises to find additional revenue sources or to make unspecified spending cuts at some later date. More important, without a real commitment to a different fiscal trajectory, the Federal Reserve cannot run the risk of inflation—which then would be a major risk indeed—from easing monetary policy while we are at full employment, if fiscal policy is actually going to remain expansionary. We must not only resolve to change our fiscal policy, but go ahead to enact the necessary legislation, including a phased tax increase as well as whatever spending cuts we are going to make, in a form to which we shall then be just as committed as we were to Kemp-Roth when we started down the path that has led us to our present unhappy situation.

Canceling nondefense programs. Making Social Security or Medicare less generous. Spending less on defense. Paying higher taxes. These are obviously hard choices, and whichever route we choose, we will have to make real sacrifices.

Successfully addressing the problems that Reagan's fiscal policy has left us will therefore be possible only if Americans not only understand why the steps we must take are necessary but also see that they are fair in how they spread their impact. Whether we cut spending by shutting down military bases or letting inflation erode retirees' incomes or paying government employees lower salaries or eliminating food stamps or farm price supports altogether will make little difference in economic terms. But it will determine who makes the sacrifices. In economic terms, what kind of tax increase to implement is also distinctly secondary to the choice of whether to increase taxes and by how much. But because there will be no public support for a tax increase that Americans think is not fair, in the end what form any proposed tax increase takes will determine whether we increase taxes at all.

The importance of these fundamentally political dimensions of the choices we now face means that there is still much to be done. But at least the basic outlines of what we need to do are clear. Unfortunately, so are the consequences of failing to do it. In his initial budget address to Congress as America's new president in February 1981, Ronald Reagan asked of those whom he identified with the tax-and-spend strategy of the past, "Are they suggesting that we can continue on the present course without coming to a day of reckoning?"[16]

The irony is that the right answer would have been "yes" in 1981, but it is surely "no" seven years later. The old policy of tax-and-spend, as the president derisively labeled it, delivered budgets that were approximately balanced by today's standards. More important, apart from wars it always reduced federal debt in relation to America's growing income. The new policy of large tax cuts not matched by spending cuts has instead delivered record deficits and a debt that is rising compared to our income. As a result, our domestic capital formation has been eroded, and for a while our international competitiveness all but collapsed. The policy of tax-and-spend at least led along a trajectory that was not fundamentally explosive. The policy of spending without taxing points a course that is clearly unstable.

If the day of reckoning that our new fiscal policy has made inevitable were likely to be concrete, sharply visible, and tangibly cataclysmic, a political system like ours that responds mostly to crisis would be better able to deal with it. But except perhaps for occasional crises in the foreign exchange markets, the costs of the fiscal policy we have pursued in the 1980s are occurring and will occur both gradually and subtly.

Without economic growth, American society will ultimately lose its vibrancy, its dynamic sense of progress, its capacity to accommodate the aims and objectives of diverse groups within the population, its ability to offer such remarkable social mobility and individual opportunity. Without a strong and competitive economy, America as a nation will watch others take its place in the world order. These are the real costs of our current fiscal policy, and for the most part they will not even be perceptible from one year to the next. Even on the occasions when discrete events do occur, like the collapse of some industry or financial institution or our abdication of a major international responsibility, it will be impossible to identify them unambiguously as by-products of our fiscal imbalance.

The best way to meet this challenge is simply to be clear about what is at stake. The issue in the first instance is one of economics. But it matters because its consequences affect more fundamental aspects of what America is about as a society and as a nation. Adopting a different fiscal policy is not just an economic desideratum but a moral imperative. If we do not correct America's fiscal course, our children and our children's children will have the right to hold us responsible. The saddest outcome of all would be for America's decline to go on, but to go on so gradually that by the time the members of the next generation are old enough to begin asking who was responsible for their diminished circumstances, they will not even know what they have lost.

NOTES

For series of economic data that are used repeatedly throughout this book, the Notes section indicates the source of each series only as it first appears in the text. In addition, the following abbreviations are used throughout the Notes section:

BC   Bureau of the Census
BEA   Bureau of Economic Analysis
BLS   Bureau of Labor Statistics
FOF   Flow of Funds Accounts
FRB   Board of Governors of the Federal Reserve System
IBRD International Bank for Reconstruction and Development
IMF   International Monetary Fund
NIPA National Income and Product Accounts
OECD Organization for Economic Cooperation and Development

CHAPTER I: BROKEN FAITH

1. Data on the federal budget in relation to national income and on net private saving are from the U.S. Department of Commerce, BEA, NIPA.

2. Productivity data are from the U.S. Department of Labor, BLS;

1.1 percent per annum is the average for the nonfarm business sector.

3. Unemployment data are from the BLS. Aggregate growth rates are from the NIPA.

4. "White House Report on the Program for Economic Recovery," *Public Papers of the Presidents of the United States: Administration of Ronald Reagan, 1981.* (Washington, D.C.: U.S. Government Printing Office, 1982), February 18, 1981, p. 130.

5. "Address to the Nation on the Economy," *Public Papers,* February 5, 1981, p. 79.

6. "Address Before a Joint Session of the Congress on the Program for Economic Recovery," *Public Papers,* February 18, 1981, p. 109.

7. Dollar figures for the federal budget are from *The Budget of the United States Government, Fiscal Year 1989* and previous years (Washington, D.C.: U.S. Government Printing Office, 1988).

8. Feenberg, Daniel R., and Harvey S. Rosen, "Tax Structure and Public Sector Growth," *Journal of Public Economics,* 32, March 1987, 185–201.

9. Stockfish, J. A., "Value-Added Taxes and the Size of Government: Some Evidence," *National Tax Journal,* 38, December 1985, 547–52.

CHAPTER II: AMERICA IN ECONOMIC DECLINE

1. Net investment data are from the NIPA.

2. Capital stock data are from the BEA. See especially *Fixed Reproducible Tangible Wealth in the United States, 1925–85* (Washington, D.C.: U.S. Government Printing Office, 1987). Employment data (here including production or nonsupervisory workers only) are from the BLS.

3. Earnings data are from the BLS.

4. Scholl, Russell B., "The International Investment Position of

the United States in 1986," *Survey of Current Business*, 67, June 1987, 38–45.

5. Trade data are from the U.S. Department of Commerce, BEA.
6. Data on net capital inflows are from the NIPA.
7. Aggregate income data are from the NIPA.
8. "Mexico After the Oil Boom," Mimeo: IBRD, 1985.
9. Data on business failures are from Dun and Bradstreet.
10. "Address to the Nation on the Economy," *Public Papers*, February 18, 1981, p. 81.
11. "White House Report on the Program for Economic Recovery," *Public Papers*, February 18, 1981, p. 124.

CHAPTER III: AMERICA'S PLACE IN THE WORLD

1. World trade data are from the IMF.
2. German and Japanese trade data are from the IMF.
3. Data on other countries' debt positions are from the IBRD.
4. Country-specific data on U.S. imports are from the BEA.
5. Nogues, Julio J., Andrzez Olechowski, and L. Alan Winters, "The Extent of Nontariff Barriers to Industrial Countries Imports," *The World Bank Economic Review*, 1, September 1986, 181–99. Also subsequent updates (unpublished) from the IBRD.
6. Weidenbaum, Murray, and Michael Munger, "Protection at Any Price?" *Regulation*, 7, July/August 1983, 14–22.
7. The Bank of Japan stated its total foreign-exchange reserves (of which roughly 90 percent is in dollars) as $75 billion as of December 1987.
8. Data on foreign purchases of U.S. securities are from the BEA.
9. U.S. price-earnings ratios are for the Standard & Poor's 500 index. Japanese price-earnings ratios are for the Tokyo Stock Exchange index.
10. *Mergerstat Review* (Chicago: W. T. Grimm & Co., 1987), and

"It's a Great Time to Be an Arb," *Business Week,* April 4, 1988, pp. 28–30.

11. Ibid.

12. *A Summary of Japanese Real Estate Investment and Development Activity in the United States, 1984–1987* (New York: Landauer Associates, Inc., 1987).

13. "For Sale: America," *Time,* September 14, 1987, pp. 52–62.

14. "Japan on Wall Street," *Business Week,* September 7, 1987, pp. 82–90.

15. Foreign direct investment data are from the BEA.

16. Herr, Ellen M., "U.S. Business Enterprises Acquired or Established by Foreign Direct Investors in 1987," *Survey of Current Business,* 68, May 1988, 50–58.

17. Ibid.

18. Scholl, Russell B., "The International Investment Position of the United States in 1986," *Survey of Current Business,* 67, June 1987, 38–45.

19. Ibid.

20. *Balance Sheets for the U.S. Economy, 1947–86* (Washington, D.C.: FRB, 1987).

21. Data on foreign holdings are from the BEA. Data on total market value are from *Balance Sheets, op. cit.*

22. Downs, Anthony, *Foreign Capital in U.S. Real Estate Markets* (New York: Salomon Brothers, Inc., 1987).

23. Data on home ownership are from the BC.

24. Schian, Dale C., and David A. Seid, *State Laws Relating to the Ownership of Land by Aliens and Business Entities, October 31, 1986* (Washington, D.C.: U.S. Department of Agriculture, 1986).

25. Scholl, *op. cit.*

26. Lipsey, Robert E., "Changing Patterns of International Investment in and by the United States," M. Feldstein, ed., *The United States in the World Economy* (Chicago: University of Chicago Press, 1988).

27. "Latin America: Debt Conversion Proliferates," *Business America*, June 22, 1987, pp. 2–8.
28. Edelstein, Michael, *Overseas Investment in the Age of High Imperialism: The United Kingdom, 1850–1914* (New York: Columbia University Press, 1982), Ch. 2.
29. Ibid. See also David S. Landes, "Technological Change and Development in Western Europe, 1750–1914," H. J. Habakkuk and M. Postan, eds., *The Industrial Revolutions and After: Incomes, Population and Technological Change*, Part I (Cambridge, U.K.: Cambridge University Press, 1965), p. 558.
30. Servan-Schreiber, Jean-Jacques, *Le Defi Americain* (Paris: Editions Denoel, 1967).
31. Japanese and German current account data are from the IMF. Net foreign investment position data are from the Bank of Japan and the Deutsche Bundesbank, respectively.
32. "Mexico Looks Better and Better to Japan," *Business Week*, June 8, 1987, p. 58.
33. See, for example, Richard Rosecranz, *The Rise of the Trading State* (New York: Basic Books, 1986). Also Robert Gilpin, *The Political Economy of International Relations* (Princeton, N.J.: Princeton University Press, 1987).

CHAPTER IV: CORRECTING COURSE

1. See, for example, the discussion of federal budget accounting in Robert Eisner, *How Real Is the Federal Deficit?* (New York: The Free Press, 1986). Also Michael J. Boskin, "Government Saving, Capital Formation, and Wealth in the United States," R. Lipsey and H. Tice, eds., *Measuring Saving and Capital Formation* (Chicago: University of Chicago Press, 1988).
2. "White House Report on the Program for Economic Recovery," *Public Papers*, February 18, 1981, p. 131.
3. Estimates of the effects of business fluctuations on federal revenues and spending are from Thomas M. Holloway, "The Cycli-

cally Adjusted Federal Budget and Federal Debt: Revised and Updated Estimates," *Survey of Current Business*, 66, March 1986, 11–17.

4. Interest rate data, as well as data on money and credit growth, are from the FRB.

5. Ratios of interest payments to corporate earnings and to personal income are computed from data in the NIPA.

6. Data on bankruptcies and debt in default are from Dun and Bradstreet.

7. Ratios of debt to equity, measured at market value, are computed from data from the FRB, FOF.

8. See, for example, the differing accounts in Milton Friedman and Anna Jacobson Schwartz, *A Monetary History of the United States, 1867–1960* (Princeton, N.J.: Princeton University Press, 1963) and Peter Temin, *Did Monetary Forces Cause the Great Depression?* (New York: W. W. Norton, 1976).

Chapter V: From Tax-and-Spend to Spend-and-Borrow

1. This section relies heavily on the chronology and data given in Paul Studenski and Herman E. Kroos, *Financial History of the United States* (New York: McGraw-Hill, 1952). Other data are from the U.S. Department of the Treasury.

2. See the discussion in Peter Temin, *The Jacksonian Economy* (New York: W. W. Norton, 1969).

3. Data on government spending in relation to national income are from the NIPA.

4. Data on Social Security payments are from the Social Security Administration.

5. Holloway, Thomas M., "The Cyclically Adjusted Federal Budget and Federal Debt: Revised and Updated Estimates," *Survey of Current Business*, 66, March 1986, 11–17.

6. Studenski and Kroos, *op. cit.*, p. 377.

7. *Conference on Inflation, September 27–28, 1974,* transcript (Washington, D.C.: U.S. Government Printing Office, 1974).

8. For example, "Statement of Hon. William E. Simon, Secretary of the Treasury," October 7, 1975, 94th Congress, 1st Session, House of Representatives, Committee on Ways and Means (Washington: U.S. Government Printing Office), p. 3.

9. George Gallup, *The Gallup Poll: Public Opinion, 1935–1971,* Vol. III (New York: Random House, 1972), p. 1777.

10. Richard C. Zeimer, "Impact of Recent Tax Law Changes," *Survey of Current Business,* 65, April 1985, 28–31, and subsequent updates (unpublished) from the BEA.

11. Calculated from "White House Report on the Program for Economic Recovery," *Public Papers,* February 18, 1981, p. 122; and *Fiscal Year 1982 Budget Revisions,* 97th Congress, 1st Session, House Document No. 97-26, March 1981 (Washington, D.C.: U.S. Government Printing Office), Tables 2, 18.

12. Zeimer, *op. cit.*

CHAPTER VI: THE REAGAN RECOVERY

1. Data on consumer prices are from the BLS.

2. Avery, Robert B., et al., "Survey of Consumer Finances, 1983," *Federal Reserve Bulletin,* 70, September 1984, 679–92, p. 689.

3. "Defense Dollars Save Many a City," *U.S. News & World Report,* May 10, 1982, 77–79.

4. Department of Defense, *Selected Manpower Statistics, Fiscal Year 1986* (Washington, D.C.: U.S. Government Printing Office, 1986), Table 1-6.

5. Data on U.S. government civilian employment are from the BLS.

6. Zeimer, Richard C., "Impact of Recent Tax Law Changes," *Survey of Current Business,* 65, April 1985, 28–31.

7. "Statement of David A. Stockman, Director, Office of Management and Budget," March 8, 1982, 97th Congress, 2nd Session,

Senate, Committee on Finance (Washington, D.C.: U.S. Government Printing Office), p. 343.

8. "First Presidential Debate, Official Transcriptional Record," October 7, 1980, Mimeo (The League of Women Voters Educational Fund), p. 2.

9. *The Effects of Deficits on Prices of Financial Assets: Theory and Evidence* (Washington, D.C.: U.S. Treasury Department, 1984).

10. Data on capacity utilization are from the FRB.

11. "Volcker Suggests Federal Reserve May Shift Tactics," *New York Times,* October 10, 1982, p. 1.

12. Holloway, Thomas M., "The Cyclically Adjusted Federal Budget and Federal Debt: Revised and Updated Estimates," *Survey of Current Business,* 66, March 1986, 11–17, and subsequent updates from the BEA.

13. Data on consumer spending are from the NIPA. Population data are from the BC.

14. Data on the labor force status of families are from the BLS.

15. Data on borrowing and asset accumulation are from the FOF.

16. Employment data are from the BLS.

17. Bluestone, Barry, and Bennett Harrison, *The Great U-Turn: Corporate Restructuring and the Polarizing of America* (New York: Basic Books, 1988), Figure 5.4.

18. Data on part-time employment are from the BLS.

19. Ibid.

20. Poverty data are from the BC.

CHAPTER VII: DEFICITS, INTEREST RATES, AND THE DOLLAR

1. Saving data are from the NIPA.

2. Data on state and local government budgets in relation to national income are from the NIPA.

3. Interest rate data are from the FRB. Inflation data are from the NIPA.
4. Bond yield data are from Moody's Investors Service.
5. Mortgage rate data are from the Federal Home Loan Bank Board.
6. Data on other countries' government budgets are from the IMF.
7. Estimated real interest rates for different countries (unpublished) are from the Congressional Budget Office.
8. Data for total imports and exports including services are from the NIPA.
9. Exchange rate data, with and without adjustments for differences in inflation rates, are from the FRB.

CHAPTER VIII: INVESTMENT, PRODUCTIVITY, AND COMPETITIVENESS

1. Output data are from the NIPA. Employment data (nonfarm) are from the BLS.
2. See, for example, R. E. Kutscher, J. A. Mark and J. R. Norsworthy, "The Productivity Slowdown and Outlook to 1985," *Monthly Labor Review,* 100, May 1977, 3–8. Also J. R. Norsworthy, Michael J. Harper, and Kent Kunze, "The Slowdown in Productivity Growth: Analysis of Some Contributing Factors," *Brookings Papers on Economic Activity,* No. 2, 1979, 387–421. Edward F. Denison, *Accounting for Slower Economic Growth: The United States in the 1970s* (Washington, D.C.: The Brookings Institution, 1979) and subsequent updates, suggested one eighth. William D. Nordhaus, "The Recent Productivity Slowdown," *Brookings Papers on Economic Activity,* No. 3, 1972, 493–536, and Edward Wolff, "The Composition of Output and the Productivity Growth Slowdown of 1967–76, Mimeo (New York: New York University, 1981) gave higher

estimates, but their work applied to the smaller slowdown that occurred after the mid-sixties.

3. Norsworthy, J. R., et al., *op. cit.*, suggested about one sixth. E. A. Hudson and Dale W. Jorgenson, "Energy Prices and the U.S. Economy," *Natural Resources Journal*, 18, October 1978, 877–897 gave a similar estimate.

4. Data on research and development spending are from the National Science Foundation.

5. Patent data are from the U.S. Patent Office.

6. Griliches, Zvi, "R&D and the Productivity Slowdown," *American Economic Review*, 70, May 1980, 343–348 suggested one tenth. M. Ishaq Nadiri, "Sectoral Productivity Slowdown," *American Economic Review*, 70, May 1980, 349–352 gave a higher estimate. The estimate given by Denison, *op. cit.*, is far smaller.

7. Farber, Kit D., and Gary L. Rutledge, "Pollution Abatement and Control Expenditures," *Survey of Current Business*, 66, July 1986, 94–105, and related releases from the BEA.

8. Denison, *op. cit.*, originally estimated one eighth, but reduced that estimate by more than half in later work. John Kendrick, "Productivity Trends in the United States," in S. Maital and N. M. Meltz, eds., *Lagging Productivity Growth* (Cambridge, Mass.: Ballinger, 1980) gave a similar estimate.

9. Data on investment in different countries are from the OECD. Productivity data are from the BLS.

10. Data (unpublished) on respective countries' capital stocks are from the FRB.

11. See, for example, Denison, *op. cit.;* Kendrick, *op. cit.;* Nadiri, *op. cit.;* Norsworthy et al., *op. cit.;* Peter K. Clark, "Issues in the Analysis of Capital Formation and Productivity Growth," *Brookings Papers on Economic Activity*, No. 2, 1979, 423–431; and John A. Tatom, "The Productivity Problem," *Economic Review*, Federal Reserve Bank of St. Louis, September 1979), 3–16.

12. Data on the federal government's physical capital outlays are from *Historical Tables: Budget of the United States Government, Fiscal Year 1989*, (Washington, D.C.: U.S. Government Printing Office, 1988) Table 9.2. For alternative estimates, which confirm the decline in recent years, see Michael J. Boskin, et al., "New Estimates of Federal Government Tangible Capital and Net Investment," D. W. Jorgenson and R. Landau, eds., *Technology and Capital Formation* (Cambridge, Mass.: MIT Press, 1988).

13. Data (unpublished) on state and local governments' capital investment are from the BEA. For alternative estimates, which confirm the decline in recent years, see Michael J. Boskin, et al., "New Estimates of State and Local Government Tangible Capital and Net Investment," Mimeo (National Bureau of Economic Research, 1987).

14. Data on the government-owned capital stock are from the BEA. See especially *Fixed Reproducible Tangible Wealth in the United States, 1925–85* (Washington, D.C.: U.S. Government Printing Office, 1987).

15. Data on spending for education are from the U.S. Department of Education, Office of Educational Research and Improvement, Center for Education Statistics.

16. Price data are from the BLS.

CHAPTER IX: BECOMING A DEBTOR NATION

1. Import price data are from the BC. Domestic price data are from the BLS.

2. Motor Vehicle Manufacturers Association of the United States.

3. Data on the U.S. agricultural trade surplus (unpublished) are from the BEA.

4. Data on different countries' productivity growth are from the BLS.

5. Data on different countries' wage rates are from the BLS.

6. Data on different countries' unemployment rates are from the BLS.

7. Data on the net international debt position are from Douglass C. North, "The United States Balance of Payments, 1790–1860," Conference on Research in Income and Wealth, *Trends in the American Economy in the Nineteenth Century* (Princeton, N.J.: Princeton University Press, 1960), Table C-1; and Matthew Simon, "The United States Balance of Payments, 1861–1900," Conference on Research in Income and Wealth, *op. cit.*, Table 27.

8. This section draws heavily on Robert Solomon, "The United States as a Debtor Country in the Nineteenth Century," Mimeo (The Brookings Institution, 1986).

9. Foreign capital inflows are estimated from current account data given in North, *op. cit.*, Table B-5, and Simon, *op. cit.*, Table 27. See also Solomon, *op. cit.* Income data are estimated from data given in Roger L. Ransom and Richard Sutch, "Domestic Saving as an Active Constraint on Capital Formation in the American Economy, 1839–1928: A Provisional Theory," Mimeo (Berkeley, Calif.: University of California, 1984), Appendix Table E-4.

10. Solomon, *op. cit.*, p. 9. Different sources present varying lists. Paul Studenski and Herman E. Kroos, *Financial History of the United States* (New York: McGraw Hill, 1952), p. 118, for example, list Arkansas with Florida and Mississippi as having formally repudiated.

11. Ransom and Sutch, *op. cit.*, p. 42.

12. *Indicative Prices for Less Developed Country Bank Loans* (New York: Salomon Brothers Inc., 1987).

CHAPTER X: ROOTS OF REAGANOMICS

1. *Statistical Abstract of the United States* (Washington, D.C.: U.S. Government Printing Office, 1987), Table 447.

2. "A Strategy for Growth: The American Economy in the 1980s," Mimeo (Republican National Committee, 1980), p. 8.

3. "Address to the Nation on Federal Tax Reduction Legislation," *Public Papers of the Presidents of the United States: Administration of Ronald Reagan, 1981* (Washington, D.C.: Government Printing Office, 1982), July 27, 1981, p. 664.

4. Smith, Adam, *The Wealth of Nations* (New York: Random House, 1937), p. 835.

5. Ibid., p. 778.

6. This rate is the median, calculated from data given in *Statistics of Income: Individual Income Tax Returns, 1980* (Washington, D.C.: Internal Revenue Service, 1983).

7. Calculated from ibid.

8. *Statistical Abstract of the United States, op. cit.*, 1982, Table 450.

9. See, for example, *Capital Gains Tax Reductions of 1978*, Department of the U.S. Treasury, Office of Tax Analysis, 1985. Also Lawrence Lindsey, "Capital Gains Rates, Realizations, and Revenues," M. Feldstein, ed., *The Effects of Taxation on Capital Accumulation* (Chicago: University of Chicago Press, 1987).

10. Calculated from Lindsey, *op. cit.*, Tables 3.5, 3.6, and 3.8, and subsequent updates (unpublished).

11. Kalachek, Edward D., and Frederic Q. Raines, "Labor Supply of Lower Income Workers," President's Commission on Income Maintenance Programs, *Technical Studies* (Washington, D.C.: U.S. Government Printing Office, 1970) derived estimates ranging from .2 to .9 for females in the aggregate. Orley Aschenfelter and James J. Heckman, "The Estimation of Income and Substitution Effects in a Model of Family Labor Supply," *Econometrica*, 42, January 1974, 73–85 estimated .87 for married females. Jerry A. Hausman, "Labor Supply," H. J. Aaron and J. A. Peckman, eds., *How Taxes Affect Economic Behavior* (Washington, D.C.: The Brookings Institution, 1981), estimated .5 for married females and .9 for female heads of

households. Michael J. Boskin, "The Economics of Labor Supply," G. G. Cain and H. W. Watts, eds., *Income Maintenance and Labor Supply* (Chicago: Rand-McNally, 1973), derived estimates ranging from −.04 to 1.6 for different subgroups of the female population.

12. Aschenfelter and Heckman, *op. cit.*, estimated zero response for all married males. Aschenfelter and Heckman, "Estimating Labor Supply Functions," Cain and Watts, *op. cit.*, estimated *minus* .15 for male heads of households. Hausman, *op. cit.*, estimated zero for all married males. Boskin, *op. cit.*, derived estimates ranging from *minus* .07 to (plus) .18 for different subgroups of the male population. Kalachek and Raines, *op. cit.*, derived estimates ranging from .05 to .30 for different subgroups.

13. Data on personal income are from the NIPA.

14. Zeimer, Richard C., "Impact of Recent Tax Law Changes," *Survey of Current Business,* 65, April 1985, 28–31, and subsequent updates (unpublished) from the BEA.

15. "Statement of Hon. Paul A. Volcker, Chairman, Board of Governors of the Federal Reserve System," February 7, 1985, 98th Congress, 2nd Session, House of Representatives, Committee on Banking, Finance and Urban Affairs (Washington, D.C.: U.S. Government Printing Office), pp. 10–11.

16. Zeimer, *op. cit.*

17. Data on Japanese government deficits are from the IMF. Data on Japanese saving and investment are from the OECD.

18. "White House Report on the Program for Economic Recovery," *Public Papers,* pp. 123, 130.

19. Feldstein, Martin, and Joel Slemrod, "Inflation and the Excess Taxation of Capital Gains," *National Tax Journal,* 31, June 1978, 107–118.

20. Calculated from *Statistics of Income, op. cit.,* various years.

21. For example, Michael J. Boskin, "Taxation, Saving and the Rate of Interest," *Journal of Political Economy,* 86, April 1978, Part

2, S3-S27 concluded that the effect was strong and positive. E. Philip Howrey and Saul H. Hymans, "The Measurement and Determination of Loanable-Funds Saving," *Brookings Papers on Economic Activity*, No. 3, 1978, 655–685 found a weak positive effect in some contexts and a weak negative effect in others, and concluded that the effect was zero for practical purposes.

22. "Address to the Nation on the Economy," *Public Papers*, p. 80.

23. *The Effects of Deficits on Prices of Financial Assets: Theory and Evidence* (Washington, D.C.: U.S. Treasury Department, 1984), p. 24.

24. "First Presidential Debate, Official Transcriptional Record," October 7, 1980, Mimeo (The League of Women Voters Educational Fund), p. 29.

25. For example, B. Douglas Bernheim and John B. Shoven, "Pension Funding and Saving," Z. Bodie, et al., eds., *Pensions in the U.S. Economy* (Chicago: University of Chicago Press, 1988).

26. Calculated from data on pension contributions in the FOF.

27. See, for example, the contrast between age-specific saving rates based on the Consumer Expenditure Survey and corresponding rates based on the Survey of Consumer Finances in Lawrence Summers and Chris Carroll, "Why Is the U.S. National Saving Rate So Low?" *Brookings Papers on Economic Activity*, No. 2, 1987, 607–635, Table 9.

28. See the summary and reference cited in Franco Modigliani, "Life Cycle, Individual Thrift, and the Wealth of Nations," *American Economic Review*, 76, June 1986, 297–313.

29. Venti, Steven F., and David A. Wise, "Have IRAs Increased U.S. Saving?: Evidence from Consumer Expenditure Surveys," Mimeo (National Bureau of Economic Research, 1987). The number of individuals who hold IRAs (as opposed to the number of separate accounts) is not reported, but thirty-five million is consistent with data from Market Facts, Inc., and the Employee Benefit Research Institute.

30. Ibid.
31. Auerbach, Alan, "Corporate Taxation in the United States," *Brookings Papers on Economic Activity*, No. 2, 1983, 451–505, Table 4.
32. Zeimer, *op. cit.*
33. Data on corporate cash flows are from the NIPA. Data on corporate borrowing are from the FOF.
34. *Mergerstat Review* (Chicago: W. T. Grimm & Co., 1987).
35. "Perot Is Removed from G.M. Board, But Has Big Profit," *The New York Times,* December 2, 1986, p. 1.
36. Data on the composition of investment are from the NIPA.
37. Data on capital spending by industry (unpublished) are from the BEA.
38. Data on venture capital financing are from Venture Economics, Inc.
39. Data on new business incorporations are from Dun and Bradstreet.

CHAPTER XI: HARD CHOICES

1. Stockman, David A., *The Triumph of Politics* (New York: Harper & Row, 1986), p. 402.
2. *Fiscal Year 1982 Budget Revisions,* 97th Congress, 1st Session, House Document No. 97-26, March 1981 (Washington, D.C.: U.S. Government Printing Office), Table 2.
3. *Budget of the United States Government: Fiscal Year 1983* (Washington, D.C.: U.S. Government Printing Office 1982), pp. 3–8, 3–12.
4. *Opinion Leader Outlook* (Cambridge, Mass.: Cambridge Reports, Inc., 1987), Table 7.
5. Estimates for spending cuts are from *Reducing the Deficit: Spending and Revenue Options* (Washington, D.C.: U.S. Government Printing Office, 1988).

6. Untitled release, March 8, 1987, Mimeo (Office of Senator William Proxmire), p. 4. Also "Another Failure to Fix the Pentagon," *New York Times*, September 21, 1987, p. A-18.

7. Ornstein, Norman J., "The Politics of the Deficit," P. Cagan, ed., *Essays in Contemporary Economic Problems, 1985: The Economy in Deficit* (Washington, D.C.: American Enterprise Institute, 1985), p. 318.

8. Data on Medicare and Medicaid payments are from the Health Care Financing Administration.

9. See, for example, Martin S. Feldstein, "The High Cost of Hospital Care and What to Do About It," *The Public Interest*, 48, Summer 1977, 40–54.

10. Data on government spending in relation to income in other countries are from the IMF for Germany, Britain, and France, and from the Bank of Japan for Japan.

11. Estimates for revenue increases are from *Reducing the Deficit: Spending and Revenue Options, op. cit.* Also *Description of Possible Options to Increase Revenues Prepared for the Committee on Ways and Means* (Washington, D.C.: U.S. Government Printing Office, 1987).

12. *Tax Reform Act of 1986: Conference Report to Accompany H.R. 3838*, Vol. II, 99th Congress, 2nd Session, Joint Tax Committee (Washington, D.C.: U.S. Government Printing Office, 1986), Table A.1, p. II-865.

13. Summers, Lawrence H., "A Fair Tax Act That's Bad for Business," *Harvard Business Review*, 65, March/April 1987, 53–58.

14. Ibid.

15. Zeimer, Richard C., "Impact of Recent Tax Law Changes," *Survey of Current Business*, 65, April 1985, 28–31 and subsequent updates (unpublished) from the BEA.

16. "Address Before a Joint Session of the Congress on the Program for Economic Recovery," *Public Papers*, February 18, 1981, p. 114.

Index

About the Author

Benjamin M. Friedman was born in Louisville, Kentucky, in 1944. After graduating summa cum laude in economics from Harvard, he received a master's degree in economics and politics from King's College, Cambridge, where he was a Marshall Scholar. He then received his doctorate in economics from Harvard where he was a junior fellow of the Society of Fellows. He is now professor of economics at Harvard, teaching courses on macroeconomics, monetary theory, and monetary and fiscal policy.

Before joining the Harvard faculty, Professor Friedman worked in investment banking in New York City. He has also worked in consulting and other capacities at the Board of Governors of the Federal Reserve System and the Federal Reserve Banks of New York and Boston. In addition to teaching at Harvard, he currently serves as director of financial markets research at the National Bureau of Economic Research.

Professor Friedman has written and edited six books and more than eighty papers in economic journals, on such subjects as the effects of budget deficits, the conduct of monetary policy, and the financing of corporate capital formation. He is a frequent contributor to the op-ed pages of major newspapers, a frequent witness at congressional hearings, and an occasional adviser to presidential candidates. He lives in Cambridge, Massachusetts, with his wife, Barbara, and sons John, age seven, and Jeffrey, age four.